Margaret Bourke-White, author of "Shooting the Russian War," who was rescued recently from a raft in the Atlantic after having been afloat for three days following the torpedoing of her ship, will describe her experiences in covering the A. E. F. in North Africa at a lecture in Town Hall at 11 a. m. Saturday. Her subject is, "With the American Air Forces in North Africa."

SHOOTING THE RUSSIAN WAR

WRITTEN AND PHOTOGRAPHED BY
MARGARET BOURKE-WHITE

SIMON AND SCHUSTER · NEW YORK · 1942

HALFTONE PLATES MADE BY EAGLE PHOTOENGRAVING CO.
MANUFACTURED IN THE UNITED STATES OF AMERICA
BY AMERICAN BOOK–STRATFORD PRESS, NEW YORK

For my sister Ruth

The White Nights of Moscow

ON THE *rim of the fifty-fifth parallel lies Moscow. It is as far north as Sitko, Alaska, and directly on the other side of the world from Pearl Harbor. It is as full of bookstores per city block as Boston and it has as many busses as Baltimore. In summer, as many Eskimo Pies are sold out of dry-ice hand trucks along its streets as are marketed by the Good Humor boys along U. S. Highway No. 1.*

In winter it is buried beneath snows too deep for either Napoleon or Hitler to endure. A low-hung sun takes a brief look at the affairs of men at lunchtime each day, and then early in the afternoon the stars rise into their positions above the pointed Kremlin towers.

But in May and June, the nights never grow completely dark. A pure white glow bathes the streets during the brief twilight which rushes hastily into dawn. At midnight the city, in its ancient and modern contrasts of bulbous and angular architecture, stands gray against a luminous green sky.

And last summer, in July, as the nights began to lengthen in their seasonal progression, the sky began to whiten with a new light. It was a light made of magnesium, of expanding nitrate compounds, of nitroglycerin. It was a man-made light, fashioned for the purpose of bringing a still-deeper night.

When we left America in the spring of 1941, we did not know how soon tracer bullets and star shells would flame their way across Russian skies, but we firmly believed that, before long, the Soviet Union would take a leading place on the stage of world affairs.

Darien, Connecticut
April, 1942

M. B.-W.

Contents

Illustrations

SHOOTING THE RUSSIAN WAR

CHAPTER 1

Halfway Around the World

I SUPPOSE it was those Irish ancestors of mine, deep-sea sailors all of them, whose sons in each succeeding generation ran away to sea when anyone tried to dry-dock them at home, who were responsible for my passionate love of seeing the world. If they were in a position to make observations, they would surely feel that it was a mistake to pass on their wanderlust to a female descendant, for in their day, as far as I have heard, the distaff side never ran off to sea. They might even think that I have an unfair advantage if they could know how quickly our flying boats take us from one part of the world to another.

In view of this ancestral roaming tendency, it was a lucky thing, I think, to marry a man who knows how to read maps. Before making this happy arrangement, I had managed to find my way with a camera through a little more than two dozen countries located on five continents, sometimes for *Fortune* magazine, sometimes for *Life*, and sometimes to satisfy my own curiosity. The only time I ever got seriously lost was in northern Canada, flying over the Arctic near the North Magnetic Pole, where compasses don't work anyway; but direction finding in the Far North was something my Canadian pilot excelled in, and he managed to find his way at last to a tiny Eskimo settlement.

However, when I come back from trips to Siberia or the Sahara Desert, my friends often marvel at how easily I can lose my way between Grand Central and Fifty-first Street while walking to the dentist. Just recently, driving home from New York to Connecticut, I managed to lose my sense of direction so completely within an eighth of a mile of our house that I had to ask the neighbors the way home. This astonished my neighbors, but it didn't puzzle me at all, for I am no good on the short hops.

But now that I am married, all is changed. My husband reads maps
the way I read detective stories. The only difference is that he follows
the clues of latitude, longitude, air and ocean currents, and topography,
and emerges with the correct deduction, while I, even though attempting
to follow that simplest of all clues—the person least suspected—rarely
guess the murderer, for I am seldom able to deduce successfully who is
the least suspicious.

Erskine Caldwell's map reading is much more than a simple matter
of finding his way from one place to another. It is a whole study in agriculture, economics, and sociology. It is as though, through the surface
of the map, he had felt the rainfall, the winds, the altitude, and the fer-
tility of the earth. When he folds up his map, he reminds me of one of
his own fictional characters, Jeeter Lester, who in the end of *Tobacco
Road* lets a handful of soil sift through his fingers. Erskine has been
feeling the land and he knows in advance what it can be expected to
produce in the way of crops and men.

When two persons who have deep professional interests marry, there
are two ways of pursuing those interests: together or separately. In our
family we do both. Sometimes Erskine is interested in writing about
America at the same time that I feel I simply must do some photography
in central Asia. The solution is simple. He does his job on one continent
and I do mine on another. Sometimes both of us feel that the time has
come to work together, in the same country, he with typewriter and I
with lens, and then we do something that we both greatly enjoy. We
make a trip together and work together.

Russia was one of the countries which we selected to do together, and
we had a joint and urgent conviction that we should get there soon, to
record in words and pictures what we expected to be the coming tide of
the war. We kept our plans somewhat secret, for we do not like to talk
about things until we are sure we are going to accomplish them. The
State Department granted us validations, although they accompanied
our passports with a dutiful and somewhat ominous letter warning us
that due to distressed world conditions, we could have no assurance of
being able to get back to our native land again. The Soviet Ambassador
in Washington promised us visas, which would be waiting for us in
Chungking, but he warned me that photographs by visitors in the U.S.S.R.

had been forbidden for some years, and I could have no certainty in advance that the camera ban would be lifted for me.

I was willing to take a chance on this, however. When I first went to Russia, in 1930, few photographs had come out of the country, and those few had been taken by Soviet photographers; foreigners had not been allowed to take pictures at all. This had sharpened my ambition to bring the first photographs, taken by a non-Russian, out of the Soviet Union. I had been successful in accomplishing this not because of any special pull, for I had none at all, but because when I arrived in Moscow and showed the Soviets the many industrial photographs which I had been taking in America, they decided that it might be a good thing after all to let an American industrial photographer record their Five-Year Plan. I was ready to take the gamble again.

Among the extremely few people who knew of our plan was the picture editor of *Life* magazine. He shared our conviction that Russia was the coming key country in the march of the war, to such an extent that he bade me good-by with the words, "Don't stop on the way to play marbles!" I had to stop and play marbles in the Gobi Desert, but that comes later.

Erskine does all his writing in a defiantly free-lance way; consequently, he made no commitments beforehand. He did, however, have an understanding with *Life* and the Columbia Broadcasting System to supply material if he got around to it.

I spent the entire month before departure planning my equipment and taking lessons in elementary mechanics so as to be able to repair cameras when I was beyond hope of assistance. Some of my most bulky photographic materials went ahead by ship to Hong Kong, where we would connect up with them at the end of our Pacific clipper flight. My quota of supplies included three thousand flash bulbs, peanut variety, a large quantity of film packs, five cameras,* twenty-two lenses, four portable developing tanks, bottles of Dk21 fine-grain developer, several papers of dressmaker pins,† duplicates of every screw found in all the

---

* Refer to Appendix for photographic data.

† The pins were to hang up films to dry after developing. They were carried along because the Russian-made pins I had used ten years before were so blunt that they could hardly be forced through the films without injuring the delicate wet emulsion. On arrival this year I was glad I had brought my own, because pins, while better made, were scarce and hard to find in the shops.

minute parts of my lens mounts and synchronizing magnets, a synchro-scope, and a jeweler's screw driver and pliers. In addition, I carried twenty-eight paper-bound detective stories.

My husband packed one small suitcase with his old corduroy jacket and a few shoes and shirts and got an extra ribbon for his portable type-writer. His professional equipment weighed seventeen pounds. My equipment weighed six hundred pounds.

At last all the preparations were completed, and in late March we took off from the West Coast. There is something about each new trip that fills me with a proud, secret excitement. Even if it is just getting on a train to go from New York to Indianapolis, I feel as if I were travel-ing toward an adventure. This was to be my first trip completely around the world, and I was walking on wings.

Our clipper's first stop, at Honolulu, should have been a matter of overnight only. It seemed like imprisonment in paradise when unusually severe weather in the Pacific forced us to spend a week in Hawaii. Honolulu had been a perfect place for a honeymoon when Erskine and I had visited it for that purpose, exactly two years before, but with our eyes directed toward a world at war, Waikiki Beach had less appeal for us.

War was closer even to this dreamy spot than anyone could know. Many of the old-time residents were uneasy. A friend of ours whose lovely home we visited at Hilo, the main harbor of the "Big Island" of Hawaii, said to us, "I want to fly to Maui to visit my sister-in-law. The flight takes only an hour, but you have to stay for five days until the return plane picks you up again. I'd hate to stay away so long and find my house had been bombed. We're so exposed here on the top of this cliff."

Bombing of Hawaii sounded fantastic to us in March of 1941, but it sounded equally fantastic when it became a reality in December.

At last, on the eighth day, the waves abated, and our clipper took off. In a few minutes Pearl Harbor was left behind us; the scalloped hills of Oahu, patterned like a textile with curving rows of pineapple plantations, vanished into the distance. We were flying into a translucent nothingness where air and water were indistinguishable, headed toward the Orient.

Our fellow passengers constituted the major portion of the Dutch government in exile; the group was headed by Foreign Minister van Kleffens, looking like a high-school boy in prim spectacles. The Netherlanders had flown from England with communications from Queen Wilhelmina to President Roosevelt and, after conferences in Washington, were now on their way to the Dutch East Indies.

Our pilot, big, burly Captain Steve Bancroft, invited me up to sit beside him at the controls, where I could watch, as though from a glass cage, the barely perceptible cloud shapes coagulate and take form over a buttermilk sea. After seven and a half hours of flying we coasted into the lagoon of Midway. Sand Island and the smaller Eastern Island make up Midway—projections of an extinct volcano two million years old, whose base rests forever unseen two miles down on the ocean floor.

Long before our giant flying ships had found this a convenient refueling point on the way to the Orient, long before the Japanese had coveted it as a valuable steppingstone toward our Pacific shore, the discovery of Midway as a halfway rest post had been made. Millions of birds, winging their way over the paths of ancestral memory on their mysterious migrations, stop here with the regularity of certain Manhattanites who return to their favorite Florida hotel during the season.

On Midway the season for visitors in wings and feathers is from November to July. The entire sanded, beshrubbed surface of the island was one huge bird nursery. Spaced at a distance of three feet, each standing singly in a primitive sandy hole which passed for a nest, stood half a million gooney youngsters demanding their suppers. Each baby gooney bird was as big as a goose, and their combined voices blanketed the island with chronic protest. Their parents were ignoring their children's wishes completely, as though their offspring should not be allowed to interfere with their enjoyment of this tropic resort. In twos and threes they circled around each other in a strange little dance, nodding their heads and snapping their beaks, like socialites exchanging polite conversation.

The goonies fascinated the clipper passengers, and I found them especially interesting, since natural history has always been a hobby of mine. We were permitted to walk only a few yards outside the pleasant little Pan American Hotel, far enough to watch the goonies, but not far enough to observe the work of the marines who were engaged in defense construction on the other side of the islands.

At dawn, as we made our way down the slippery pier, the half-million goonies bowed with equal politeness to us and to each other. I hope that when their hour of trial comes they will not show such courtesy to the Japanese.

After seven hours of flying over a sea like shimmering cellophane, we saw below us, suspended in translucent light, a slender little horse-shoe, Wake Island. We stepped out on a sand bar, wild with wind and waves. On the fringe of the atoll, which surrounded the island like the rim of a cup, the breakers rose into fountains of spray.

"I always go swimming when I get to Wake," said Captain Bancroft. "They have the most gol-darned fish here you ever saw."

We jumped into bathing suits, and the Captain strapped heavy glass masks over our faces. I took a deep breath, plunged down, and found a miraculous pink coral world which opened up just below the surface of the water. I had to keep my fingers and toes out of the way of giant clams which, embedded forever by their own growth in rocky pockets, still were able to reach for me with their thick scalloped lips of purple velvet. Suddenly I realized that I was being watched by hundreds of eyes. A school of transparent fish, almost invisible except for their coal-black eyes, was staring into my face. Soon I felt like a fish myself as exquisite creatures, some sapphire, some indigo, and some smart black ones with red circles on their tails, began swimming along with me. A flounder, looking like an old tire, flapped its way along the ocean floor. Then ahead of me the disembodied leg of a giant with five human toes swam into my vision. I came up, gasping for breath, and identified it as the magnified foot of my husband, who was lost in the exploration of a little cave just ahead of me.

In the morning, while the clipper's motors warmed up, the Dutch Foreign Minister and I took a last walk along the beach and watched the love terns maneuvering themselves on and off their eggs. The tern, who lays her single egg on a slender branch, where it remains balanced despite constant winds, executes her take-offs with miraculous precision so as not to knock off her egg.

The perfection of Captain Bancroft's take-off from a choppy sea also had something ternlike about it, and after seven hours he deposited us gently at Guam. On this hot, lush island we sipped cool drinks with navy officers, who complained, with more prophecy than any of us could know, about Senators who refused to vote appropriations for adequate armaments, for fear of offending Japan.

During our dawn departure we were witnesses to a small dispute between the A and D nations. The Dutch Minister protested heatedly that he had diplomatic immunity when asked to conform to the blanket rule that all passengers open their baggage for examination before boarding the clipper.

"What do you think I have in my dispatch case," he stormed, "a time bomb?"

"We're not taking any chances," replied the Captain. "Someone else might put one there."

As his ruffled excellency stepped down the dock, the Captain said, "The Japs make the most trouble on this rule. We had one of those special Japanese diplomats a while ago who continued making a scene during the whole time the ship was warming up. 'He says he doesn't have to open his brief case for inspection,' said the dispatcher. 'No, he doesn't have to,' I answered as sweet as sugar, 'and I don't have to take him along or take his brief case either.' At which I took off, leaving the Jap on the pier to reconsider until the next clipper arrived."

At Manila our clipper was met by a flock of Filipino correspondents, eager, well-informed young people, hungry for news of the mainland. What were people reading? What was being done about this or that social problem? These natives showed a surprising amount of knowledge about the United States. Several of the Filipino correspondents were endeavoring to get assignments in Free China, whose struggle they greatly admired, for they all had a deep-seated distrust of the Japanese.

One more day of flight above the truly china blue of the China Sea, and we descended over rocky coves patterned with groups of sampans like floating wheat grains, circled over a city rolled out across hills and valleys and beaches, and finally swung into Kowloon Harbor. We were in Hong Kong, and we had flown halfway around the world.

CHAPTER 2

The Three Graces of China

EVERYONE HEARS about "The Three Graces" immediately upon reaching China. However, it is only slangy Americans who would dream of calling them that. To the rest of the world they are the Soong sisters: from eldest to youngest, Madame Kung, Madame Sun Yat-sen, and Madame Chiang Kai-shek.

The names of all three of their dazzlingly eminent husbands are treated with deserved and justifiable reverence throughout China. This does not prevent some of the resident Americans, who admire the ladies but still are not easily overawed, from referring to the two younger sisters as, respectively, the widow of God and the bride of Christ.

Madame Kung, the eldest of the three, is the wife of Dr. H. H. Kung, Minister of Finance and Executive Vice-President of the Bank of China. Madame Kung is said to keep a guiding iron hand on the finances of her wealthy family. Her understanding of industry is rather remarkable, and she holds the position of Adviser of the Chinese Industrial Co-operatives. The second sister, Madame Sun Yat-sen, is head of the China Defense League. Although both these ladies are very active, their executive positions had an absentee character until the fall of Hong Kong sent them on to Chungking. During our visit to Hong Kong, they had residences there, where they held in effect the odd position of refugee guests of the British government.

Madame Kung is self-effacing almost to the point of invisibility. She is rarely seen and almost never photographed. When I heard that the last time she had consented to sit for a portrait was twenty years ago, I was especially eager to make a new portrait of her.

It was through Madame Sun Yat-sen that I finally reached her. Madame Sun is not very accessible either, but her interest in her China

Defense League made her listen to my arguments that submitting to have her portrait taken was the best way to publicize her cause in America, since Americans take such an interest in personalities. I found her plump, jolly, and gracious, and so shy that I think the very fact that she had overcome her timidity sufficiently to be photographed made her willing to talk her elder sister into doing the same thing. The next day, Erskine and I received an invitation to dine at the home of Madame Kung. Madame Sun would also be a guest, and I was allowed to bring my camera.

I had heard various guesses as to the age of the eldest Soong sister, ranging from fifty to a little over sixty. When I saw her, I thought she looked hardly forty. She had that smooth, enameled slimness which makes many Chinese women ageless. She wore the typical dress which the women of China wear like a uniform—a straight-cut tube, slit up the side, of identical cut for rich and poor, and made of fabrics ranging from the faded blue cotton of the coolies to heavy black silk embroidered in pearls. Madame's was embroidered in pearls. As she walked into the room I was startled to observe that even this modest lady's dress showed the expanse of well-shaped slender leg, from ankle to a bit above the knee, that flashes out through slit skirts all over China.

During the portrait, she was so bashful that all the servants and even my husband were sent from the room. I was grateful that she allowed her sister to stay, for I needed someone to help me hold reflectors, a job which Madame Sun Yat-sen performed with evident pleasure at the novelty of the operation and with many exclamations over the miraculous quickness of flash bulbs. Madame Sun powdered her sister's nose at intervals and straightened her coiffure, although it was already as sleek as polished bakelite. When I had finished, the two promised to write letters to "little sister Mei," so that on arrival in Chungking I should be able to make portraits of her and of her husband, the Generalissimo.

Then Erskine was permitted to return, and we were led in to what appeared to me, in my inexperience, to be an unusually well-loaded table. As we took our seats, Madame Kung expressed regret for the inadequacy of the meal.

"I am not serving bird's-nest soup or shark fins," she explained, "because I don't feel it is right to have such delicacies in time of war."

She spoke with the same faint trace of a Georgia accent that my husband has, for she had received her early American schooling in Macon, which happens to be not far from the town where my husband was born.

I tried, in an experimental spirit, all the peculiarly flavored dishes. They included the peppered sinews of fowl, and other items less recognizable, but delightfully seasoned and served in bewildering array.

Course after course was served, but each time an exotic-looking dish was brought in, Erskine waved it aside and asked for another serving of rice.

Madame Kung was perturbed.

"Rice is peasants' food," she said, "and I served it tonight only because I wanted you to sample truly Chinese dishes."

"That makes me a peasant then," Erskine gulped, "because I was raised on rice in Georgia and I like it. This is the first time I've been able to find any since we reached Hong Kong."

Madame was speechless for a moment and then she called the maids and ordered them to bring in all the rice in the kitchen. She and Erskine ate nothing else during the remainder of the dinner.

We came to find out later that it is surprisingly difficult for a foreigner to get rice in China. Foreign travelers are expected to prefer more elite fare.

Hong Kong had the unreality of stereopticon slides. Its streets showed three dimensions, but even as we were rolled through them at breakneck speed in rickshas they still retained that insubstantial quality of one picture succeeding another. The hillsides were piled high with crowded houses. Decorative Chinese-lettered signs were strung across the alleys, and fabulously plentiful flowers were sold under all the archways. The stores were spilling out into the streets with their stocks of Swiss watches, English woolens, carved ivories, and embroideries at fantastically low prices. Everything was cheap, because Hong Kong was a free port for foreign articles, and coolie labor made native products cost next to nothing.

We were astonished when a tailor arrived unsolicited with our breakfast tray. He quickly talked my husband into ordering a suit, which he copied from one of Erskine's old ones—for the Chinese can copy anything—and it was delivered with our morning paper the next day, perfectly tailored and finished down to the last hand-stitched lapel.

We were startled but delighted when, the following morning, the instant we woke up, a shoemaker was at my husband's bedside with a pencil to draw the outline on a piece of paper when his foot first hit the floor. A pair of Erskine's old shoes served as a model, and by noon my husband had a beautifully finished pair of new shoes.

I gave the shoemaker some jobs, too. I ordered cases of chamois leather, closing with zippers, for each of my five cameras, for each flash gun and chromium reflector, and for all of my filters. When they were finished they fitted each piece of equipment like a glove and acted as perfect dust protectors. When it came to final packing of supplies, I tore off and discarded all the cardboard protectors of my three thousand peanut bulbs. The bulbs themselves I packed into two large wicker baskets such as Chinese peasants carry. Merely removing the wrappers saved one third of their weight. I knew that it risked a great deal of breakage, but space would be at a premium as we flew across China. During my work later in Moscow, in that vast quantity of flash bulbs I found only six that were even cracked.

The luxurious Chinese world which Hong Kong presented began swinging toward the opposite extreme when we started our flight to the war capital of Chungking. We were taken to the airport at midnight to wait for an unannounced departure time. Since three hours of the flight were made over Japanese-held territory, the take-offs were planned when two layers of cloud would offer the best possible chance for the Douglas to pick its course between them, unseen from the ground, and with the hope of being undetected by enemy planes that might be scouting above. Since there was always the chance that we might have to make a forced landing back in the wilderness, in case an air raid over Chungking should make it impossible for us to land there, we were told to carry a couple of sandwiches.

We were flown by an American pilot and co-pilot, volunteers flying for the Chinese National Airways, who have since become famous in

the group of American "Flying Tigers" who attacked the Japanese during the invasion of Malaya.

We flew in a plane laden with bales of money freshly printed to pay
the Chinese soldiers, and every kilo of extra luggage brought for us,
every camera and every film pack, displaced its weight in money. We
sat on stacks of Chinese dollars, we tucked our legs around them, and
I believe that if we had actually had to land in the wilderness we would
have warmed our hands in front of fires built of money.

But the Japanese stayed out of our way that night, and after circling
over intricately sculptured mountains, carved into whorls and ara-
besques by the agriculture of thousands of years, we darted down
between two towering peaks and stepped out on a narrow landing field
at the bank of the Yangtze.

At first I could hardly believe I was in Chungking; in the early-
morning light it was difficult to see a human habitation anywhere. Then
we began climbing the stone steps on the north bank—446 steep, by actual count—toward the capital on the mountaintop. Halfway up we
began seeing people, hundreds and thousands of people. They were
carrying little baskets of cracked rock out of the newly blasted dugouts;
they were squatting in the road, dipping chopsticks into bowls of rice;
some of the luckier ones were riding in sedan chairs carried up the
breathlessly steep streets by two human beings. The roads were lined
with dugouts carved out of solid rock, dugouts not only for humans, but
also for automobiles and trucks. Everywhere there was the never-ending activity of building.

The Kialing House, our hotel, in addition to being filled with its
usual foreign population, was overflowing with a fashionable Chinese
wedding, proceeding in the midst of much starched pink tarlatan and
massed artificial flowers. The many cell-like bedrooms were being
utilized by the gentlemen guests, who were changing to swallow-tails
and tuxedos, the last costume that we expected to see in war-torn China.
However, a corner cot was found for us, and depositing our luggage on
it we made off to the Soviet Embassy.

Our journey up the precipitous path was one of extreme anxiety, not
only because it seemed that our swaying sedan chairs might be pitched

off our coolies' shoulders at any instant into the gorge below, but also because of acute worry as to whether our visas would really be there. People were delayed weeks, sometimes months, for Soviet visas—often to find that they were not getting them after all.

We saw the Soviet Ambassador after a wait of only five minutes and received our Russian visas after only fifteen. While our credentials were being stamped in our passports, we talked with him over glasses of Russian tea and munched little chocolate candies in wrappers stamped "Red October Candy Factory, Moskva."

Over our tea, we commented on what a target the Soviet Embassy must make, situated as it is on the highest point in Chungking. We knew that most of the diplomatic staffs of other countries had moved to the South Bank, which is much less frequently attacked than the main part of the city.

"We stay here," said the Soviet Ambassador, "because we think that if the Chinese people can stand the bombing we can share it with them."

This expression of solidarity with the Chinese people was demonstrated again a little later, when the Ambassador's secretary led us down to our waiting coolies. As we were hoisted in our sedan chairs to the shoulders of these human beasts of burden, the Russian said, "None of us in the Soviet diplomatic service ever use sedan chairs, because we do not feel that it is right to exploit the back muscles of other men."

It was not a pair of exploited backs, however, but a body by Buick that called to take us to the residence of the Generalissimo and Madame Chiang Kai-shek.

Their house might have been built for a well-to-do resident of Kansas City, Missouri. It had a square frame, regularly spaced windows, and mission furniture. The living-room suite, complete with sofa, was the same overstuffed style that has been multiplied time without number throughout the United States. There was nothing either beautiful or exotic about the house or its furnishings. The only Oriental touches lay in a few Chinese scrolls hanging on the walls.

But when Madame Chiang Kai-shek entered, it was immediately evident that there was nothing ordinary about her. I doubt if one would find that complex assortment of characteristics anywhere else. She has a combination of purpose and of glitter, of capacity for intensive hard work with a dash of the theater thrown in.

She spoke in a voice so soft-timbred and low that one had to listen carefully to hear her. Her spare but graceful gestures seemed studied, her beauty was of a restrained sort held back under an enameled exterior and glowing out of a pair of hot eyes. She was dressed in that severely cut tube dress which is so becoming to the slenderness of Chinese women; hers had tiny flower patterns woven in the black fabric, picking up the color notes of the emerald, sapphire, and diamond clips that gleamed in fashionable smartness on her tiny ears.

After a few minutes of conversation with her, the overwhelming impression of theatrical perfection was forgotten in the feeling that here was a person with a will like a stretched steel band.

While tea was being served, Madame Chiang and Erskine entered into such an absorbed conversation that I set down my half-empty teacup and got my camera into operation as quickly as possible. It is always a help to me when my subjects are interested in conversation while I work, because it gives me a chance to record a varied succession of facial expressions while they forget the camera. Madame's beautiful face was very expressive as she talked.

Erskine was telling her that she should visit the United States as soon as possible, in order to convince the American people that it was to America's interest to send more military supplies to China.

"But I have written a book for publication in the United States," said Madame Chiang. "That will do more good than anything else."

"A book will help some," Erskine said, "but your personal appearance would help China more than a dozen books at this time."

Madame Chiang was silent for several moments.

"I suppose that's true," she said, "but I can't leave China now. There is so much to do here that I wouldn't feel right if I didn't stay here every minute."

"Just the same," Erskine told her, "I wish you would go for a quick visit. Americans haven't been able to keep up with the world. They don't know what it's all about any more—and they probably won't find out until it's too late—or almost too late."

"But Americans should know that by helping China they are contributing to the defeat of our enemy, and theirs—Japan."

"The average American thinks this war is taking place on another planet," Erskine said.

At which point the photographs, which were progressing with the conversation, were interrupted by the entrance of the Generalissimo, who came in to have a cup of tea.

Generalissimo Chiang Kai-shek is a masterpiece of monotone. His hair and mustache are the texture of straw, his skin is the color of dried grass. He is as immobile as a wheat stack, and his general impassiveness contrasts with the striking personality of his dynamic wife. But here, also, one has that feeling of hard, strong purpose, and one hears constantly that the men fighting under him are ready to die for him.

I asked the Generalissimo's permission to take his portrait and went on working again: it seemed odd to photograph a general holding a teacup and sitting on a sofa with a lace antimacassar behind his head, but when you are a photographer you learn to take what you can get. While Chiang did not speak English, he gave the impression of not missing a single thing when English was spoken. At rare intervals he smiled, and I was able to catch a startling mouthful of false teeth, gleaming in his otherwise impassive countenance. When he talked with Erskine, Madame Chiang interpreted.

My husband asked Chiang if China was getting sufficient military supplies from the United States and England.

Chiang was quick to say that he was satisfied with American help to the extent that it had been promised, but that very little had been promised at that time.

"What about England's help?" Erskine asked him. "Is it enough?"

"No! no! no!" Chiang said. "England has done very little. England does not understand. England is afraid of offending Japan. The British should realize that Japan will eventually attack them."

Erskine told Chiang of the crated warplanes he had seen on the docks in Los Angeles Harbor, waiting shipment to China.

"Did you see many of them?"

"Very many," Erskine said.

"Good! good!" Chiang said. "Were there any big bombers?"

"I am quite sure there were," Erskine told him. "We saw several shiploads of all types of bombers and fighters."

"Good! good! good!" Chiang said. "It is heartening to hear of planes on their way from America. That is what we have always needed. We can defeat Japan only with planes. Japan cannot be defeated without planes."

Every facility was to be provided for Erskine and me if we could take time to fly to the front, but since our destination was Russia we decided to take the first plane available to the U.S.S.R.

"But before you leave, you must surely photograph my war orphans," said Madame, and the next day I set out into the hills across the Kialing River to visit the "Warphanage," as it is called.

There are hundreds of thousands of Chinese orphans whose parents were killed in bombing or fighting. When great areas had to be hastily evacuated, too, countless children became hopelessly lost and separated from their families. In Madame Chiang's various "Warphanages" 30,000 children are cared for. In between climbing into dugouts, which air raids make a frequent necessity, the children are taught to raise their own vegetables and care for their own pigs and are given their arithmetic lessons just as are the school children of any country.

Arithmetic was in progress when I made my visit. I was interested to see that the children in learning to count use symbols of the war which has become such a part of their lives. Under *1* on the blackboard was pasted a cutout of a bombing plane; under *2* were two antiaircraft guns. The other numbers were illustrated by rifles, tanks, Chinese sabers, and so on, through *9*, which was represented by nine bombers. But under *10*, I was pleased to observe that the children had pasted up cutouts of ten butterflies.

However, there is more of bombing than of butterflies in their childish lives. Bombs enter even into their songs. They put up their fists to their ears and chant, "The enemy planes are coming"; then they crouch down, ducking their heads, and sing, "So you must crouch down quickly," and at the end of their song, when the raid is over, they jump up, clapping their hands and singing, *"Chan tong kawai,"* which means, "Very, very happy."

When the air-raid alarm comes, the orphans wind their way, double file, over jagged cliffs to their shelters a mile away, the two leaders carrying a stretcher that may be needed before the raid is over, and the other children carrying little stools so that they will not have to sit on the cold stone floor of their cave dugout. This stool has become as much a companion to each child as a doll would have been in a happier age, and he calls it his "sister-in-law." The war orphans have a song even for their little stools:

> My sister-in-law she drinks and gambles
> So she pawns her socks and sells her sandals.

From these rocky peaks, over which the war orphans must hurry many times a month, one can command a fine view of Chungking. Down in the valley, near the broad and always misty Yangtze, there are factories —if you know where to look for them. Their smokestacks are camouflaged like trees, draped with green-dyed nets and newly covered every few days with fresh branches. Under some of the terraced gardens are factories set up in caves, their machinery installed after having been dismantled and moved laboriously across the country ahead of the invading Japanese.

It is this constant moving on coolie back, moving things in river sampans and in hand cars, moving everything from a dismembered dynamo to the family teapot; it is this constant excavating, mending, and building that tells the story of China at war.

Chungking is like the movie lot at Warner Brothers' in Burbank. The Hollywood store fronts seem real, but look behind them and you see a wasteland. The hastily erected shop fronts of Chungking seem solid; but walk behind them and you see piles of blasted ruins like waste piles of a deserted stone quarry.

Yet in the midst of all this devastation the work goes on: a constant tapping and splitting of rock and carrying away of spoonfuls of earth, a steady rebuilding of houses and shelters at the slow continuous pace which has been typical of the Chinese for centuries.

On our last day in Chungking there was an air-raid alarm, and we watched a curious sight from above the great stone steps that lead from the center of the city down to the Yangtze. When the warning sounded, the great staircase suddenly overflowed with what looked like little black ants, so densely matted that it seemed as if an enormous black curtain were being pulled down the white steps to the river. The people near enough the water to escape the city got into little sampans and rowed across the swift stream, and in half an hour thousands of them had evacuated to the hills.

The next morning, we left the Kialing House, which, sooner than we knew, was to be blown to bits. We had arrived in a wedding and we departed in a funeral. As we stacked our six hundred pounds of luggage into the providential truck that the Soviet Embassy had loaned us, the procession swept past us. The Chinese love American tunes, and the mourners were singing unintelligible words to "Massa's in the Cold, Cold Ground."

While the bags were being tied firmly on the truck, we started ahead on foot down the steep road toward the airfield. It was a long funeral procession, and as we pushed our way through the dense ranks of mourners, they began chanting their dirge to the unmistakable lilt of "Happy Days Are Here Again."

CHAPTER 3

Lanchow—the Gobi—Hami—Moscow

IT IS a complete puzzle to me why all the planes in China, with the exception of the new ones coming from the United States, do not fall to pieces all at once, like the One-Hoss Shay. Many of them are Junkers purchased from Germany ten years ago, and no one knows how many years they were in use before then. The only reason why we finally reached the Soviet border was that our plane did not fall to pieces all at once—only bit by bit.

The disintegration process started when we were circling over some extremely high mountains. Our pilot managed to bring down the plane successfully on a landing field in a bend of the Yellow River, at a town called Lanchow, in central China.

Lanchow is an old historic city at the end of a branch of the Great Chinese Wall. It is of great interest to students of medieval China, and I am quite willing to leave it to the historians. We went into the walled city to find a place to stay, and settled down in an arrangement that was called a hotel but more closely resembled a pigeon coop. We set up a hand-to-mouth existence in a little cell which had an earth floor, no windows, and two benches against the walls, which could serve as cots. The sanitary arrangements were a kind of every-man-for-himself idea. Despite the primitiveness of our "hotel," each morning as soon as we were seen stirring we were brought cups of tea with the regularity with which the better American hotels deposit the morning paper outside your door. These first cups of tea we sprinkled on the floor in order to settle the dust, and then called for two more cups. These we used to brush our teeth, a ritual we performed in tea after being unable to identify certain bits of foreign matter we had seen floating in the water;

the tea, we felt reasonably certain, had been boiled. If we were lucky enough to obtain a third cup each, we used it to take a bath. When I was a child, I had been told that a Chinese can take a bath in a teacup. I now am able to state from experience that this is possible.

Every day, we would ride out in rickshas to the airport and watch the mechanics attempting to fit pieces from other dismantled planes of varying sizes into the gaps of our Junkers, and when twilight fell we would go back to our pigeon coop.

Finally, the airport manager telegraphed to Hong Kong for repair parts. It was a happy day when we loaded our bags into Lanchow's one bus and went out to the airport to see the Hong Kong plane come in. It was a matter of only a few hours to repair our plane with spare parts that fitted; but when it was done, our plane and the repair plane both took off and flew back to Chungking and back to Hong Kong, leaving us still in Lanchow. The reasons for this curious maneuver were never explained to us.

There was nothing for us to do but go back to our pigeon coop. It was at this period that we cultivated the acquaintance of a young Chinese named Show King.

Show King was the cook boy, and he stepped into an important place in our lives. He was a refugee from Shanghai, where he had worked in a fashionable tourist hotel. When the Japanese had come uncomfortably close, Show King had escaped, carrying one of his most valuable worldly possessions—an enormous cookbook with the recipes written in an elaborate hand in Chinese and the titles translated neatly into English. There were ninety-six ways of fixing beef, one hundred and eleven ways to prepare chicken, forty-seven salad dressings, eighty-four meat sauces, and twenty-eight different kinds of soufflés. Every morning, in consultation with Show King, we would choose our menu for the day, though no matter what we ordered we almost always got stewed chicken.

Each day, we took a little shopping tour along Lanchow's teeming Main Street. We bought crude rings of hammered silver, and bracelets jingling with little bells; and after each buying orgy, Show King, in his limited English, scolded us for letting the Lanchow merchants take advantage of us. However, in terms of American currency translated from Chinese dollars, it was seldom that we could spend more than twenty cents.

Whenever we saw them for sale, we would purchase the intricately carved little gourds, about the size of a walnut, which are a specialty of Lanchow artists. These are exquisite pieces of workmanship, with tiny figures carved with extreme delicacy, illustrating episodes from Chinese history. Once, when we brought a handkerchief full of these back to our cell, we examined them closely and several of them turned out, surprisingly, to be pornographic.

It was a happy day when we found, in a bookstore hollowed out in a thick stone wall, an enormous map of Asia with the place names in Chinese characters. While Erskine was paying for his purchase, I explored the shelves, deep in dust, and found a textbook for students of English literature. It contained short stories by Conan Doyle, Chinese on the left-hand pages and English on the right. Thus even in Lanchow I was able to buy detective stories.

We used to sit out in the sun on a box in the courtyard, following our respective studies of map examining and mystery reading. The map of Asia was so large that Erskine needed the whole courtyard to open it up in.

Then one evening the airport manager called at our cell, with the happy tidings that a plane was coming through the next morning on the way to Inner Mongolia and would pick us up. We were almost too excited to sleep that night, and the cold dawn light found us standing at the roadside outside the hotel, with our bags and cases strapped up beside us, so that the bus could not possibly miss us when it went to the airport.

Suddenly people began running in two directions to the tune of a rising sound which we reluctantly recognized as an air-raid siren. We didn't have to be told that no Chinese Airways plane would land in Lanchow that day.

We dragged our bags to shelter and stood at the door and watched. It seemed that all the residents of the north end of the city wished to reach the mountains on the south side, and all the people who lived in the shadow of the South Hills preferred the shelter of the slopes toward the north. The speed of both contingents was very swift, and the effect, to one who stood still, was dizzying.

Storekeepers closed the blinds of their doll-house shops, snatched the advertising signs off the outsides, locked their shutters with lightning speed, and were off. Soon the upper classes, easily distinguishable because they proceeded in rickshas, began making for the mountains, urging their coolies to pull them at a faster and still-faster pace.

As we stood, absorbed in this lively scene, a voice behind me said, "Missy take her coat off. Missy be arrested. Red color against the law in air raid."

It was Show King watching out for us. Appreciating the reasonableness of this position, I turned my coat inside out so that only the black lining was visible.

The Japanese dropped their loads that day on some near-by villages. The cessation of the alarm brought the people promptly back to town, opened like magic the doors of the shops, but did not bring our plane to the landing field.

The next day it was a raid over Chengtu, some three hundred and fifty air miles away, that detained our plane; but on the day following, the good news was true news. We paid for our pigeon coop, which, complete with stewed chicken and tea and an occasional soufflé thrown in, averaged the equivalent of fifteen cents a day; we accepted with thanks the parting gift of a bag of hard-boiled eggs from the airport manager; and we swept up into the air, leaving Lanchow, its segment of Chinese Wall and its venerable history, behind forever.

At Süchow, just across the border of Inner Mongolia, where we spent the next night, we began to notice the beginning of Russian influence. The airport hotel, which was laid out like an adobe tourist camp in the Arizona desert, was hung with Soviet posters. My husband slept under a portrait of Lenin, and over my bed hung a map of Spain, with pins still in place indicating the Loyalist lines during the battle of the Ebro front.

In the Gobi Desert, sandstorms began blowing toward us. Frequently the sand became too thick for flying, and as our plane descended for a forced landing, the co-pilot faithfully followed military regulations— drawing the blackout curtains so the passengers might not look out.

Once we managed to reach a small airfield, but usually we landed in trackless wasteland; nevertheless, the curtains were always faithfully drawn. I have yet to discover what military secrets there are in the shape of a sand dune, but there must be some.

So that the hours might pass more pleasantly while we sat in our sealed plane on the hot desert floor, Erskine brought out his Chinese-checkers set, his favorite game. It was in the Gobi that we made the discovery that Chinese checkers are unknown in China. At least the game was unknown until we taught the Chinese how to play. The pilot and the co-pilot were fascinated by the board with its bright-colored marbles and entered into the game with such zest that frequently I would have to remind them to look out and see if the sandstorm had died down so that we could be on our way.

As we continued on our course, it was easy to believe the geographers who say that the Gobi is the largest uninhabited portion of the globe. After the sandstorm belt was left behind, we flew over huge level areas as polished as agate and over vast tumbled precipices as dead as the mountains of the moon, until at last a group of little rooftops took form on the horizon and we swept down on the windy airport of Hami.

Hami is in Sinkiang, the border province between the Soviet Union and China. Freight is carried through it on trucks and camels. Here we were to leave our venerable Junkers for one of the newer Douglases of the Hami–Ata Russian-operated line.

It was completely in key with our record of airplane delays that no attempt had been made to connect with the weekly Russian plane. It did not therefore surprise us, although we certainly were not pleased, to discover that the plane to Alma-Ata, the nearest large city on the border of the Soviet Union, had taken off only two hours before. We looked with envy at the three passengers who had disembarked from Russia just that morning and who were to connect miraculously and immediately continue across China to their destination. And then our envy was momentarily forgotten in curiosity. The three were stout middle-aged women, in sensible black coats and old-fashioned pancake hats. Since it was impossible for us to guess the business of three plump ladies in the middle of the desert, we forgot politeness and asked them. They were Dutch missionaries who had taken the long journey through the Reich and across the Soviet Union and were on their way to central China. They chattered to us in eager German about how poor the food had been in Germany and how delighted they were to find plenty of butter and cream on their trip across the Soviet Union.

Our pilot came up to bid us good-by and to write down the particulars of our Chinese-checkers set, so that he could order one at Hong Kong. He copied the lettering on the board carefully into his notebook: "Chinker Chek, the Game for All Ages." We helped the trio of decorous ladies embark and wondered if there might be some deep reason why missionaries journeying on their benevolent errand should be more speedy on their travel than journalists and photographers. We stood quietly on the field and watched the ancient German-born vehicle which had brought us rise on its tired wings and return the way it had come.

During the interval in Hami I attempted to enlarge my meager Russian vocabulary by practicing with the cook and the little boy who waited table, only to discover later that due to the mixed dialect spoken in this border province I had laboriously committed many lengthy words to memory which turned out to be unintelligible in Moscow because they were Chinese.

It was an American-made Douglas, containing a smartly uniformed Russian pilot and co-pilot, that carried us across the border into the Soviet Union. Alma-Ata, the southeastern doorway into Russia, was reached after a total of thirty-one days spent in crossing China, from its Pacific gate at Hong Kong to its western border in central Asia. Within this month of travel across China, the mileage was covered in a mere twenty-four hours of actual progress through the air.

In Alma-Ata the Soviet customs official made an unbelievably minute examination of my equipment, even prying open the cans of hypo and probing with a stick to make sure nothing was hidden inside. The carved gourds from Lanchow he examined with a magnifying glass and removed all the naughty ones. "Censored!" he explained.

One and a half days more of flying over great red smudges of poppies in the wheat fields of Turkestan, along the marshes of the Aral Sea, where peasants who have never seen a train or automobile get their letters by mailplane, over a city called Kuibyshev (soon to become the secondary war capital) sprawled within loops of the Volga. On we flew to Moscow, and when we landed on its crowded Dynamo airport we had traveled fifteen thousand miles, almost two thirds of the distance around the world, in a total flying time of one hundred hours.

CHAPTER 4

The Last Days of Peace

IN THE middle of the Red Square, on the first day of June, hailstones pelted down on me while I attempted to take pictures. All through the month of May it had been snowing fitfully. Never in the memory of the oldest peasant, everybody was saying, had there been such a spring in Moscow. I was shivering and coughing in the heaviest coat I had, which I wore with equal impartiality at chilly breakfasts in our room or outside in the Red Square. It was the same red coat which had been frowned on during air raids over China, but here, at least, it was the right color.

We had been in Moscow for a month. On our arrival we had been greeted cordially by the Union of Soviet Writers, some of whose members had helped select and translate Caldwell stories for the U.S.S.R. and were eager to welcome the author in person. VOKS, the Society for Cultural Relations with Foreign Countries, which knew my Russian photographs from my three earlier visits, had obtained permission for me to take pictures again. There were many restrictions, but still I was happy that I could work.

The occasional limitations on subjects that I wished to photograph troubled me much less than the weather. It was the kind of weather that drives photographers alternately to ecstasy and madness. Piles of dazzling clouds let through the sunlight in short quick stabs, and before one could so much as whip out a yellow filter the skies became overcast and gray.

Not only did the weather delay my photographs; it retarded the crops as well. This did not worry the Russians as much as might have been supposed. War fears were growing. There was an ominous feeling that harvesttime might bring fighting with it; and when the unnaturally cold weather delayed the harvest of spring wheat for several weeks, everyone began repeating the favorite Soviet quip—that the Bolsheviks had learned to control even the weather.

While it was evident that uneasiness was growing, no one was discussing openly from which direction the war clouds were expected to gather. The nonaggression pact between Germany and the Soviet Union was in effect; Germans were to be seen in all the leading hotels; the Soviet press, which is government controlled, contained not an anti-German word.

Still, I was interested to observe that if the man in the street opened his morning *Pravda* or *Izvestia* and read that a British ship had been sunk, he felt very bad about it, almost as though one of his own ships had been sunk. And if, on another day, he read that British pilots had downed an unusually large number of German planes, he was apt to tap his neighbor on the arm and show him the good news.

It made me feel that the Russian people recognized the pact as a marriage of convenience, designed to give their new industries more time to turn out needed munitions while their country remained at peace. In recent history, as short a time ago as 1918, the Germans had invaded the Ukraine, only to be driven out by the Russians, and the people had not forgotten. In the thirteenth century, the Huns had invaded the Ukraine and were driven out by angry peasant hordes led by the great Russian hero, Alexander Nevsky. And the people of Moscow had this invasion clearly in mind, too, because a vivid moving picture about it had been released in 1939. It had played to packed audiences throughout the city until the very day when the German-Soviet pact was signed, at which time it was withdrawn so suddenly that some of the movie audiences were left in darkened suspense as the Huns and the Ukrainians, clashing at saber points, faded from the screen. They were not even given the "Continued Next Week" slide, which American movie theaters run as the thriller breaks off at its most exciting point. If some omniscient theater manager could have run such a sign, it would have read, "To Be Continued After Two Years." Its director, Sergei Eisenstein, however, had a bit of that kind of foresight. When we arrived in Moscow, he got the reels out of a safe where they were stowed away and gave Erskine and me a private showing.

"We think," he commented sagely, "that it will not be much longer before *Alexander Nevsky* will be shown in public cinema theaters again."

Although technically, in early June, 1941, Germany was the friend of Soviet Russia, there were other rumblings. The most significant, to us, was a report that came to our ears about an address that Stalin had made to the graduating class of the Military Academy. Stalin's speech had already been printed in the Soviet papers, but we learned through one of the underground routes by which news sometimes reaches journalists that the printed version was merely the preamble to his fateful address. The main theme of his talk to the Red Army graduates had been: "Germany is our real enemy."

This was so sensational that some of the foreign correspondents who heard it tried to cable it out; but such a statement, not even published within the borders of the Soviet Union, could not be expected to pass the censors. One foreign correspondent who smuggled the story abroad was deported within a week.

The American Ambassador, Laurence A. Steinhardt, had been preparing for weeks for the emergency he thought was impending. A second embassy was being established in the country about thirty miles north of Moscow in a *dacha,* or country house. He was importing tents from the United States and preparing to set them up under the birch trees to house needy Americans who might be blasted out of their hotels if action started.

He did not know until it was too late to change that the spot selected for this safe retreat was close to a group of munitions factories. More dogfights were to be held over those tents than if they had been pitched in the middle of the Red Square.

Mrs. Steinhardt was very busy making the *dacha* homey and comfortable. She was choosing harmonizing wall colors and fabrics and was hanging curtains in attractive color tones and heavy enough to be drawn for blackout purposes. A perfectionist down to the last pleated valance, she had curtains matched for fringes and chenille edgings by the courier who carried the pouch to Stockholm each week, as the Swedish capital afforded a wider selection of drapery trimmings than could be found in Moscow.

Ambassadors' wives were faced with extraordinarily complex problems in the social field during those last confusing weeks that the German-Soviet pact was in force. Protocol was assuming such proportions that it could be tackled only by supertechnicians. Within diplomatic circles each dinner called for divisions for which Solomon would have needed an advisory committee. How many Axis or Allied plenipotentiaries could be mixed, if any, and in proportion to how many neutrals?

Many embassy hostesses expanded their operating budgets by giving all entertainments in twos. But even when this was done, which of the neutrals could be trusted to speak to which of the belligerents? Some brave ambassadresses flung everyone together and continued to smile glassily while the room coagulated into sections, with floating icebergs, unseen but plainly felt, bobbing in between. One of the Scandinavian ministers evolved a superb handling of the situation. He gave a reception in which two great rooms judiciously divided up the Axis and Allied guests. These salons were not adjoining, but were connected by a short hall through which the waiters and the more fancy-free of the neutrals circulated impartially.

Lady Cripps flew into Moscow from Stockholm in the same plane which carried the wife of the French Minister, who had been her intimate friend for many years.

"It was too dreadful," she told me. "We were the only two women on the plane and we felt so silly, not even being able to look toward each other. When the plane stopped at Riga, I found I didn't have enough Russian currency in my purse to phone my husband. There was no way to change it at the airport, and when I saw my dear friend go to the telephone and ring her consulate in Moscow, it would have been so convenient if I could have asked her simply to tell them to call up the British Embassy and let Sir Stafford know when I was coming."

The diplomatic colony was buzzing with a story which had recently leaked out, concerning the departure of Molotov earlier in the year for his visit to Berlin. The pro-Ally members of the diplomatic colony had been lucky in getting a long laugh at the German Ambassador, and long after the event the laugh was still good.

The station authorities had been notified, when it was time for Mr.

Molotov to leave on a special train with the German Ambassador, that no one without the proper credentials would be allowed to pass the train gates. This was a routine rule in such a case. The Soviet Commissar for Foreign Affairs had already gone on board when the German Ambassador reached the train gate, closely followed by an attendant carrying his bags. There were, of course, credentials for His Excellency Count Friedrich von der Schulenburg, but no one had thought to make out a pass for the attendant.

The fidelity with which Soviet citizens obey orders is one of their most admirable and, sometimes, most exasperating characteristics. His Excellency, of course, wanted his bags. Courteous regrets were expressed, but certainly the station guards could not be expected to break a ruling, particularly when such important personages were involved!

Hastily, because the train was due to pull out any moment, the German Ambassador decided to make the best of it and carry his bags himself. But how could this be permitted? No papers had been issued authorizing these articles to be carried within the gates.

Zero hour arrived, and Count von der Schulenburg, complaining in two expressive languages that he would not even have a clean shirt in which to disembark at Friedrichstrasse Bahnhof, sprinted for the train and jumped on it as it moved out.

Hurrying through the moving train, he at last found Molotov in an observation car, beginning to worry about the nonappearance of the Ambassador. As soon as the Commissar understood the difficulty he issued an order. Immediately, not only the diplomatic train, but all trains coming in or out of the station on near-by tracks were stopped, and in twelve minutes a trouble engine had brought up the German Ambassador's luggage.

During these last weeks of Russo-German peace, Erskine and I were living in a plain but comfortable room on the top floor of the old National Hotel. It was much like any European hotel room, but the service was greatly improved over Moscow hotel service as I remembered it nine and ten years ago. The bathroom plumbing worked, which it had not always done during the Five-Year Plan, and I was pleased to see small cakes of soap supplied daily with the fresh linen, for soap had been an almost unobtainable luxury in earlier years. At that time such efforts were being made to bring machinery from abroad that consumers' goods were forced to sink to a low ebb.

Our windows looked over Gorky Street, which is the Fifth Avenue of Moscow. It was a very different-looking Gorky Street from the narrow alley which I remembered from ten years ago. Whole rows of buildings had been pushed back on rollers to make an extremely wide thoroughfare, and modern office buildings and new shop fronts gave the effect of a complete face-lifting program.

From our windows we could see the names of a block of shops; there was a Cheese Shop, a Champagne Store, a Children's Store, with toys and frocks and suits designed for little boys and girls. Next to it was a new shop of which Muscovites were very proud. It was the Ice-Cream Parlor. We found that Eskimo Pies, which the Russians liked particularly because they considered them a symbol of Western culture, could be purchased there. But the store to which we paid the most frequent visits was the Dietetics Shop. Just inside the entrance was a door leading to the office of a doctor, who could be consulted free of charge by ailing customers who wished advice on diet. In the intervening years between the comparative famine of my last visits and the comparative plenty of this one, the Russians had discovered the vitamin and pursued it with unbridled enthusiasm.

While we were happily free from those ailments which made shopping at the Dietetics Shop necessary, it was interesting to see the array on sale. There were partially cooked meats and specially blended salads, prepared for people with specific diseases. There were thirty-two kinds of breads with various ingredients omitted or included for sufferers from ulcers, diabetes, and other illnesses. Then, there was one invalid product which we used to buy. We had discovered that an ordinary chocolate bar, at our disadvantageous rate of exchange, cost us the equivalent of $2.50; but in the Dietetics Shop, where prices were kept low for the benefit of invalids, their specially prepared excellent chocolate cost only thirty-five cents. So we became steady purchasers of diabetics' chocolate.

During our early weeks in Moscow we had many visitors and we made many Russian friends. We were singularly fortunate in the kinds of contacts we had with the Russian people because it is not easy, as

a rule, for foreigners to mix with Russians. The changes in ideology—
for example, like that which was then going on in regard to the Germans—were too unpredictable to the average Russian for him to want
to take a chance on being seen too much in the company of foreigners.
But our work, my photographs and my husband's writing, gave us a
kind of immunity which was one of our greatest assets in learning to
know the country.

The people we saw most often were members of the Writers' Union.
The assistant to the editor of the foreign-literature department, young
Elisaveta, who spoke almost perfect English, became one of the best
friends I have had in any country. She was small and fragile-looking,
with blue eyes and a cloud of black hair which she held back from
her pale, sensitive face by a narrow ribbon tied Alice-in-Wonderland
style. She had a warm curiosity about everything American and an
almost fanatic patriotism about everything Russian. She went with me
frequently while I took photographs, to act as interpreter. Each photographic expedition became at the same time a Russian lesson, for I was
trying hard to increase my Russian vocabulary. I could understand
short phrases, but I wanted to learn to follow longer conversations.

Erskine was busy collecting material for the book he planned to
write and he often was accompanied by the young editor, Eugene
Petrov, whom I had met six years before in New York City. Petrov
and his collaborator Ilf, joint authors of a humorous book about the
Soviet Union called *The Little Golden Calf*, had visited America in
1935. They had driven about the United States in a Ford car, studying
what to them was a strange and mysterious land, and returned to Moscow to write a book which they entitled *Little Golden America*. This
book became one of the greatest best sellers the Soviet Union has ever
known. From Siberia to Samarkand, Soviet citizens by the hundreds
of thousands alternately marveled and split their sides with laughter
over the humorous adventures of Ilf and Petrov among those quixotic
and delightful Americans. Since the book was written, Ilf has died,
and Petrov, as stern and grave in appearance as are most humorists, is
now editor of the weekly picture magazine, *Ogonyok*.

Interest in American magazines, whenever the Russians could get
their hands on them, was tremendous. One day when I was unpacking

some delicate pieces of camera equipment, Elisaveta came in and carefully smoothed out the sheets of old magazines that I had wrapped them in. When she saw that they were pages I had torn from *Vogue* and *Harper's Bazaar,* she exclaimed: "We must carry these to the House of Fashion Models."

She took me to visit the House of Fashion Models, on Gorky Street, and we found a fashion show in process of preparation. The chief designer received my old magazine pages eagerly. "We are improving on the American models to suit the needs of Soviet women," she explained. They were also adapting native peasant dress for city wardrobes. This latter effort I found the more commendable of the two, for with the coming of modern clothes, peasant handiwork is too easily lost.

A "bathing costume," as the institute's staff called it, was being prepared for the style show. This was a more radical innovation than the "costume" itself might seem to indicate, for it marked a new interest in mixed bathing. Russians have always been enthusiastic swimmers and have carried on the sport in a monastic segregation of the sexes, in a universal costume which has needed no designing from the House of Fashion Models. However, I could not imagine the weather ever getting warm enough for bathing with or without costumes.

No slacks were designed for the fashion show, a surprising thing in a nation of women workers. The first day I put on mine, for I always wear them if I am planning to do any particularly strenuous work with a camera, Elisaveta exclaimed: "Are you going out in that costume?"

FOOTBALL CROWD AT DYNAMO STADIUM

THE STADIUM is enormous—Ambassador Davies gives its capacity as 100,000, which sounds large but is probably right. A game is played every Sunday all through the spring and summer. It is not true football. Although the Russians use our word football for it, actually it is a kind of soccer. Russians are overwhelmingly proud of this "American" sport which they have adopted. They emulate our love of sports and have placed great emphasis, in their new society, on the development of healthy bodies.

Most interesting point to me is that they have never learned our American way of cheering. I think they would go cheer wild if they ever heard it. The crowd is rather solemn, follows the game intently, and shows its enthusiasm by clapping.

The teams wear brilliant uniforms of glistening satin. The Dynamo team wore bright-blue satin, and the Red Army team wore red tops and short blue pants.

"And why shouldn't I go out in this costume?" I asked.

"Because you will be so stared at," said Elisaveta.

"I've been stared at in so many countries," I replied, "that I might as well add one more to the list."

However, a natural reluctance to be stared at by a whole stadium caused me to abandon my more convenient slacks for a skirt, on the day that I went out to photograph a football game; but my camera attracted an amount of attention that proved painful to me, nevertheless.

On a Sunday shortly before the war, when the Dynamo team played the Red Army, I took my place with the Soviet press photographers. It was with some pride that I brought out my new Speed Graphic, which had been built especially for me by the Folmer Graflex Company in Rochester. It has range and distance finders for five interchangeable lenses, and when a 30-cm. telephoto lens is used, on a $3\frac{1}{4}$ x $4\frac{1}{4}$ film, it is an excellent camera for sports. At least the Rochester technicians and I thought so. But the Soviet photographers all use the Russian Leica. It is made in one of their new factories, and while the lenses are ununiform, the camera itself is fairly well constructed, and the Russians are exceedingly proud of it. Any camera larger than the palm of your hand is something they think an antique. "Why does she use such an old-fashioned camera?" I could hear them say about my beautiful treasure, so newly designed that there was only one in existence.

No photographer likes to look old-fashioned in front of one hundred thousand people. I could not stand up and make a speech to the stands, explaining that in America practically all pressmen use Speed Graphics, and most of them a size larger than mine. It was even worse when, after I had photographed a few touchdowns, I turned my camera on the crowds, who interested me more than the game itself. Their incredulity—that the American photo-correspondent should turn her back on the game—was audible.

I shall probably never be able to redeem my reputation with the football fans, who perhaps think that in the United States we are still using wet plates; but I am happy that before I left the country I was able to vindicate my cameras before the Russian photographers. After watching on repeated occasions, with some amazement, what a peanut flash bulb could do, they requested me to show my equipment before a mass meeting of photographers, and they left in ecstasies over what were, to them, entirely new developments in camera construction and flash synchronization.

But some of the elements of our culture which they chose to borrow surprised me exceedingly, principally the cocktail. Its evolution, by the time it reaches Gorky Street, is something to astonish anyone who had been inadequately trained on Fifty-second Street. The new palatial Koktail Hall serves a Kowboy Koktail which would frighten into a stampede the cowboys after whom it is named. Several layers of brightly colored liqueurs, combined with gin and topped with brandy, are separated by the yolk of an egg into something that looks like a rainbow parfait and tastes like everything behind the counter.

I suggested to Erskine that maybe they were trying to symbolize the dawn of civilization, with a rising sun and everything, but he was busy murmuring under his breath, "Which came first, the cowboy or the . . . ?"

The Kowboy Koktail has a little cousin, The Beacon, also designed like a prism: a layer of chartreuse below the egg yolk and an inch of brandy above. These masterpieces are swallowed in one gulp (it was one gulp or not at all, I discovered) by actresses, literati, and Red Army soldiers on leave, to the tune of four rubles and ten kopecks a cocktail, or ninety cents. But these evidences of foreign culture are discarded by most Russians for vodka, which tastes like kerosene until you get used to it but usually turns out to be the best idea after all.

During those prewar weeks, whether we were attending a writers' banquet with Petrov, or whether I was photographing schools and factories with members of the staff of VOKS, or whether I was just walking along the streets or sitting in a little restaurant with Elisaveta, I noticed that the jokes people told were beginning to take on a political significance. I have often thought that one can tell more about what the people are thinking by the anecdotes that they tell than any other way. Many of these stories were aimed at Hitler.

In one of their favorite anecdotes, Hitler goes to the edge of the English Channel and stands there looking longingly across the water. He decides that the problem is too much for him and summons the

oldest rabbi in the countryside, who, he believes, can give him expert advice.

Hitler explains his problem, and the rabbi says, "Oh, that's not so difficult. Moses had the same problem three thousand years ago."

"What did Moses do?" asks the Führer.

"Oh, he solved it very simply," answers the rabbi. "All he did was to pick up a certain stick, strike the waters, and everything was handled."

"That's just what I wanted to know," exclaims Hitler. "Where is that stick?"

And the rabbi replies, "It's in the British Museum."

Another indication of the drift of international relations was a new rule that was passed, forbidding foreigners, even diplomats, from traveling outside Moscow without a government permit. This meant that even members of the diplomatic corps could not travel down to

---

KOWBOY KOKTAIL
(Pronounced Covboy: there is no true w in the Russian alphabet)

KOKTAIL HALL is a surprising innovation of Gorky Street, the Fifth Avenue of Moscow. The Russians are very proud of it, and aside from its most obvious attractions it serves the only really good coffee in Moscow. The American cocktail idea is new and exciting to Russians, although nothing will ever displace vodka, which is drunk at all parts of a meal, but mainly before, as we would drink cocktails. The proper way to drink vodka is in thimble-sized glasses, holding in your left hand a thick slice of black bread spread with plenty of butter and caviar, which are supposed to absorb the alcohol. Vodka must be downed in one gulp. The Kowboy must also be downed in one gulp as that is the only way to handle the egg. It costs about ninety cents.

Kowboy Koktail is prepared in the following sequence:

1. apricot liqueur
2. benedictine
3. egg yolk
4. gin
5. cognac (a special kind, with pepper)

The barmaid, whose hands are shown, is Olga Alexievna Vakalina, earns five hundred rubles a month. Her husband is an engineer earning eight hundred and fifty rubles a month. They live in a flat for which they pay forty rubles monthly. Both of these are good salaries.

Koktail Hall is a tall, white-marble-pillared place with an American type of bar (it is a new experience for Russians to sit on bar stools), with a red carpet, great windows looking out on Gorky Street, and a winding marble staircase. It is still open despite war, though less well attended. The huge windows are partly blocked up with sandbags, and the outsides of the sandbags have been boarded up to prevent the snow sifting in and freezing there. The coatman at the door adds an air of elegance, with his uniform and great whiskers.

Another variety of egg-yolk cocktail is The Beacon. Both Beacon and Kowboy look as though they were painted by Dali to represent the sun coming up.

the Black Sea for a vacation without a special permit, which was not often granted. This annoyed the diplomatic colony at first, but soon they guessed that it was a measure aimed at the Germans, to keep them from seeing too much.

However, it was essential for us to break through this regulation if we were going to do our work properly, and with the help of the Writers' Union and VOKS, which felt it was all to the good to permit us to do a thorough reporting job of their country, in words and pictures, we were given permission to travel. Early in June we left for an extended trip through the wheat fields of the Ukraine, factories in Kharkov, Rostov, the Donbas Coal Region, the Caucasus, and the Black Sea.

CHAIRMAN D. V. NERIVNY, HEAD OF THE SOVIET OF COLLECTIVE FARM "105"

THIS FARM, near Kharkov, was named after 105 peasants who were killed fighting the invading Germans in 1918. When the German invasion of 1941 occurred, Chairman Nerivny called on the members of the collective to use all their forces to speed the harvest and resist the invaders.

By his side is Chief Milkmaid Nititchenka. On the table is a prize goose, mounted in a glass case, and on the walls are certificates from the government and from various agricultural exhibitions, testifying to the excellence of the work done by Collective 105.

Collective-farm workers are rewarded according to the number of their workdays per year. In the beginning of the collective-farm movement, all shared equally, the industrious and the lazy. This brought about a radical change by Stalin providing that workers be paid according to the amount of work done.

The working day is an arbitrary measurement, based on an average day's work; the superior workers do more and earn more. Chief Milkmaid Nititchenka does 620 working days, produces 400,000 liters of milk a year from her cows. One of her cows gave 8000 liters in a single year, and she was decorated for the high production of her fine cow.

Chairman Nerivny does 860 working days a year. Pay is partly in products which vary depending on the harvest, and a small part in money. For example:

Milkmaid's pay (most of them work from 500 to 550 days): four and a half kilograms of grain for each working day, plus a specified amount of vegetables and sunflower seeds. (Sunflower seeds are valued in the Soviet Union for oil; and peasants chew them, spitting out the seeds.) These amounts are voted by the local soviet of the collective.

In addition to these goods each milkmaid receives one and a half rubles per working day. However, in the Moscow area this pay in hard money ranges between eleven and fourteen rubles.

The products they receive as pay may be consumed or sold. Each district has its farmers' bazaar, busiest on Sundays, where collective farmers gather to sell their products and buy store goods.

Chairman Nerivny is a specialist on insecticides. "We used to have so many grasshoppers," he said, "that when they sat on the railroad tracks the trains couldn't pass. Now the aviation is against them, and we have liquidated the grasshoppers."

It seemed advisable to have Russian traveling companions, as our limited knowledge of the Russian language was hardly adequate for such a trip, and we asked Petrov and Elisaveta to come along. We were delighted when they were able to arrange to come with us.

A crowd of Soviet writers saw us off at the station with baskets of wine, vodka, chocolates, and packages of fresh caviar to eat on the train.

As the train pulled out of the station, Elisaveta took me aside. There were two compartments, and she felt a conference was in order.

"How shall we divide up?" she asked. "We two girls together, or what?"

"What is your preference?" I inquired.

"Preference doesn't enter into it," she said, using the phrase I had heard before in the Soviet Union. "An interpreter is a sexless person."

"In that case, I have a preference," I said. "I'd like to stay with my husband."

And so it was arranged.

CHAPTER 5

Way Down South in Georgia

AN UNNAMED Mason and Dixon's line separates Georgia, in the south, from Great Russia. Georgia was the last of the major republics to come into the Union of Soviet Socialist Republics, and its people are independent and proud. They have the same superiority in their attitude toward Russian northerners that our old Southern families have toward Yankees. The large-eyed, handsome Georgian people show the touch of their sunny climate: they sing more and joke oftener than their countrymen to the north, and their southern hospitality is fabulous.

In 1932 I had ridden on horseback through the Caucasus, accompanied by a group of Georgian soldiers and commissars. As we rode, they taught me a song which the Georgians have been singing for many years; the words of the chorus are, "Mamma, I want to go to America, to bring back an American girl who will come and sit beside you." It was unprecedented for them to have an American girl to sing it to; therefore, this fact warranted celebration. Every time we came to a new village, we dismounted and sang the song over the local wine. Each district in Georgia makes its own wine, of which it is justly proud, and which is drunk not from glasses, but from wine horns that are drained at one gulp. Whenever a toast is proposed, the toastmaster and the person to whom the toast is addressed must drain their wine horns, letting the last drop drip out on the thumbnail to show that the horn has been emptied. After the song to the American girl had been sung, with many improvised verses, and in the elaborate barbershop harmony of which the Georgians are masters, the toasting over wine horns began. Since I was their guest, toasts were addressed, not only to me, but to my father and my mother, my aunts, my uncles, my grandparents, and to my husband-of-the-future. Politeness demanded that I down a horn after each toast. This quantity of wine horns was only possible because it was spread out, usually, over the greater part of the day and accompanied by huge wooden platters of *shashlik* (lamb cut up and roasted on a skewer) served with rice and pomegranate seeds. Usually it was sundown by the time my hosts reached the final toast: to the husband they hoped I would have.

And now, after nine years, I had returned with that husband. The fact that he was also a Georgian was a never-ending source of inspiration to the makers of toasts. Parallels between the Georgia of Russia and the Georgia of America were recited in improvised verse, were sung in barbershop harmony, were celebrated in liquids both golden and red, dry and sweet, still and sparkling. As our excursion was conducted by the local Writers' Union, our escorts included the leading poets of Georgia, who turned their considerable talents toward rhyming every comparative feature between that "Paradise" of America and that "Garden Spot" of the Soviet Union. Both Georgias grew cotton. Both were famous for corn and oranges. Both had golden sunshine. Both produced beautiful women. But, best of all, both Georgias were noted as the birthplaces of the greatest writers in the land.

I whispered that *Tobacco Road* had never seen anything like this, but Erskine whispered back that they were just a lot of Georgia crackers here, same as back home.

Erskine, who likes to learn about a country by the see-but-don't-be-seen method, succeeded in being as inconspicuous as a presidential candidate on a campaign tour. Nothing was too much to do for Amerikanski Kaldvell. Whenever he thought he had drunk the last toast and consumed the last feast, and could be permitted to vanish into the obscurity of a disinterested observer, a new committee of honored writers wearing the Order of Lenin and the Badge of the Red Banner would rise up out of the earth and thrust bouquets of flowers into his reluctant arms, and another banquet would appear, spread out on a table under the trees as though it had grown out of the fertile Georgian soil. This happened even at breakfast time, for it is a Georgian practice to break one's fast with small glasses of vodka instead of orange juice.

Their attentions reached a climax when they discovered that Erskine had broken his little toe. My husband will never forgive me for letting them find out about it. He had broken it one night when we reached the little hotel where we were staying in the mountains, after a day spent visiting the vineyards of the enormous state farms near Zinandali. Samplers had been drawn from barrels of each variety of wine in the great wine cellars, and it was only natural that when we got home Erskine should walk right into the bedstead. His toe, however, was healing rapidly and didn't hurt him very much.

It was a few days after Erskine's abrupt meeting with the bedstead that we were taken to visit a group of rest homes in the North Caucasus, where the workers who have shown special efficiency in filling their factory quotas were given vacations as a reward. We had stopped at Mineralnye Vody, in a sanatorium for the Baku oil workers, when I let out the news about my husband's toe. The sanatorium was as full of specialists as a baseball crowd is of peanuts. It seemed a shame to waste all this science when my husband had a broken toe, and I said so. Erskine's reaction made me glad that Reno wasn't handy, but everything was forgotten in the bustle that ensued. Thermometers were thrust simultaneously under his arm and under his tongue. His pulse was taken, and he was tapped with hammers. An X ray was made of all ten toes, his shinbones, and his kneecaps, and the laboratory did not miss the opportunity to look at his lungs and watch all four chambers of his heart. And, as I shall never forget as long as I live, they placed him in a wheel chair.

After two days tucked in the wheel chair on a balcony facing the mountains, Erskine was able to escape from the ministrations to his little toe, and we went on to Tbilisi,* deciding that we must flee the hospitality of the North Caucasus. My husband and I make poor visiting firemen on a trip meant for work. Too many banquets in the middle of the day are hard for me, particularly, to take with good grace: a point is soon reached where all I can do is count the hours of sunlight lost, and suffer. When the toasts begin, too, I have to pray for strength to be able to focus a camera after the last wine horn is emptied.

At Tbilisi we spent several days which were fairly productive of work. In the morning we usually divided forces. Eugene Petrov took my husband off to talk with writers and other people, as Erskine was

* Tiflis, the capital of Georgia, is now officially designated throughout the U.S.S.R. by its Georgian name, Tbilisi.

busy collecting material for his book; and Elisaveta accompanied me while I took pictures in near-by wheat fields and villages. Once we went to Gori, thirty miles away, and photographed the shrine which has been newly erected in honor of Stalin's birthplace. On these trips, I practiced my new Russian words with Elisaveta; and she, fascinated with such expressions as "tear jerker," "cracked ice," and "sob sister," studied American slang. When we came back to the hotel, Petrov and I compared notes to see who had learned the most new words during the day, for he was also trying to increase his English vocabulary.

The Georgian newspapers began breaking out with a lot of translations of Caldwell short stories, and we had great fun picking out the names of Erskine's characters in Georgian letters, which are much different from the Russian alphabet and closely resemble Arabic characters. On our last evening in Tbilisi, a large meeting was held with Georgian writers and poets who wanted Caldwell to tell them about the current work of American writers. Their questions showed them to be

---

REST HOME FOR LOCOMOTIVE WORKERS AT SOCHI ON THE BLACK SEA

REST HOMES are a very special Soviet institution where workers go for vacations. Each home is a sanatorium, complete with doctors, specialists, laboratories for taking X rays, and solariums for sun-baking on the roof. The Soviet government is very careful about the health of its workers and gives each one a vacation varying from one to two months during peacetime. Anyone with a tendency toward tuberculosis, heart trouble, and so on is sent to a sanatorium where he is treated and watched.

The dressiest of the rest homes are rewards for the most efficient workers. Probably many exist which are infinitely more modest than this one. The most elegant are in the Caucasus or Crimea or on the Black Sea. Workers who overfulfill their quotas do not have to pay transportation or even the rates charged by the homes. These are paid for by their trade-unions. The unions also pay or help pay for a selected number of workers who have large families and could not afford otherwise to bring them along. Besides the locomotive workers' rest home there were other sanatoria at Sochi: one for Arctic workers (scientists and meteorologists), one for coal miners, one for newspaper employees of *Pravda*, and the largest of all for the Red Army. Others than employees of these industries may still vacation there at regular rates. Artists, writers, and actors will often choose their own favorite spots. Stalin has a rest home of his own in Sochi as well as in other parts of the Caucasus.

Union members pay at their own rest homes in proportion to their salaries. Outsiders pay 1300 rubles ($260) a month, which covers any treatment that may strike their fancy. This makes the homes available to artists, writers, and other people high up in government service.

Anyone who comes for a night must have his temperature taken and a brief physical examination to make sure he is not bringing in any contagious diseases. The Russians are crazy about vitamins, sun baths, and sea baths, and have gone hygiene mad.

surprisingly familiar with contemporary American literature, some of which has been translated into the Georgian language.

The next morning, we boarded a plane at Tbilisi, and the group of poets and authors of the Writers' Union of Georgia, who had been our guides, saw us off. We flew over spectacularly beautiful mountain ranges until we came down in the midst of tropical vegetation by the Black Sea. It was, had we known it, the last civilian flight to be made in the Soviet Union. The next day all civil planes were withdrawn from service. Upon landing at the resort town of Sukhumi,* we went swimming, coeducationally and in "bathing costumes," along the black gravel shores of the surprisingly salty Black Sea.

The next day was the twenty-second of June, and it brought an event of such magnitude that the whole course of our work was changed.

It was Sunday, and there was a peculiar tension in the atmosphere. Crowds of peasants gathered in knots around the loudspeaker in the public square. An important announcement from the government was expected, no one knew just when. (All over the Soviet Union, dance music, news, and government proclamations come over the government-controlled radio through a loudspeaker which blares out constantly in the center of each small town.)

We drove from one village to another, through the tropical vegetation that bordered the Black Sea, and in each public square stood knots of people, restlessly grouped about the loudspeakers, waiting uneasily for they knew not what.

We went back to our hotel and had tea, and at four o'clock Petrov went out to the square again to see if the news had come through. When he came back, Elisaveta ran down to meet him. For a long time we could see them from our balcony, walking back and forth in the garden below.

"I think the war has caught up with us," remarked Erskine.

"If it really has, I wish they'd come up and tell us something," I said.

"It's their war," said Erskine. "Let them talk it over first."

When they came into our room they were smiling, not with joy but with relief.

Molotov had spoken from the Kremlin. Before daybreak, German

---

* The Georgian Sukhumi is now considered correct usage throughout the Soviet Union, rather than the Russian form, Sukhum.

planes had flown over the Soviet border and dropped bombs on Kharkov, Kiev, and other Soviet cities. Troops were being rushed to the border, and the indications were that the most intense warfare in history had begun.

We drove from one collective farm to another that afternoon, and everywhere there were scenes of the most enthusiastic patriotism. Collective farmers were pledging their support, their work, their lives, to victory of their country. But everywhere there was one question on everyone's lips: where did Great Britain stand?

How could they, as Soviet citizens, guess what would be the policy of capitalistic nations? Could all this be a frame-up between England and Germany? Financial interests are powerful, the collective farmers kept reminding one another, and might swing the tide against the will of the people. The Russian people admired the brave citizens of England, who had showed so much courage during the bombings, and if they were to be together in the struggle it could mean much.

It was almost dusk when we reached a large citrus-fruit collective farm on a hill overlooking the Black Sea. The collective farmers had gathered in a clearing in an orange grove, where a loudspeaker had been mounted. Just as we arrived, the amplifier blared out a second announcement from the government: Churchill had made a speech, and the translation was being read from the Kremlin. Churchill had stated that Great Britain would stand with the Soviet Union to meet their common enemy.

I saw tears of joy stream down the cheeks of those farmers. "With Great Britain and the Soviet Union together against the invader," they began to shout, "the bloody Fascists will be crushed."

We packed our bags and drove from Sukhumi to Sochi, where we hoped to get a train back to Moscow. We were fortunate that the head of the district Party Committee had been able to lend us a car. All along the way, whenever we paused for petrol or water, dozens of people pressed up to us, wishing to engage our car if we could spare it. They were all trying to find transportation from their vacation spots so they could get back to enlist.

In the jewel-like resort of Sochi, steeply banked above the sea, the rest homes were emptying rapidly. Its principal street, twisting through flowering groves and over cliffs, was lined with resthouses: the sana-

toria of the Arctic workers, of the Donbas coal miners, of the *Pravda* newspaper staff; the Red Army House, and the rest home for locomotive workers. This last, where we stayed, was a Pompeian, pillared structure, run according to the plan we had found in Mineralnye Vody—giving reduced rates or free vacations to *otlichniki*, the most efficient workers. But the *otlichnik* locomotive workers were leaving as fast as they could get room on the trains.

The Red Army House had been emptied before we arrived. It is a colossal glass and concrete structure, startlingly modern, and with a private funicular to shuttle vacationing soldiers down the dizzy grade to the beach. Now its pair of little cars stood idle on their sloping tracks.

Reaching the station, we found a crowd that pressed about it for blocks. Petrov forced his way into the throng, and the fact that he was able to return with tickets was evidence of the influential place which writers are accorded in the Soviet Union.

Our two-day train trip back to Moscow was an hour-by-hour struggle to get news. During each stop, we tried to listen to the station radio, but troop trains roaring in the opposite direction drowned out the loudspeakers. In the larger stations, Petrov would be out on the platform before the train stopped, trying to get a newspaper. But the papers vanished, the instant they appeared, into hundreds of outstretched hands.

The dining cars had been taken off all trains, and at each stop we bought whatever food we could find, usually black bread and cucumbers. While we shopped, during what minutes were available, Elisaveta tried to collect news by word of mouth. She would approach groups of soldiers first and then civilians and then run back into the

---

COLLECTIVE FARMERS HEAR WAR NEWS

SHORTLY AFTER the declaration of war, Erskine and I were at the collective farm, Lenin's Path. This picture was taken when the radio announcement came through of a British-Soviet mutual-assistance pact. The farmers were overjoyed. When the provisions were read they said, "The great nation of Britain fighting side by side with our glorious Red Army is a very good thing. Together we will annihilate the Fascist bandits."

We had dinner with these farmers—the meal consisting of jumbo strawberries, big hothouse cucumbers, fresh black bread, plenty of butter, and delicious sour cream.

train to give us what scraps she had found out. The Germans were bombing points in Bessarabia, attempting to break through to Odessa. At the next station, she would hear that they had been repulsed but were reported bombing fortresses near Leningrad.

At Rostov, a long stop, she walked up and down the platform with an old man in a Santa Claus beard, until the train started; whereupon she ran around to everybody in our car to tell them that during the first three days of the war the Soviets had brought down three hundred enemy planes.

Trainloads of naval guns and sailors passed us, headed south toward the Sea of Azov. Freight cars packed with motorbusses rolled by, directed west, to expedite the movement of troops on the front. A long line of cars carrying tractors—of the charcoal-burning type, to save gasoline—were being unloaded to hasten the harvest in the Kuban region, where the rye was growing as tall as a man's head.

At many stations along the way, we picked up copies of Churchill's speech, translated into Russian, Georgian, and Ukrainian and evidently printed by the hundreds of thousands. And at last, when we were within a few hours of Moscow, we saw our first newspaper. We still had not been able to buy one, but soldiers in a troop train moving in the opposite direction on the next track passed their paper through the window of our train. The newspaper traveled through our entire train, where it was read aloud in every car. Some dispatches were read more than once. These favorite items were cables of sympathy from various organizations in America, expressing friendship for the Soviet people and admiration for the way they had met the Fascist attack. As each of these cables was reread, the whole carful of Russians would burst into cheers. "With the friendship of the great United States," they cried, "and the solidarity of Britain, we will drown the Fascist head-hunters in their own blood."

We reached Moscow in a pouring rain the evening of June 27—the old chilly weather back again. Petrov asked us to forgive him for leaving us to rush out to the country. He had left his wife and two children at his *dacha* while we took our trip and he wanted to be sure that they were safe. Elisaveta hurried off to her apartment to find her mother.

At the National Hotel we were reinstalled, not in our old room, but in the vast corner suite that had been occupied, during the time of the nonaggression pact, by the leading German trade representative in Moscow. The hotel had previously been full of Germans, who had been seen at their best gloating over meat soups and saucers of sour cream and of butter in the hotel dining room.

The suite we inherited from the Nazis possessed a czarist magnificence that dazzled us. Cupids swung from the chandeliers. Cherubs winged their way across the murals on the ceiling. The rooms were so filled with tables covered with vases, lamps with china bases, inkstands of Ural Mountain stone, and ash trays mounted on the backs of lions that I wondered how our Teutonic predecessor in all his plumpness had made his way about without knocking off an art treasure at every step. In the adjoining bedroom the immense bed was piled high with quilts of yellow satin. The bathroom was a vast tiled cave. The drawing room was equipped with grand piano and great white bear rug, and its finest feature was a gold-fluted pillar bearing on its summit a blue cloisonné vase with the picture of Napoleon.

It was a month later when we discovered that we could swing Napoleon around on a socket joint and reveal the Empress Josephine on the other side. Erskine adjusted the vase after each military communiqué. When the invaders were doing well, he allowed Napoleon to face the world. When the Russians seemed to be beating the enemy back, he turned Bonaparte's face to the wall.

All this splendor cost us no more than we had been paying for the narrow room we had occupied before we left. Ninety-six rubles— eighteen dollars at the current rate of exchange—had seemed exorbitant when we didn't have a grand piano and Napoleon thrown in. But when I walked through the double doors and stepped out on the balcony, I called back to Erskine, "This balcony alone is going to earn that eighteen dollars a day when I get a camera out on it."

Opposite us was the Kremlin, Lenin's Tomb, and the Red Square— a magnificent Moscow panorama. If the *Luftwaffe* did any work on the Kremlin, I knew we would have the best viewpoint in the city to photograph it. Against the lemon-yellow night sky stood the onion-shaped domes of St. Basil's and the five-pointed stars which topped the Kremlin towers. These stars were of ruby glass holding lighted lamps in peace-

time, but now the city lay in complete blackout. Above this silhouette
of domes and towers the sky gleamed unnaturally bright. It was the
time of the "white nights."

I went back into the room. "Do you realize this hotel is so old it
trembles every time a streetcar goes past?" said Erskine. "What's it
going to be like when they start pounding the Kremlin?"

"Perhaps its very flexibility will help," I ventured optimistically.

The head chambermaid came in to show us how to adjust our blackout curtains, and as she chatted we learned that our hotel suite possessed certain elements of history. Trotsky had stood on our balcony,
addressing the unheeding Trade-Unions at the time of his fall from
power. Lindbergh had stayed in our suite during his visit to Moscow.
(Later, after we moved out of it, Lord Beaverbrook moved in, while
attending sessions of the American-British Economic Conference.) But
its most recent occupant had been the chief delegate of the "Fascist
bandits," the chambermaid stated specifically.

"When did the Germans leave?" I asked.

"It was an odd thing," she said. "They had been checking out of
the hotel all week, and Saturday night they were all gone but two, that
thin Gestapo one and the fat one who had these rooms. At seven in the
morning they went running out of the hotel without their suitcases and
even without their breakfast. We wondered where they were going so
fast, and later, when we heard Comrade Molotov over the radio, we
knew that we would never see them again."

"Did they pay their bills?" I inquired.

"No," she replied. "Not a ruble from those Fascist reptiles."

CHAPTER 6

The First Days of War

I WOKE up the next morning to find that the military authorities had issued a ukase proclaiming that anyone seen with a camera should be shot on sight. Here was I, facing the biggest scoop of my life, an opportunity so great that a photographer would conceive it only in an opium dream: the biggest country enters the biggest war in the world, and I was the only photographer, on the spot, representing any publication and coming from any foreign country.

The anticamera law was decidedly inconvenient. But I had only to reflect on the supreme convenience of being within the country's borders at all, at a time when all sorts of other news photographers were hammering vainly on the gates, to be willing to face almost any difficulty, even that of shotguns. I did think, however, that to have to face German bombing planes and Russian firing squads on the same side of the same war was rather a lot for even a photographer to do.

But a greater inconvenience even than the military law was the fact that we were supposed to be evacuated. When a war breaks out, an ambassador always has to evacuate somebody, and there was hardly anybody left but us. All the embassy wives and half the embassy staff had been sent out even before the invasion took place. Mrs. Steinhardt had boarded the last crowded plane to Stockholm, with only that percentage of her wardrobe which she was able to wear directly on her own little figure, and her worried husband was still hoping that some miraculous way might open up to get her suitcases to her.

The telegrams of distress that began coming in from *Life* magazine in New York made me guess that our evacuation had already been reported in the American papers. And yet, surely, I thought, anybody would know that I would start throwing my lenses like hand grenades at anyone who tried to carry me away from such a scoop as this.

When Mr. Steinhardt called us to the embassy, Erskine counseled me, "Don't talk too much. Let the Ambassador feel that he's doing his duty. The less we argue, the better chance we have."

The Ambassador warned us that it was his duty to protect the lives of American citizens. "No one knows how soon Moscow will be bombed," he said. "And when it begins, the loss of life and the destruction are bound to be terrible. There are still two seats left on the train to Vladivostok. It might be your last chance. Later, after bombing starts, there may be no means of getting you out. You may be trapped. Yes, I really have to point out that to stay will be to risk the greatest danger."

"Don't forget we came here to work, Mr. Ambassador," we reminded him.

"However," he continued after a meaningful pause, "if after thinking over the perils to which you are exposing yourselves, and if after seriously weighing the dangers involved, it is your considered decision to stay, our embassy will help you in every . . ."

He had no chance to finish, for within the next instant the United States Envoy and Plenipotentiary Extraordinary found himself being kissed by a photographer.

We tripped out of the embassy and walked back to our hotel, and as we passed through Arbat Square the marquee of a cinema theater caught our eye. When we had left on our trip for Georgia, the theater had been playing *The Great Waltz* to capacity audiences which had thronged in for the rare chance to see an American moving picture. Today a long queue waited for seats, and the title on the marquee was *Alexander Nevsky*. Eisenstein's anti-Nazi picture had been brought out of its two-year retirement.

As we entered the hotel, we found Elisaveta waiting for us. She had come to tell us there were meetings being held all over the city. From the lobby we could hear a roar of voices sounding down the stairwell, and we hurried up to the second floor, where, in the large dining room, a clamorous meeting of chambermaids, chefs, and waiters was in progress. The speakers were jumping up on the tables, and the long room rang with oratory.

The hall maid for our floor was shouting: "When we heard the words of Comrade Molotov about the barbarous attack on our country, we remembered the saying: 'They that take the sword shall perish by the sword.'"

The cheering of the hotel workers drowned out her voice now, and the second-floor supervisor leaped to a table, snatching a feather duster from the nearest chambermaid and waving it over her head until she could be heard. "We will wipe Hitler's fiends off the earth," she called, waving her feather duster as though to show how it was to be done. "The hangman hordes shall perish!"

A resolution was passed providing that the women workers of the hotel would take over the tasks of the men in addition to their own, whereupon the hall porter jumped to a table and called for volunteers to the Red Army down to the last waiter and dishwasher, at which the male personnel broke into cries that resolved into a chant: "We shall meet the Fascist bandits with a wall of fire."

"Let's get out and see things," I said, and we went out into the streets. We were swept along with the throng until we reached the October Railroad Station. The freight yard was jammed with locomotive engineers and mechanics, rallying for active and reserve service in the army. A red-draped tribune had been hastily set up at the end of the yard, and a brakeman was calling through a megaphone, "We volunteer to fight not only for the life of our fatherland but for the whole of progressive humanity."

In the Red Night Rubber Factory we found the women volunteering to take over the work so that the men could go to the front. At the Stalin Auto Works the pressure of volunteers was so great that a restraining speech was being made, explaining the necessity of keeping key men at their jobs until women could fully take over the production. The head of the pattern shop, who had been requested to stay at his post, jumped to the platform and shouted, "The motors we turn out shall be better than those of our enemy, for ours are made by free men and theirs by slaves."

During those first dramatic weeks of the war, you could go into any factory, and side by side with almost every man there was a woman standing. Sometimes it was his wife, sometimes it was his sweetheart;

or it might be a woman brought from a less important industry; but the man was teaching that woman his job. Realizing that it is not an easy thing to take over a skilled job, the women were going to night school to increase their factory technique. They took great pride in keeping production up to the level that had been maintained by their husbands and brothers.

And the women, who wanted so much to go to the front, too, dramatized their jobs as only Russians would think of doing, by referring to their tools and industrial processes with military names. Even in the meat-packing plant, the girls were happier if they could refer to a "spearhead attack" on their masses of beef and if they could speak of the cutting operations along the conveyor belt as a "bayonet advance."

Soviet citizens, who have always taken the principle of work earnestly, undertook the work of defense with the utmost seriousness. Everyone began studying to do something new or something better. Salesgirls were learning to be truck drivers, schoolteachers were studying shooting. I talked with a group of algebra teachers who were learning to operate and to clean machine guns. Factory workers of all kinds were studying in their spare time to be nurses. I visited a cinema theater which had been turned into a school for delegations from apartment houses, who were organizing classes in their homes for instruction in various defense tactics. In the first-aid section an anatomy class was studying a very animated-looking skeleton. At a signal from the director they began bandaging up each other's heads with an amount of energy that would have bound up a whole wounded army. Near by, a group of high-school girls were studying the internal con-

---

"SANITARY TRAINING," SOVIET EQUIVALENT OF FIRST AID

THE "COMMANDER," shown giving a bandaging demonstration, is Klavdia Hakina, twenty-one years old. The student being bandaged is Sidjykina, nineteen years old, who works in a scientific laboratory.

This is one of the home-defense schools established at the beginning of the war to give instruction to instructors. These students are being trained to lead the work of their apartment units. The instructors receive forty hours of training and on alternate nights teach what they have learned to the folks back home. These, in turn, must take a minimum of fifteen hours in first aid, fire fighting, and other defense subjects.

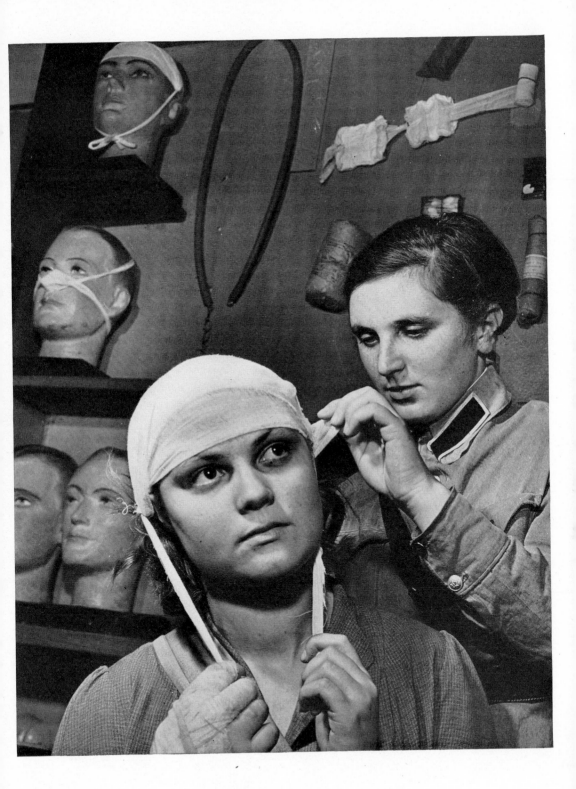

struction of a fire extinguisher, in a room lined with ladders, fire hose, buckets, and fire helmets.

Children patrolled the streets at twilight to warn householders who allowed threads of light to leak through their blackout curtains. It was the special function of children to keep sandbags and water pails constantly filled in case of incendiary raids. The Young Pioneers volunteered to do the marketing and help with the housework for the many women who had gone into the factories to replace the men who had left for the front.

Petrov and Elisaveta dropped in every day to tell us what was going on. Petrov had desired keenly to go to the front, but he had been requested to stay at his desk and take over the editorship of a second publication. His office was in the *Pravda* organization, and in addition to the magazine *Ogonyok*, of which he was editor, he now had charge of *Crocodile*, a humorous weekly. He always had anecdotes and bits of news to tell us before they were published, valuable material for Erskine's writing; often he brought in colleagues from the Russian newspapers, newly returned from trips to the front, whom Erskine could interview. Petrov had been promised that he could go to the front later.

Elisaveta had a similar ambition. "I just hate medicine," she told me. "I loathe the sight of a bandage. But I'm taking night courses in first aid because I know that's the only way I'll ever get to the front, and I simply have to go."

She took me to visit the medical-training centers which had sprouted

---

CLASSROOM DEMONSTRATION ON THE CONSTRUCTION AND USE OF FIRE EXTINGUISHERS, GIVEN IN THE SCHOOL FOR INSTRUCTORS

THE COMMANDER is Dzelodkov, forty-one years old. His classes frequently wear gas masks, for practice, while listening to lectures. The walls of the classroom are lined with fire-fighting equipment—hose, ladders, boxes for sand, iron pikes, grappling hooks, hammers, and axes. Girls in class are all factory workers taking night courses in antiair-raid defense. Part of their duty is to see that their apartment houses are equipped with the necessary fire-fighting tools, that children keep the water pails and sandbags filled, that each member of the fire brigade knows his or her duty in an emergency.

In addition to learning how to tend the wounded and how to put out fires, these instructors learn how to "behave in shelters," and enforce the necessary discipline: "Don't be frightened, don't cry, don't talk loudly, always sit down."

up at every street intersection, like the corner drugstore. Schoolgirls, housewives, and working women were going to night classes, and the applications for front duty as "medical sisters" were stacking up like mounds of snow. I was glancing through them one night, with Elisaveta looking over my shoulder.

"Why, that's Lenin's adopted daughter," she exclaimed as we came to the name Barbara Alexandrovna Armand.

"I can no longer stay out of the struggle," the letter ran. "I have had a good education and can do either nursing or cultural work at the front. I beg you not to refuse me."

Her wish to serve was granted, I found later, but not to nurse the wounded. She was sent into the country to take care of children who had been evacuated.

Evacuation of children was never announced as a fact, even with the growing tension of German front lines moving steadily closer to Minsk, steadily closer to Smolensk. It was announced that twenty thousand school children were being moved during their summer vacations "for scientific research in the Arctic regions," that fifty thousand youngsters were going on an expedition to central Asia "to make geological surveys."

As the Germans drew closer to Moscow, the streets around the railroad stations were narrowed into lanes by the overflow of thousands of mothers with their children, camped on their sacks of belongings and living within sight of the station gates until space could be found for them on the trains.

When I went into the hotel barbershop for a shampoo and a manicure, I was met with the announcement, "There are no more manicurists left in the city of Moscow."

"Why not?" I asked.

"They have all been sent to the country to take care of the children."

There was no more nail polish either. I brought down my own little bottle of lacquer, which, after its long voyage from America, retained only a small sticky residue in the bottom, and the cashier obligingly helped me to apply it. This became a weekly practice, with mutual benefits, for when she had given me my coat of polish she would dab the brush back into the few drops that remained and apply a coat to her own fingers. In Russia the use of lipstick and nail polish is considered "cultured," but the red capital has only introduced the most flaming shades. The softer tone of "Cyclamen" was quite a novelty for her.

Day after day, underneath our balcony, passed those husbands whose wives had taken over their machines. We used to see them marching to the railway stations en route to the front. Often their womenfolk walked quietly at their sides. The process of volunteering had been stopped for the more efficient procedure of mobilization. Theatrical performers and opera singers who wanted to enlist were not accepted as soldiers but were sent instead to the mobilization offices, where enrollment went on to the tune of arias. As the mobilized groups were moved outward, the concert and theatrical troops followed and continued their entertainment tours right up to the front lines.

No one knew where these front lines were. According to the Soviets they were far to the westward, with small forward thrusts being permitted the Germans only for the purpose of allowing the Soviets to capture the enemy in the pockets thus formed. According to the German radio, to which we foreigners but not Soviet citizens had access, the Nazis were on the outskirts of Smolensk.

"When Smolensk is taken," said Mr. Steinhardt, "the bombing of Moscow will begin, because the Smolensk airport will make a convenient hopping-off point only an hour away." (It turned out later that he was right.)

The war was not quite two weeks old when we went to a garden party at the Spazzo House, the Ambassador's residence. We were attending what was probably the most exclusive reception to be given by any embassy, any time, anywhere. It was exclusive because there were so few Americans in Moscow left to go to it. The kindly Ambassador, worrying over the safety of his small flock of Americans and overworked with detail because of his greatly reduced staff, had still not forgotten that it was the Fourth of July.

A long table was spread under the trees, with bowlfuls of small disks which had become strange to us. Some were marked Sunshine and some NBC. Cocktail sausages were served on toothpicks, and Scotch and soda instead of vodka; but the guests crowded mainly around a big central dish steaming with baked pork and beans. Erskine, who has never become acclimated to raw cucumbers, eaten like apples by Russians all over the Soviet Union, was holding a corner on the sweet pickles.

"There's only one thing that hasn't been served," he told me.

"What's that?" I asked.

"No firecrackers—yet!"

As though the Ambassador had the same thing on his mind he was moving quietly from group to group, calmly saying that all of us should keep our bags packed, ready to leave on two hours' notice. He intimated that the government might leave at any time and that the diplomatic corps had to be ready to follow the government wherever it went. He thought it would be somewhere in Siberia, or possibly Sverdlovsk, or Kazan; no one knew where. There were some who believed that Moscow would crumple like a house of cards when the Germans started bombing the city; undoubtedly, he said, it would be wisest for all foreigners to follow the government. But there was no way of telling whether arrangements would be made to take the journalists along. The city might be too congested, if bombing started, to get to a railway station or airport when the exodus began. It might be impossible to give the warning over the telephone, for something as significant as moving the government would have to be kept strictly secret until it was an accomplished fact: a leakage on the telephone lines could not be risked, a hint would have to be enough. In the meantime we should stick close to our telephones and keep our suitcases packed. And, above all, be prepared to travel light.

Travel light, I thought. Four of my five cameras could be left behind. I would sacrifice all changes of clothes. But that epic hegira must be recorded, and to do so I would have to take some tools. The films and flash bulbs, I would need, and, if we were to be trapped in Siberia for an unknown period, the chemicals and spare parts—these could not be reduced to something light.

I motioned Erskine, who was still hovering over the pork and beans, to the end of the garden, and we discussed the flight plans that were in the air.

"I have a hunch," I said, "that the Caldwell family will never have time to pack suitcases!"

"And I have a hunch," said my husband, "that the Russians are not going to let their city fold up like a pack of cards."

Before leaving the party, I asked the Ambassador: "If we should decide to stay, even if the city risks capture, what then?"

"It's hard to say," he replied. "The next two weeks will tell a lot about whether they are going to be able to stave off the Germans. But if the Germans take the city they will bring their own press along. You won't be able to get permission from the Nazi army of occupation to take pictures when you've been photographing the other side. And in the meantime the destruction of the city will be terrible. You won't be able to do a thing while that goes on—if you come out alive!

"If you can go with the government, you would have a historic set of pictures. But, on the other hand, no one knows when you would be able to get your pictures and yourself out of Siberia."

Erskine and I walked home along the west wall of the Kremlin. Over the wall, swirls of a kind of gray dust were blowing, and charred bits of paper swept down about our feet.

"Why, they must be burning their records!" I exclaimed.

"They must have plenty to burn," Erskine replied, "the way they keep tabs on everyone. I'd like a look at your dossier before they put it in the furnace. It must have been plenty interesting on those three trips you took here before you were married to me!"

When we reached our room the sound of singing brought us out on the balcony. A long column of trucks was streaming below our windows, moving westward up Gorky Street. I counted them as they passed. There were thirty-eight trucks and they held thirty soldiers each. The men were singing the "Internationale."

As the voices died away, the loudspeaker, which was mounted on the corner of the hotel roof directly above our balcony, began blaring out a communiqué. In German-occupied Poland, the report stated, guerrillas hiding under the cover of woods were shooting holes in German gasoline tank cars as they passed along the railways. In some sectors the Russian peasants had heaped burning trees on the tracks to block German artillery trains, and in others the rails were torn up altogether and hidden away in the swamps.

"Fierce fighting," the communiqué concluded, "continued today in the Pskov, Porkhov, Smolensk, and Vitebsk directions."

"In the direction of a sneeze!" I exclaimed. "That's all we know about where the front is."

"We'll know where the front is when it catches up to us," said Erskine. "Or when we take the subway to the last station on the Gorky Street line and find it there."

Then an event took place which raised hopes in the hearts of all journalists. The first press conference was announced. To a member of the fourth estate who has struggled to collect news in this secretive capital, the first press conference ranked in importance with Benjamin Franklin's kite and the maiden voyage of Robert Fulton's steamboat.

The government spokesman, Mr. Solomon A. Lozovsky, Assistant People's Commissar for Foreign Affairs, who worked directly under Molotov, received us in the recently vacated Greek consulate building, which had been renamed the Soviet Union Information Bureau. His pale-blue eyes twinkled at us above a luxuriant chestnut-colored beard. We sat in fragile gold-ornamented chairs around a long red-felt-covered table and were invited to partake of fruit-flavored soda pop and Narzan, a charged water bottled in the Caucasus. When we inquired about the front, Mr. Lozovsky would say, "Where is the front? The front is un-

---

SOLOMON A. LOZOVSKY, THE ASSISTANT PEOPLE'S COMMISSAR FOR FOREIGN AFFAIRS

MR. LOZOVSKY, the government spokesman in charge of press conferences, works directly under Molotov. Witty, clever, he was always ready with a joke when the questions of the press got too explicit. The bigger the news was and the more eager the correspondents were to hear about it, the more time Lozovsky would spend telling us about German propaganda. His favorite pastime was to disprove German claims and call them "just some more lies out of the gossip factory." Of German claims and boasts that they would conquer Moscow he said, "The only way Hitler will ever see the Kremlin is in a photograph."

He has an Old World charm and is very shrewd. Though he speaks good English and excellent French, he conducted his press conferences in Russian—which only a small percentage of the press understood fluently enough to follow. Our secretary, Tatiana, had remarkable speed in translating and writing his words in English for our benefit as he talked. At the end of each conference we were permitted a question period.

Mr. Lozovsky has a reputation in London with the Ministry of Information for being the smartest propaganda dispenser alive. He was popular with the press, although we never could get out of him as much as we wanted to know. Still, we felt he understood the problems of newspapermen and was not afraid to act on our behalf.

stabilized." When we sounded him out on the claims from Berlin, he would reply with the good old Russian expression, "Just another fried duck out of the rumor kitchen."

But still, it was a press conference after all, and we regarded it as the opening of a new era—especially when Mr. Lozovsky invited suggestions from correspondents about how their work could be facilitated. The Japanese correspondent was first with his suggestion. "In as much as ours is such a difficult language," volunteered Mr. Hatenaka, "the Japanese correspondents should be given the news dispatches two hours ahead of the other newsmen. Also it would be well, in the case of our cables, to omit the practice of censorship altogether because of the language difficulty."

Mr. Lozovsky, we were soon to discover, possessed a highly developed faculty of listening to this and other requests without committing himself.

Outside of the Foreign Office—Narkomindel, as the Russians called it—a large rusty bathtub had been placed, filled with water in case of incendiary attack. Every time I passed through the Narkomindel courtyard I tried to picture what a similar tub would look like on Pennsylvania Avenue on the front steps of the State Department.

I had reason to pass this particular tub often, for I was making a concentrated attack on the People's Commissariat for Foreign Affairs in the effort to get my cameras into operation again. Every day for two

---

A PRESS CONFERENCE AT NARKOMINDEL, SOVIET FOREIGN OFFICE

FROM LEFT to right are two men from Reuter's News Agency, a Czech correspondent, Erskine Caldwell, Mr. Lozovsky, Mr. Polgunov, Chief of the Press Department, Henry Shapiro of United Press, and others.

The night this picture was taken, we had been called together in a special evening session to see important documents captured from the German army. Mr. Lozovsky loved captured German documents and he was kind enough to call me and invite me to bring my camera. When I finished with the documents, I turned my camera on the press conference itself and was so absorbed that I did not hear the siren. Mr. Lozovsky laughed and said that that would have to be the last picture. I did not understand why, and suddenly all the correspondents had jumped up and fled before I could guess what was going on. My cameras went with me to the shelter where I took more pictures. The correspondents were envious because I was the only one who was able to go on working. They could get nothing passed in the shelter, even though the three censors were present. Everyone said that the censors couldn't work because they had left their dictionary behind.

weeks I called on various Foreign Office commissars. Sometimes I not only called on them, but telephoned as well. Often, in addition to visits and phone calls, I wrote letters. These communications were prepared both in English and Russian, to facilitate matters, and carbons were submitted to other officials of influence: to the President of VOKS, to the Commissar in charge of Protocol, to the Mayor of the city of Moscow.

The letters began with a sentence something like this: "May I respectfully point out that these are historic times," and continued with all the arguments I could muster in favor of having our great American nation receive an unbiased view of the Soviet Union through the lens of an American photographer.

At last a day came when the resistance of all the commissariats and all the bureaus wore down, as anything will, I suppose, under a continual frontal attack; and on the fifteenth of July, I emerged from the doorway of Narkomindel with a precious little bit of folded pasteboard in my hand, my photographer's "passport." A small child was leaning over the bathtub with a jar of pollywogs in one hand and a tiny turtle in the other, and as I passed he permitted his turtle to go in for a swim. I was so happy that I could have dived in with the turtle.

Our own bathtub, one of the finest in the land, took on an important function. We did not use it for air defense, but turned it into a photographic laboratory. The maids brought me cut-glass salad bowls and

---

GERMAN ARMY DOCUMENTS CAPTURED BY THE RED ARMY

THESE WERE exhibited at Lozovsky's press conference. The one on top gives explicit directions as to when and how to use poison gases.

Part of the page shown reads: "Gas also inflicts great emotional damage because it is hard to estimate the extent of the danger zone. If gas is used by surprise before there is time to put on gas masks it can have great effect."

Document continues with "Preparations for Gas Attack."

In showing us this evidence that the Nazis planned gas attacks Mr. Lozovsky said, "Let these knights of the great highway not think that they alone possess poisonous substances. The Fascist bandits will be annihilated together with their artificial poisons."

At a later press conference Lozovsky startled everyone by saying that "injurious" substances had been released by the Germans in trenches, causing coughing, stomach sickness, and other harmful effects. We could get no details, but evidently some kind of poison gas had been tried out by the German army.

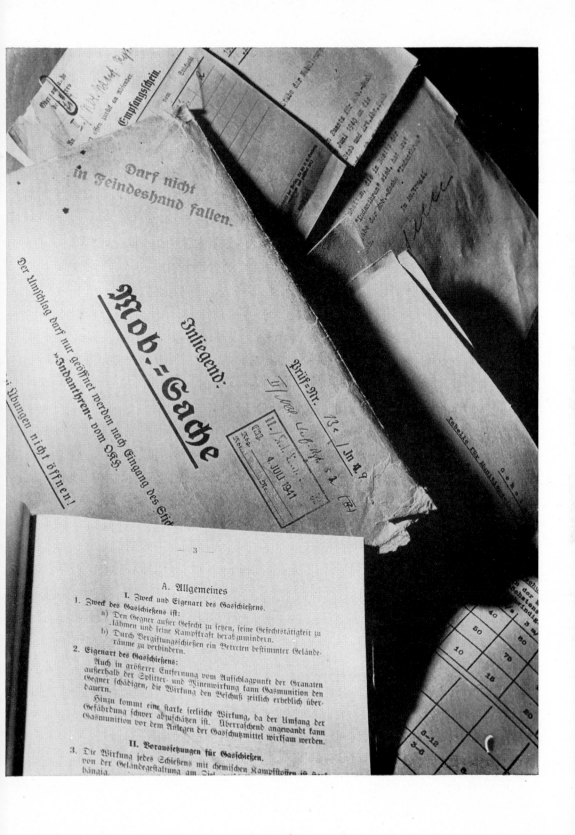

soup tureens to use for developing trays. On Saturday nights, like the good country boy that he is, Erskine would say plaintively, "Don't you think you can clear out the bathtub for a little while?"

During this time we had succeeded in obtaining the unprecedented permission to broadcast "live"—that is, directly into the microphone to America, without making a previous recording to be broadcast from a phonograph. In the month of July I broadcast irregularly,* and Erskine went on the air regularly every other night and every afternoon.

Just before dawn one morning I happened to be leaving the studio after speaking to America for an evening broadcast, which, with a difference of eight hours, meant early morning in Moscow. I was just putting on my hat and coat when I was told that an important speech was coming through in a few minutes from the Kremlin. I walked home sleepily, in the conviction that nothing of real importance could be broadcast at such an hour, and had just stepped through the door of our hotel room when I heard the loudspeaker over the square blaring out. I hurried onto the balcony. From the amplifier mounted on the roof over my head a strong voice spoke out: "Comrades, citizens, brothers and sisters! Men of our army and navy! I am addressing you, my friends!"

Wondering what leading official could be speaking at six in the morning, I ran for the hall porter and brought him out on the balcony.

"Who is that speaking?" I asked.

"The enemy is cruel and implacable," continued the voice. "He is out to seize our lands watered with our sweat, to seize our grain and soil secured by our labor."

The porter was listening like one transfixed. "He has a Georgian accent. Yes, I am sure of it! That is Stalin's voice."

Stalin had not spoken to the people since 1938. "Imagine President Roosevelt giving an unannounced fireside chat before breakfast!" I thought.

I hurried into the bedroom and woke up my husband. The coming night would be his turn on the radio, and I knew he would want to report on the reaction of the people at first hand. When I was finally able to convince him that it really was Joseph Stalin who was making a dawn

* See Chapter 10.

speech, he leaped into his clothes and we hurried into the Red Square.

Small knots of people had stopped near the amplifiers and were listening in dead silence. "A grave danger hangs over our country," Stalin was saying, as though preparing the people for news of losses. "In case of forced retreat of Red Army units, not a single engine must be left to the enemy, not a single railway car, not a single pound of grain or gallon of fuel." Larger and ever-larger crowds gathered around the loudspeakers as the voice continued. My Russian was not good enough to get all that he said, but Stalin spoke slowly and I could catch the drift of the "scorched-earth" tactics which were later to become famous. "Diversionist groups must be organized to blow up bridges, roads, telephone lines, and set fire to forests and stores." As I looked at the determined faces around me I could tell that here were people willing to burn their homes, destroy their crops, give their own lives, before one iota of comfort or help should fall to the enemy. "Our cause is just," concluded the voice. "The enemy must be crushed. We must win."

When he had finished, an old woman standing near us spoke her thoughts aloud, and what she said so manifestly expressed the sentiments of the crowd that it sent Erskine back to the typewriter to use her words as a lead for his evening dispatch. "He works so hard!" the old woman said. "When does he sleep? I worry about his health!"

When Stalin spoke at dawn it may not have been timed to be heard by the greatest number, but it was certainly planned to be read. *Pravda* and *Izvestia* devoted their entire front pages to the speech. Queues a block long moved steadily toward the newspaper kiosks as people waited in line to buy copies. By midafternoon, reprints of the speech were pasted up on walls and billboards throughout the entire city. There they hung, through sun and rain, faded but still readable, throughout the difficult months that were to follow.

During the whole of July the tension continued to mount. Specific news became scarcer. The lines of trucks filled with soldiers poured, more frequently day and night through the Red Square, past our windows and westward up Gorky Street in the direction of the front. Trucks camouflaged with branches carried ammunition westward every evening and returned empty at dawn, to go back with new explosive loads the next night. A squad of men on ladders mounted the gleaming Krem-

lin towers and painted each gold onion-shaped dome a battleship gray. Work trolleys rolled in from the country, laden with sand, which was unloaded to the pavement under our balcony, where women shoveled the earth into bags for barricades. Householders contributed their extra petticoats and blouses for sack material, and the mounting walls of sandbags had all the gaiety of patchwork quilts. Follow-up squads coated the stacks of sandbags with wavy gray and black bands like the armored sides of a cruiser. Moscow went paint mad. Rooftops began appearing in flat wash tones in all squares and plazas. Imitation windows were painted realistically on the pavement, with shadows indicated around the edges to give the illusion of depth. Little artificial villages were erected in unexpected spots here and there and moved about from time to time, to distract the enemy from their real objectives. Artificial rooftops were thrown across the banks of the rivers to mislead enemy planes that might try to follow the rivers from the air. The Bolshoi Theater disgorged its mammoth backdrops, and these were hung on the outside of office buildings throughout the city. One of my Russian friends arrived to see me, with her white dress splashed with green. Trees were being painted as a disguise against the walls of a row of apartment houses, and a painter had overturned his pail from the twelfth story.

CAMOUFLAGING MOSCOW

IN ALL the squares of Moscow, squads of women with pails of many-colored paint filled in areas which, while meaningless from the ground, took on the illusion of rooftops when viewed from an upper window. Later windows were drawn in perspective with painted shadows increasing the illusion, until every open space in the city was filled with imitation rooftops and buildings. This was to confuse the German pilots who might be looking for specific objectives. Sometimes actual toy villages were erected and these were frequently moved from place to place. The paintings in the squares were periodically altered to prevent the enemy pilots from getting their bearings.

While the paint was still wet, the militia directed all traffic around it with the exception of one car I watched. This automobile, a large black Packard accompanied closely by an escort of two cars, streaked at top speed through the wet paint. It was Stalin on his way to the Kremlin.

CHAPTER 7

The Half-Ton Bomb

IT WAS a thrilling day for Erskine and me when the American Ambassador came to visit us for tea. This was not only because we liked Mr. Steinhardt very much, but also because we were always enthralled by his escort of secret police.

The ambassador of a major power is allotted six members of the NKVD, as the former OGPU is now called, who act as bodyguard. Lesser diplomats receive an escort in diminishing size, depending on their importance. The stated purpose of the guard is protection, but the prevailing opinion is that though fifty per cent of the reason for their assignment may be protection, the other fifty per cent is the fact that whatever a foreign diplomat does is bound to be interesting.

Mr. Steinhardt seldom had any conversation with his guards, but he told us that he had become so accustomed to them in the two years he had been Ambassador to Moscow that he had grown to like the boys and would miss them if they weren't around. They were referred to by Americans as the Four-Letter Boys or, more often, the YMCA.

They went with the Ambassador to the theater and to the opera. Once he took us to a restaurant which happened to be the best dining place in Moscow. Since it happened to be the most expensive as well, I was interested to observe that the diners at the table next to ours, without a question or a protest, got up immediately, leaving their meal half finished. The partly eaten dishes were carried away, and the bodyguard ordered a new and lavish dinner. Who paid for the unfinished meal and who paid for the new one, I was never able to discover.

On the Saturday of July 19, when Mr. Steinhardt visited us (it was after the Germans had been hammering their way into the Ukraine for four weeks), the NKVD followed their customary procedure. Two of them stayed in the street to watch the Ambassador's car and one guarded the door of the hotel. Three came up to our floor, and of these, one watched at the head of the stairs and two stationed themselves outside the door of our suite. They fared less well with us than they had at the restaurant, for they received no tea.

As the Ambassador and Erskine and I sat sipping our glasses of tea we discussed the question which was on everybody's lips: "When would the first bomb fall on Moscow?"

A ukase had appeared, compelling everyone not on active watch duty to go into a shelter when the siren sounded. Blackout was enforced so strictly that anyone allowing even a crack of light to show from his windows at night was subject to fines and imprisonment. During the preceding ten days there had been several alarms. We had gone into shelters, and after a few minutes the all-clear had sounded, and we had been told that it was just a practice alarm.

As we sat drinking our tea we heard the loudspeaker in the square outside our window blare an announcement. We opened the window to hear more clearly, and suddenly the voice of the announcer was swallowed up in the rising wail of the siren. We looked at each other and said: "This time it's the real thing."

We hurried out of our room, down the steps, and out of the hotel. As we crossed the street to the subway I looked over my shoulder and observed that precisely two paces behind us the secret-service men were following us, with military exactness.

Thousands of people were pouring into the great entrance of the Metro. In orderly fashion they were guided to the escalators, on which they descended to the safe depths a hundred feet below. It was interesting for us to watch this human stream, and here our secret-service squadron proved of aid. The YMCA boys cleared a vantage point for us beside a soda-pop stand at the head of the escalator and formed a cordon to keep the crowds from our corner, so we could watch everything that took place.

After forty minutes, the all-clear sounded, and we came out to the streets, where we were told that this was another rehearsal.

"Perhaps," said Mr. Steinhardt, "it's not just we who are rehearsing. Perhaps the Germans are rehearsing."

On the following Tuesday night, July 22, at exactly ten o'clock, the alarm sounded, and Erskine and I went across the street into the subway, hoping that we would not have to stay in the shelter very long, as we each had a great deal of work to do. I was mixing chemicals preparatory to starting a quantity of films through the developer, and Erskine was polishing off a radio script.

The Moscow subway is something very special, war or peace, as visitors to the New York World's Fair in 1939 will recall. The platforms in the stations have multicolored marble pillars, the ceilings are decorated in gold and blue mosaic, and some of the stations are finished with archways bound in stainless steel. Eisenstein, the Soviet moving-picture director, remarked to me, "The Metro is exactly what Metro-Goldwyn-Mayer would think an air-raid shelter should look like."

SUBWAY SHELTER

THE SUBWAY makes the ideal shelter. Most of the stations are incredibly deep—average probably one hundred feet. There was news, however, which the censor never allowed us to send, of a direct hit on one station, unfortunately one of the few shallow ones, where several hundred people were killed.

The subway-shelter job was excellently handled. Cots, stacked up in the daytime, were set out on the platform at night for children and women. The trains were stopped at eight o'clock, and sick children were allowed to sleep in the cars in seats especially reserved for them. Some of the subway stations installed movie screens; all of them had an excellent first-aid section curtained off with sheets at one end of the platform, with doctor and nurses. During the long hours of raids saleswomen came around with hot breads and the modern little pushcarts which have become a feature of Moscow, containing "baked Alaskas" on dry ice and soft drinks. It took a little time to get all these comforts started, but by mid-August the subways were pretty fine places to be in.

Even the track space was used. The platforms were reserved mainly for children and their mothers.

In peacetime the subway trains never ran between one A.M. and six A.M. This was to give the staff time to clean up the subway, which was kept as neat as a kitchen. The Russians are very proud of their Metro, which they built with their own hands, volunteering their extra hours of labor while it was under construction.

Raid or no raid, mothers and babies could come in after eight at night, and long queues formed in the streets, waiting to be admitted. These crowds usually went home at four when curfew was lifted.

During the day, when trains are in operation, fare is thirty kopecks (about six cents), but admission for shelter purposes is free. There are many women dispatchers and conductors. Once during the day I saw a peasant woman get separated from her party when her friends got on a train and left her behind in the crowd. A woman platform guard phoned to the next station and the party was notified. Lost children get instant attention through this system.

This enormously long station is in Mayakovsky Square, named after one of the country's most famous poets. It is very striking: stainless steel binding the pillars, and mosaics on the ceiling. Between the lighting fixtures are inlaid mosaics showing airplanes, Kremlin towers, parachutists.

Going into the subway was in itself an adventure, for a triple set of escalators raced downward at a speed three times as fast as that to which New York's underground system has accustomed a Manhattanite. As we coasted down the escalator to the lower platform, we discovered that the trains had been stopped and the power turned off from the tracks. People had been conducted to the tracks, where they sat, uncrowded, several thousand strong. Sitting on the tracks in the Moscow Metro is something you can do in your best clothes, for Muscovites are so proud of their subway that it is kept as clean as a whistle.

Erskine stayed on the platform, where he could try to talk his way out if the all-clear did not sound before his broadcast time, and I went back into the tunnel with the crowd. I sat on the tracks and counted the hours. It hardly seemed that a practice alarm would keep us there so long. Down the tracks, a man wearing overalls and an embroidered Kazak cap read an illustrated edition of the poems of Pushkin. I pulled out of my pocket the Russian textbook I always carried, and that night I added to my vocabulary a number of words which I might never have acquired if the alarm had been shorter. I glanced at my neighbor and noted that she was a schoolgirl doing crossword puzzles. "When I can do a crossword puzzle in the Russian alphabet," I thought, "I'll feel that these hours spent in shelters are worth while."

SPAZZO HOUSE

SPAZZO WAS the Ambassador's residence until the war started, when it became the embassy proper. The reason for this shift was that the embassy, which is exactly across the street from the Kremlin (and next to our hotel, incidentally), is in the best possible position to catch any bombs that miss their primary objective.

Spazzo House was built in czarist times by a sugar baron who immediately upon moving into the house, so the story goes, was assassinated by his illegitimate son. The building is said to have cost $2,000,-000, and Ambassador Steinhardt says, "The chandelier must have cost $1,900,000 of that amount."

After the Revolution, when all such places were taken over by the govern-ment, the building was used as the *spiridonovka* (Foreign Office place for entertainment of distinguished foreigners). Whenever foreign visitors to Moscow were distinguished enough, they were put up here. Litvinov, when he was head of the Foreign Office, used to give great entertainments here. In 1931 I attended a party here given by Mme and Mr. Litvinov, where people, including Russians, actually wore evening clothes.

When the United States recognized the Soviet regime, Spazzo was leased to the American government as a residence for its ambassadors. This was a handsome gesture on the part of the Soviets toward America since it is supposed to be the finest residence in Moscow.

Finally, after five and one half hours, the all-clear sounded, and the downward movement of the three escalators was reversed, shooting the thousands of us quickly up into the street. The early dawn light hung green in the sky. People were running toward the Kremlin, and I ran with them. There, beside the Kremlin wall, and within only a stone's throw from our hotel window, was a huge bomb crater. The first bombs had fallen on Moscow.

Hundreds of people crowded up to look. Immediately trucks carrying repair squads arrived and dozens of men set to work to fill up the hole. "They can't hit our Kremlin," a familiar voice beside me exclaimed. It was the reception clerk from our hotel. She grabbed me by the hand and led me running toward the Red Square. "They can't hit our Red Square either, and they can't get Lenin's Tomb."

The Germans had undoubtedly tried very hard to hit the Kremlin that night, and while they did not succeed they did do a thorough job of smashing up both the Italian and the Japanese embassies.

The next night, knowing we would be forced into air-raid shelters by zealous citizen guards whose job it was to see that everybody made for cover, Erskine and I went to the Spazzo House. This was the Ambassador's residence, now being used as an embassy, and here we knew no one would prevent us from having an unimpeded view of the spectacle in the heavens. On arriving we found that the Ambassador had left early with his entire staff for the *dacha*, his country house. It was very plain that the Germans had designs on the munitions factories along the Moscow-Leningrad road that led to the *dacha*, and he wanted to get his people home before raiding started.

DINING ROOM ON MOVING DAY

In 1934, it was decided that the beautiful oval dining room of the Spazzo House, which accommodated only eighteen couples, was not large enough for American Embassy entertaining. So this great dining-room wing was added.

Ambassador Steinhardt is lunching with his staff while furniture is being moved in from the regular embassy opposite the Kremlin. Staff members who had been living in apartments over the embassy offices were now spending their nights at the *dacha*. Their mattresses, bedsteads, bureaus, and desks were being stored at Spazzo.

The servant carrying the tray is known as Gin Fizz. He is Chinese and was retained by Ambassador Steinhardt from service with a previous ambassador.

My husband and I felt a little thrilled at taking charge of the American Embassy for a night. The two or three Russian servants who had been stationed there to put out fire bombs, if necessary (three had fallen on the embassy grounds the night before), made us comfortable and brought us tea in the garden.

"I'll make a bet with you," said Erskine. "I bet that they come again at ten o'clock, just as they did last night."

He sat with his watch in his hand, and it was exactly five seconds before ten o'clock when a hum in the sky from the north told us that German planes were on their way.

We went up to a convenient stretch of roof just outside the Ambassador's office windows and began our watch through what will always be one of the outstanding nights of my life. I have seen bombings before in other cities, but I have never before seen the entire heavens filled with shooting stars, with hanging parachute flares, with dot-dashes of tracer-gun fire, with red, white, and blue Roman candles, and streamers like the tails of red comets shooting out into space. Around the complete circumference of the horizon the beams of searchlights swung restlessly, as though a horde of insects turned over on their backs were waving their luminous legs in the air. Once while we watched, these shafts of light came together in a knot and caught in their focus a plane which glowed like a silver moth against the sky. For minutes the knot of light kept the moth imprisoned as it dipped and turned, trying to escape, until suddenly it twisted violently and fell; we had seen our first German plane shot down.

THE BEGINNING OF AN AIR RAID

WHEN THE enemy approaches, the searchlights sweep the heavens for oncoming German planes. Each battery of searchlights, like the one shown rising from left center, patrols its portion of the sky.

The lines slanting at a low angle toward the right are from short bursts of machine-gun fire which contain one luminous tracer bullet in every ten. The high-rising lines, farther right, are tracer shells from heavy guns. Notice how one line of tracer shells has broadened out. This was because a heavy wind that night was blowing burning residue from the tracers.

The short slanting dashes are hard to identify. Probably they are part of the course of some tracer bullets.

The star-topped tower in the distance is the Spasski Clock Tower, part of the Kremlin wall. This clock chimed the quarter hour regularly throughout the heaviest air raids—an eerie reminder of peaceful days.

At a quarter after one my husband had to leave to go to the radio station. I found out later that the car from the studio, the only one at that time with authority to be on the streets during a raid, had been hit by a bomb. So Erskine had to make a dash for it in our car, racing not only through falling bombs, bricks, and shrapnel, but rushing past militiamen who might have machine-gunned him had they discovered that the car did not have air-raid credentials.

Left alone on my roof, I began putting my camera to work. Incendiary bombs had begun falling now, so the horizon was bright enough to aid in focusing. Spasmodically, flames began shooting up in scattered spots where fire bombs had found enough timber to work on. The drone of planes sounded more frequently directly overhead, and the beams of searchlights swung upward, crossing and recrossing until the whole heavens were covered with a luminous plaid design. I had not realized that there is so much music with an air raid. The most beautiful sound is the echo of the guns, which returns on a deeper note, like the bass of a Beethoven chord. The total effect is as though two types of music were being played together—formal chords with overtones of jazz thrown in. The peculiar whistle, which one soon learns to recognize, of bombs falling in the neighborhood is like a dash of Gershwin against a classic symphonic background.

I cannot tell what it was that made me know the bomb of the evening was on its way. It was not sound, and it was not light, but a kind of contraction in the atmosphere which made me realize I must move quickly. It seemed minutes, but it must have been split seconds, in which I had time to pick up my camera, to climb through the Ambas-

---

FROM THE ROOF OF SPAZZO

I HAD just completed this picture when the big bomb fell, breaking all the embassy windows.

The direction of the German parachute flares at the lower left shows that a strong wind was blowing. The slight curlicues at the beginning of the flare path indicate where the flare package exploded in its metal container, allowing the parachute to open.

The bright spots high in the heavens are "flaming onions"—antiaircraft shells which explode with a brilliant orange light.

There were so many things happening at once that night that it was impossible to identify everything. However, the distant lights clustered low to the right probably were rockets, as many of them—red, white, and blue—were being shot into the sky.

Low, luminous clouds that night shone with a red glow, reflecting the fires which had been started on the ground.

sador's window, to lay my camera down carefully on the far side of the rug, and to lie down beside it myself. And then it came. All the windows in the house fell in, and the Ambassador's office windows rained down on me. Then something else came down on me, which I did not recognize at the time to be a Japanese screen. Fortunately, a heavy ventilator blown out of the window had missed me by a comfortable margin. I did not know until much later that my finger tips were cut with glass splinters. I only knew that the basement would be a very pleasant place in which to be.

Getting there was the longest journey of my life. My cameras went too, of course, and with my arms full I started toward the stairway but lost my way so completely that I elbowed around the Ambassador's bathroom three times before I reached the stair. Here I had the hardest job, for each landing was ankle-deep in glass, and with the house spasmodically trembling I had to try to choose moments for each crossing when I would be less apt to slip on the glass. When I finally achieved my three-flight descent I found the basement not only a pleasant but a sociable place. The A.P. and U.P. correspondents had arrived to sleep in the comparative safety of the cellar shelter, and at dawn my husband got back from the radio studio.

The all-clear sounded, and we were about to start home when it suddenly occurred to me that I was leaving a lot of good news pictures behind. It was too dark then to photograph the wreckage, so I made my way about the house and on each of the biggest piles of glass I left a note: PLEASE DON'T SWEEP UP GLASS TILL I COME BACK WITH CAMERA.

Home we went, and I fell into such a sound sleep that it was only with difficulty that I aroused myself sufficiently to answer the loud jangling of the telephone. It was Mr. Steinhardt's secretary saying,

---

EMBASSY TABLE AND FLOOR AFTER BOMBING

THE MORNING I returned after the bombing, my attention was caught by the Ambassador's table. Directly back of the water jug, and upside down, was the Coca-Cola slogan, "The pause that refreshes"; the book at the bottom of the pile is *Nationality Laws*, published, oddly enough, by the Carnegie Endowment for International Peace. I wondered whether the *Style Manual of the Department of State—1937* contained a protocol for behavior in the midst of burning bombs.

It was fortunate that I picked the far side of this rug to lie on when the glass shattered. I didn't get a major dose and was lucky to escape with cuts on my hand only.

"You'd better come over here at once if you want to take pictures of this glass, because Mr. Ambassador wants to get the house cleaned up." For which I could hardly blame him; and I hurried over without my breakfast and began to photograph the wreckage.

The bomb, a thousand-pound one, had fallen on the Vachtangov Theater fifty yards away, completely demolishing the building. Muscovites grieved because its beloved director, Kuza, had chosen that night to do his patrol duty on the roof and had been lost, along with a popular actor, Christiakov. Of its two underground shelters, filled partly with theater workers and partly with passers-by who had taken refuge from the street, one was completely destroyed and many in it killed. In the second the occupants escaped without a scratch.

When I returned to the hotel with my films I began immediately to develop them in the bathtub; but no sooner were the cherished results of my work immersed in the developer than another air raid started. The only chance of saving my films was to stay with them, something not so easy to do in a hotel where a dutiful patrol shepherds all tenants into the shelter. As a knocking sounded on the door I found that the space under the bed fitted my measurements very exactly. I could hear the guards enter and go through our rooms until they had satisfied themselves that everyone was absent. And as their steps echoed down the corridor, and the symphony again sounded over Moscow, I completed the developing, hypoing, and rinsing process well known to all photographers.

WINDOW OF SPAZZO FOYER AFTER BOMBING

THIS STAINED-GLASS window was one of the finest features of Spazzo. When it was knocked out in the bombing, Mr. Steinhardt said he was glad to get it broken and over with, for sooner or later it was bound to fall out anyway. When the window broke, the stained glass from the colored panels lay in patterns on the rug like a loosely put-together jigsaw puzzle. One long spear of glass stuck like a dagger in the side of the sofa.

CHAPTER 8

Daily Schedule

IN THE morning the bathroom always resembled the inside of a cave, the ceiling bristling, as though with stalactites, with dripping films that hung from cords stretched between the water pipes. I usually slipped out of bed a little ahead of my husband to take out of the bathtub any additional films that had been rinsing there all night. If the ceiling was too full to accommodate these they were pinned on the edges of all available towels except one, which was carefully reserved for Erskine's use.

As the Spasski Clock Tower chimed nine from the Kremlin, Alexander, our day chauffeur, arrived. These chimes were reminiscent of my college days, for the Kremlin clock marked the hours with the same melody as the Library Tower on the campus at Cornell.

Alexander's arrival necessitated my slipping back into the darkened bedroom to rifle my husband's pockets. My search was not for change but for slender slips of lavender paper, called "talons," which permitted us to buy a total of two hundred liters (fifty gallons) of petrol a month. Erskine had threatened to shoot anybody who spent more than three talons at a time, because once our gas tank had been drained during the night; and the chauffeur and I had to be careful. The talons seldom lasted through more than two thirds of the month, so it was Alexander's constant duty to conserve our supply and add to it in any way possible.

With the departure of Alexander on a petrol hunt Tatiana, our joint secretary, arrived. The size of our establishment awed us—a day and a night chauffeur, for our work carried us practically around the clock; a secretary (in addition to Elisaveta, who acted almost as a second

94

secretary to us) ; and, most impressive of all, a car. This purchase had become a necessity when other means of transportation evaporated with the beginning of the war, and it was a small miracle to be able to buy a secondhand car at all. The Ambassador had helped us find a six-year-old Plymouth, which we bought by cable from an embassy clerk who had left it behind when he was evacuated to Stockholm. After the deal was made, Mr. Steinhardt said that now that he had turned secondhand car dealer he knew better than to let his customers push their car home through the streets, so he searched his pockets for a few talons to throw in with the deal. Not finding any, he drained several liters of precious petrol out of his own Packard and poured it into our gas tank.

Tatiana, our secretary, was a big motherly woman with a plain, kindly face and dark hair marcelled in the regular little rows which are the specialty of Russian beauty shops. She always wore voile dresses decorated with big flower patterns. She typed in English as though it were her native tongue, though there was always a quaint foreign wording to what she wrote.

By the time Erskine was out of bed Tatiana had gone over the military communiqué which Narkomindel furnished daily to correspondents, and typed it out in translation so he could refer to it quickly. While we ate breakfast, she read aloud from *Pravda* and *Izvestia* (except when the papers were late, which was often).

The hotel's part in our breakfast consisted uniformly of eggs, bread, butter, and coffee, which routine fare cost five dollars each. The day's food, even omitting luncheon—which we seldom had time to eat—averaged from twenty to thirty dollars for each of us, for although food was plentiful the exchange must have been set by some Bolshevik who still believed all Americans were millionaires.

We often had surprises for breakfast. The Ambassador sent us frequent gifts of shredded wheat from the embassy commissary, on the principle that all Americans like reminders of home. Alexander usually returned from his gas hunt with a jar of iced orange slices or a handkerchief full of peanuts, an unusual delicacy in Russia. Once he brought gooseberries from the market, and when these proved too tart

for us Tatiana took them home and returned next day with some excellent jam which she had made in her own copper kettle.

Tatiana was the kindest person who ever stepped into a human skin.

EDITORIAL CONFERENCE AT *PRAVDA*

THIS TAKES place every day in the strikingly modern-looking *Pravda* building. I was directed to turn my back to the enormous plate-glass windows for fear of catching a glimpse in the picture of factories outside for which no specific photographic permit had been arranged.

This particular meeting was interesting as an example of *Pravda* procedure. Every day at three P.M. the entire contents of that day's paper are criticized from all points of view. Literary and political critics come to give their opinions. For example, on this day *Pravda* was late on the streets because it ran an article dealing with the raising of production in which many figures had to be verified. The critics praised the article in question for its good literary style and accuracy but mentioned in mild terms that the paper should not be late.

The lateness of the papers was a constant source of distress to us, for we needed them as source material for our radio broadcasts. *Izvestia* was usually equally tardy.

A second article in this day's *Pravda*, a review of battles in the Atlantic, was attacked by the critics because the news was two days old. Nevertheless, it was highly praised for its literary style.

High rivalry exists between *Pravda* and *Izvestia*. At each of these daily meetings the critics vote which was the better paper that day. When I was present *Pravda* received the vote.

The picture magazine, *Ogonyok*, and the humorous magazine, *Crocodile*, both of which our friend Petrov edited, are printed at *Pravda*. Two magazines for young people are also printed here: *Young Bolshevik* and *Stalin's Falcons*.

During the whole time we were in Moscow *Pravda* was running a continued story. This was an extraordinary event because it was a detective story, the first ever offered to Russian readers. The setting was the Moscow Hotel (the big new hotel across the street from ours) and the opening event was the mysterious death of an elevator operator.

Publication figures:

1. *Pravda*—two million circulation
2. *Young Communist Pravda*—600,000
3. *Pioneers' Pravda*—900,000
4. *Teachers' Gazette*—300,000
5. *Red Fleet*—200,000

Papers are mailed to points outside the city and are received a day or more after publication date.

Fourteen cars of paper are used a day, each car containing from twelve to fourteen rolls. It takes three hours, from six to nine A.M., to print the two million copies of *Pravda*. There is no city desk, no local news as we understand it: nothing about fires, arrests, etc. Even during the fire bombing there was no such thing as a report of where the biggest fires took place and where they were put out. The nearest approach to this was in the periodic stories of patriotism and heroism which appeared after the event, undated and without specific data about locations. Our best sources of information for local happenings were our two chauffeurs and Tatiana, who reported each morning what they had seen on the way to work.

Pravda, although consisting of eight or less pages, is more than a newspaper. It is a whole community. The staff have their apartment houses in the *Pravda* group, the stores where they shop, their cafeterias and dining rooms, a hospital; nurseries, schools, and playgrounds for their children, and recreation grounds for grownups. They have their own rest home in Sochi opposite the home for locomotive workers where we stayed.

This type of organized living is characteristic of home life in Moscow, where each industry or business activity is a social unit.

Also she had a quality, hard to find among Russians, of understanding an American's point of view. Tatiana's experience had come from working with many American businessmen and engineers during the American influx that occurred during the Five-Year Plan. Colonel Hugh L. Cooper, who built the Dnieper Dam, and Samuel Untermyer were among the people for whom she had worked. When the Russians blew up Dnieper Dam, to keep it out of the hands of the Germans, Tatiana wept. "We can't let the Nazis get our dam!" she said. "The Colonel would feel so bad if he were alive now and could know about this!"

Tatiana had come to us with something of an aura of mystery about her, and one day at breakfast she told us her story. During the time of the purge, in early 1938, she had been arrested. This apparently had amazed her rather than frightened her. "I didn't worry," she said. "I knew I had done nothing wrong. I spent two years in central Asia, on a prison farm near Alma-Ata. In the winter I banked up the snow with boards, in narrow furrows, to conserve the moisture; and in the summer helped cultivate the fields. During the whole time I had faith that I would be set free. Then I was sent in a sealed train to Moscow, where

---

DEPARTMENT OF LETTERS AT *PRAVDA*

PRAVDA IS a clearinghouse for complaints of all sorts—a sort of secondary government bureau. Files for years back are kept, containing letters of all sorts from people who want something changed in their offices, who think they deserve a better apartment, who observe something they think is wrong in the offices of others. *Pravda* refers the matters to the proper government departments. Many of the letters are from citizens who find spelling mistakes in the paper.

Thousands of letters are written about people's personal affairs. The three shown:

1. Man at left foreground—a disappointed writer who cannot get his work published, thinks he is being discriminated against, expects *Pravda* to help him place his writings. (He is reading *Pravda*.)

2. Woman in center—a Red Army wife who wants to move to a larger room in a new apartment building. She thinks she deserves this because her husband is a sol-

dier. (Red Army wives *do* get the best apartments.)

3. Woman in background, right—from Town Council of Tambov, Siberia, the Financial Division. She feels that there is too much red tape in the finances of her small town. She has been trying for years to accomplish small things, without success. Now that it is wartime she feels the red tape must be cut without delay and she comes to *Pravda* to see what can be done with her Town Council.

This last is a typical complaint, for bureaucracy has always been the enemy of efficiency in Soviet Russia. Recent improvement has been very considerable.

As for the apartment difficulty, this is one of Moscow's main problems. Almost everybody is trying to get a larger apartment. The rent is regulated according to salary. The family's total income and the number of children are taken into account. Moving to a larger apartment is mainly a matter of privilege.

I waited six months in prison while my case was investigated. That was the hardest part. I grew despondent and couldn't eat. Those prison guards were certainly good to me. They kept fixing special dishes for me, and urging me to eat, and telling me that everything would work out all right.

"Finally my case came to court. It came out that a certain commissar had been maneuvering to get the most efficient office workers imprisoned, as part of a scheme to sabotage various offices and thus slow up the work of the country. He was liquidated, and all the people he had attempted to incriminate were set free."

"How did your old friends act?" I inquired. "Were they afraid to be seen with you?"

"Oh, no," she said. "When people are the victims of a mistake, everyone tries to make it up to them. They couldn't do enough for me and were always inviting me to parties and taking me to the theater."

PAVEL F. YUDIN, HEAD OF STATE PUBLISHING HOUSE—OGIZ

OGIZ IS an affiliation of the Gosizdat, the tremendous State Publishing Organization. This gives Yudin the highest position in the publishing world.

Yudin has been head of Ogiz for two years; before that he was secretary of the Writers' Union. He is a member of the Academy of Sciences, author of many books, principally *Dictionary of Philosophy* and *History of Philosophy*.

Ogiz has the following departments: Political Works, Technical Literature, Encyclopedia, Social and Economic Literature, Agricultural Literature. And the output of Military Literature is enormous, including all sorts of textbooks, many of them on the art of sniping and various techniques of guerrilla warfare (for the partisans).

Recently the first volume of a *History of World Diplomacy* was put out in an edition of 500,000 copies. In ten days it was sold out. If there had been enough paper they would have published a full million. About 111 million volumes are published a year. A *Philosophic Dictionary* was published in an edition of two million copies. A technical encyclopedia of twenty-six volumes was published in an edition of 32,000 copies.

Here Yudin is in his office, which is lined with maps. He is the jolliest, wittiest man imaginable. He is also fearless in his opinions, a good executive. The writers who work with him adore him, and everywhere he is greatly beloved.

Whenever I arrived, he would always order from the Ogiz cafeteria a chicken dinner which he served in his office with bottles of Orange Fruit Water, of which he is very fond.

Yudin has a shelter under the Ogiz building, with desk, telephones, cot, and ventilator, so as to be able to continue working during raids. He likes to do his own cooking over an open fire in the country near his *dacha*. He drives a Soviet-made ZIS, which is their better car, modeled after our Buick. His car is lined with carpets thrown over the seats—a fashion which appeals to Russians.

Yudin made frequent trips to the front lines to keep close touch with the progress of the war.

"Did your experience make it hard to get a new job?" Erskine asked her.

"No, there is a state regulation that people who are cleared must be given back their old jobs and all the salary they have lost must be paid up to date. The government gave me a new apartment, much bigger than my last and looking out over a park."

These chats at breakfast were our last quiet moments in the day—although not even breakfast was pure leisure for me. Mealtime had to be synchronized with developing time. My processing was done in tanks by the time-and-temperature method. For four minutes I could eat, and on the fifth minute run to the tanks and agitate the developer.

AMBASSADOR STEINHARDT

HIS EXCELLENCY Laurence A. Steinhardt arrived two years before the beginning of the Russo-German war to take over his post as Ambassador Extraordinary and Minister Plenipotentiary of the United States to the Union of Soviet Socialist Republics. He had come direct from a year's service as Ambassador to Peru, and previous to that had been stationed for four years in Sweden as American Minister.

Mr. Steinhardt, before entering the diplomatic service, had been a leading New York lawyer, accustomed to hard work. He worked no less hard when he reached Moscow, for this post requires personal attention to an enormous amount of detail, and this detail increased greatly at the beginning of the war, for the embassy staff was cut in half so that part of its members could be evacuated to safety.

The Ambassador followed a daily schedule which kept him at his duties from fifteen to eighteen hours of the twenty-four. He was frequently called to the Kremlin for a conference at two A.M. This is typical of Russia, where the Kremlin officials do almost all of their important work at night. Even Stalin works until four A.M., at which hour his big Packard can sometimes be seen shooting out of the Kremlin gates, taking him home to sleep at his *dacha*.

Ambassador Steinhardt was well liked by the Russians, who considered him honest and shrewd. To his flock of Americans he was generous to a fault.

Shortly after the garden party described in the text, the Ambassador established an emergency embassy in Kazan. It was not until after we had left the country in the late fall of 1941 that events forced the evacuation of embassy staffs and all foreign newsmen from Moscow. It was then that the Ambassador's meticulous attention to detail bore fruit. When the temporary war capital was finally announced as Kuibyshev, all he had to do was inform his skeleton staff at Kazan to float all supplies to Kuibyshev on rafts on the Volga River. Thus, when all the refugees from Moscow arrived in the bleak city of Kuibyshev, the American Embassy was fully equipped, even to the point of lending sealing wax for official seals to the embassies of other nations.

After a short term in Kuibyshev, the Ambassador flew back to America by way of Iran, Egypt, across Africa, across the Atlantic, and finally to America, where after a brief Christmas vacation he was sent back to a new post as American Ambassador to Turkey.

Then back to my food, and back to the tub. Developing is like washing dishes—one of those jobs that never end.

Our rooms took on some of the aspects of a factory. Erskine's literary output rose almost to production-line levels. The scarcity of correspondents had brought us both a wave of offers. For the first few weeks I was constantly cabling refusals to write from the "woman's angle," to news agencies, to magazines, and even to movie companies who wanted me to make newsreels. In the publication field my work was exclusively for *Life* (though in the early stages of broadcasting I alternated with Erskine on the microphone). After each photographic subject was completed I wrote out extensive pages of data to identify the negatives, from which the editorial office at home could make up captions. Erskine's work kept two typewriters in use constantly. On his own machine he turned out articles for *PM*, for a newspaper syndicaté, for *Life*, and always one and sometimes two broadcasts a day. On a second typewriter, borrowed from the embassy, Tatiana copied everything in triplicate for the censors. As fast as the dispatches left the typewriter the chauffeur took them to Narkomindel, to be passed by the Press Bureau. Then back the copies came to us so we could see how much they had been mutilated by the censors. Then the chauffeur took cables off to the post office to be telegraphed to America, and carried the broadcast material to the Radio Center, to be passed by a second set of censors called Glavalit. In between these expeditions Alexander usually found time to drive to the market and find us a watermelon or whatever fruit was in season.

My day had its literary labors also. All the requests for photographs I wished to take were made in the form of carefully composed letters, with copies in both English and Russian and with carbons sent to various commissariats, both military and civil. This system was adopted when I discovered that verbal requests never went through, while written ones sometimes did. The intricate network of co-ordinating arrangements was in the hands of VOKS, the Society for Cultural Relations. When arrangements dragged I would call on Mr. Lozovsky and beg him to speed the cultural-relations machinery.

The task of VOKS was not an easy one, in as much as using a camera without specific permits was forbidden even to Russians, and I was the only foreigner with photographic privileges. Often my photographic entourage occupied a caravan of three cars, containing a VOKS official, a VOKS interpreter, several military officers, someone from the Mayor's office, and a representative of the Central Governing Committee. When all these had been gathered together, and permission finally obtained, I photographed whatever had been arranged even if the sky spilled pitchforks. There is no such thing in wartime Russia as dashing out to get a picture just because the sky and sun are right.

Even a photograph of the lobby of my own hotel had to be arranged, complete with escorts. Once I had asked to photograph a bookstall, one of the many which spring up all over Moscow streets in the summertime, selling everything from textbooks on how to recognize the silhouettes of enemy planes to Russian fairy tales. My entourage conducted me to the bookstall, for which permission had been granted, and it happened to be on the shady side of the street. Across the way was an identical bookstall, beautifully situated in the sun and set against a splendid background of sandbags and war posters. It was useless to attempt to transfer our operations across the street, for we did not have the correct permit. When the document was finally obtained, with all its necessary stamps and signatures, the sandbags had been boarded up and the bookstall moved to another street corner.

Whenever, in the evening, I would speak a few complaining words about these incidents my husband would say, "Just picture those news photographers sitting in Chungking, Ankara, and Cairo, waiting for their Russian visas." We were always hearing about them, so a reminder was enough.

The Soviet photographers don't always have such an easy time with their permits, either, I found, for only those who are members of the Communist party are given the good assignments. Of the Soviet Union's 194 million inhabitants only about two per cent are actually in the Communist-party ranks. The fact that the photographers who are party members may cover more important subjects than their fellow workers is taken as a matter of course in Moscow. Soviet pressmen were amazed

when I told them that Republicans are allowed to take pictures in the White House, along with the Democrats. When I explained that their ability to focus a camera counted for more than their politics, they were incredulous. "Isn't Mr. Roosevelt a Democrat?" they exclaimed.

There was one occasion, I remember, when I broke unexpectedly through the red tape. The press had been invited to view a German scouting plane brought down in the country near the town of Istra. When I arrived at the entrance to Narkomindel, to start with the party, I was told that no permit had been arranged for me to take pictures. "But a German plane that has been brought down by Soviet pilots!" I protested. "Surely you will want pictures of that published in America!"

"The Soviet photographers will photograph it," I was told by the Press Chief. "We shall see that some of the pictures reach your home-land."

At that I burst into oratory. "Do you realize," I addressed the throng gathering on the steps, "what the great American public will think if I am not allowed to photograph this plane? Americans know that Russians are masters of stage effects! Whenever they see Soviet pictures of wrecked German planes, our people will believe that these alleged Fascist planes are built of papier-mâché, and that your theatrical designers have painted them with swastikas. How will you convince our great public that your glorious Red Air Fleet is really bringing down German planes unless their own American photographer is allowed to take such pictures?" I probably sounded rather silly, but the censors got into a huddle and my lenses went along.

When we reached the wreckage of the Junkers 88, I set to work, only to glance up and see Mr. Hatenaka, the Japanese correspondent, bene-fiting by my victory. He had simply pulled his camera out of his pocket

---

STREET BOOKSTALLS ON KUZNETSKY MOST

RUSSIANS ARE avid readers, and bookstalls spring up all over Moscow in the summer —on sandbag piles, in doorways. Books range from *Manual of Guerrilla Warfare* and *Encyclopedia of Aviation* to children's books, including a great number of fairy tales.

One of the most popular books shows silhouettes of German planes so that citizens can learn to spot them. Books of exercises and diet are in demand.

Steinbeck's *Grapes of Wrath* came out in a paper-bound, inexpensive edition at sixty kopecks (about fifteen cents), and 50,000 copies were sold the first day.

and was taking snapshots, in the matter-of-course way in which the Japanese have photographed the whole world.

All three censors accompanied us on this expedition—two young ones, whom we had found quite pleasant fellows, and an older man, whom we called "the Chinese Professor" because his English sounded like Chinese to us. Several correspondents who had decided that they had too much work to spare time for the trip into the country waited all day with their correspondence unsent, because there were no censors left in Moscow to pass it. When we were shown Soviet newsreels, too, no regular news dispatches could be sent by the more diligent correspondents who stayed home to work, for all the censors always went with us to the movies. What they expected to find censorable in their own newsreels I was never able to determine.

My husband has his own system of grammar and spelling. His grammar was always carefully corrected by the censor, but the search for a word which Erskine had spelled "skamper" nearly wore out the Narkomindel dictionary. When Erskine once reported that there had been a "picayunish" raid, and picayunish could not be found in the dictionary, the censors thought it was code.

Supper was our most amusing meal, for it was usually about suppertime that Erskine's broadcast scripts were being censored, and each course was punctuated with a telephone call from Narkomindel. I would sit back and enjoy our hundred-ruble dinner of caviar and chicken cutlet à la Kiev while Erskine explained what it meant to "crawl out on a limb," "keep your fingers crossed," and no matter "which way the wind was blowing," not to "let the cat out of the bag."

GERMAN PRISONER OF WAR

I VISITED German infantry prisoners in a large hospital in Moscow. Most of them were in their early twenties—none of them were officers. On the whole they were unintelligent, inclined to be surly, and took their part in the war in a fatalistic way. They seemed neither ardent for the war nor enough against it to rebel. This impression may have been heightened because they were wounded and prisoners of war.

Their demeanor made me appreciate the current Russian quip that German soldiers are politically undeveloped.

My secretary had a long chat with this infantryman, Georg Verler, and tried to discover something of his cultural background. She discovered little. He did not recognize the names of Kant, Schopenhauer, or any others of a long list of prominent German philosophers and scientists.

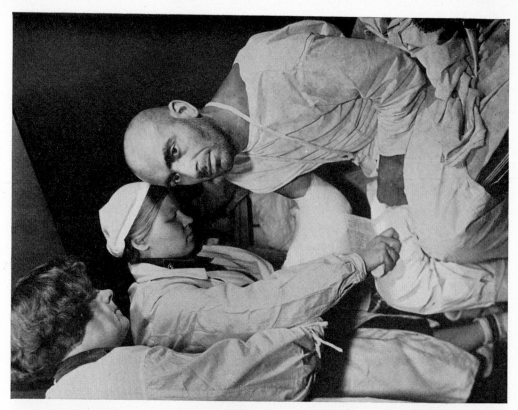

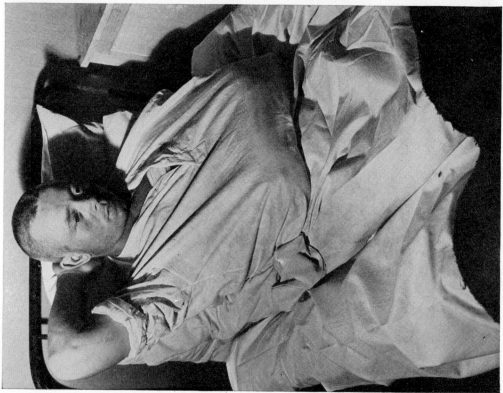

"Pouring water down a rathole" required a minute analysis, for the censor couldn't understand why anyone would want to pour water down a rathole; and I shall never forget the night when Erskine tried to cable that Hitler had "stirred up a hornets' nest." Hornets in Russia were despised insects, he was told, and the censor didn't want his countrymen to be called that. The hardest line Erskine ever had to argue through was "Hitler is a good lid-sitter." The censor couldn't bear to have Hitler called a good anything.

The task of interpreting many of these phrases fell on Henry Shapiro, the United Press correspondent, because he put in such long hours at the Press Bureau that he was usually at hand when the dictionary failed. After Henry had reassured the Chinese Professor one evening that Cald-

---

NAZI INFANTRYMEN

THIS IS infantryman Stefan Dorisch, having his wound dressed by a Russian nurse. Dorisch was older and more alert than the other prisoners. He watched me attentively while I was photographing him.

The nurses are known as medical sisters. The one at the extreme left is Head Nurse Sedinkina in charge of the prisoners' ward.

The head of the hospital told me they make a point of treating prisoners well and talk ideology to them. "But when the Germans were drawing closer to Moscow, it was hard," he said, "to keep everybody treating the German prisoners gently." During air raids the prisoners are brought from the fourth down to the second floor of the hospital, where they stay with the other patients, who are Soviet soldiers. The German soldiers feel very uncomfortable in the proximity of their own bombs.

EUGEN NEUNERT, twenty-four years old, was born in Frankfurt-am-Main and worked as a roof slater. He has been in the army since 1938. He was in a trench near Smolensk when the orders came to retreat. Although he tried to be careful during the retreat, he was wounded. The phrase "tried to be careful" came out because my secretary was questioning him along the lines of the theory that many Germans prefer to be wounded and captured so that they can stop fighting. This may sometimes be true. At any rate, we heard constant tales of Germans holding up their hands and crying, "Russki, Russki!" when they were fright-ened beyond endurance in hand-to-hand bayonet battles. We were constantly told that Germans cannot stand bayonet attack.

Neunert said that all he wanted was to get well and get back in the army again. My observation was that he was quite willing to fight, but took it as routine work, carried on with little enthusiasm. Neunert seemed to me something of an automaton. He had taken part in the campaign against France. We asked him whether the German people were tired of war. He said that he didn't know, but added enigmatically that they would stand it as long as necessary.

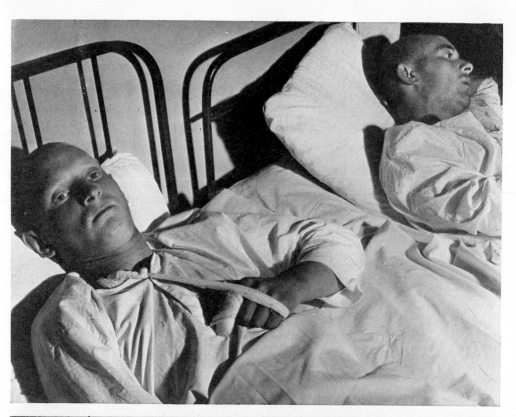

well really was not trying to give information to the enemy but was simply talking straight American, the censor said, "I don't know why it is! Both Caldwell and Gorky are great writers, but I have no difficulty at all in understanding the writings of Gorky."

GERMANS IN MOSCOW

EHRHARDT WAS born in 1920 in Stuttgart and worked in a chinaware factory until he was mobilized in October, 1940. He arrived in the Moscow hospital with a wound in his hand and seemed to be delighted to be out of the fighting for a while. He expressed the wish that his old father might know that he is only lightly wounded. He reported that he and his fellow soldiers had expected the Russians to be much weaker than they proved to be, and when the bayonet charge came, he and a group of his friends tried to run and save their lives. He wishes he were back in his china factory.

Spahn, a year older than Ehrhardt, was a corporal. He had been a metalworker until he joined the army in 1940. He had fought in France and left there on June 26, 1941, when he was sent to Russia. Two days previously he had heard about the Russian war. But it was only after he had arrived on Russian soil on August 3 that he knew he was no longer in France. We asked him how he felt about being in Moscow under bombing. "It is good," he replied, "that we are hidden from our own bombs." Spahn apparently had never thought much about the ends or the aims of the war. Very little was told him or his friends, he said, about the reasons for the war. He said he would prefer not to fight anybody "but just to sit home."

SPAHN IS having his Russian cigarette lighted by Georg Hammerschmidt, twenty-nine years old, of Frankfurt-am-Main. Hammerschmidt was wounded on August 11 and captured the following day near Smolensk. He said the Germans attacked and the Soviets counterattacked with a battle in which the Germans were surrounded. He had fought in France and said this was the heaviest war he had ever seen and wished he were back home. He has a wife and four children and wished he could let them know he is still alive and treated well by the Russians. When we asked what he thinks about the war, he replied, "It seems to be necessary to fight, but I do not know the reasons why. That is up to the officers. I am too small a man to know whether the war will be over soon or who will win it."

The hospital supplies "Box" cigarettes for prisoners. They are a cheap brand costing thirty-five kopecks a package of ten.

CHAPTER 9

Moscow Air Raid

THE OPENING air raids over Moscow possessed a magnificence that I have never seen matched in any other man-made spectacle. It was as though the German pilots and the Russian antiaircraft gunners had been handed enormous brushes dipped in radium paint and were executing abstract designs with the sky as their vast canvas.

This spectacular quality was due to the intensity of the ground barrage. London, for all the severity of its blitz, had more scattered ground defenses: inevitable because of the large size of the city. But Moscow is smaller, and its defense rings were concentrated. Also, the Russians were so eager to keep the Germans back that they flung an enormous amount of ammunition into the air, at what must have been prodigious cost. During that last week in July and through the first half of August, the prodigality of the barrage continued. Later, even on nights when bombing might be heavier, there was usually less to see. There were fewer searchlights used, and the Russian ground crews had learned to employ their defenses more economically.

AIR-RAID WARDEN AT ENTRANCE TO BOMB SHELTER

It is impossible to overestimate the importance of the duties of these citizen watchers. For twenty-four hours of the day and night every doorway, every alley, every rooftop has its watchers who work on four-hour shifts. A woman like this has great authority while on duty. She may challenge any stranger whose passport and documents she wishes to see. If anyone asks his way, thus showing that he is unfamiliar with the neighborhood, she may regard him as a suspicious character and call the militia.

A fifth columnist wouldn't have a chance. At night, watchers exactly like this one challenge the pedestrian every few steps to show his *propusk*, or night pass. When the alarm sounds, the watchers stationed near the entrance to shelters see that children get safely underground. If fire bombs fall they set to work with the other "spotters."

The words above the watcher read BOMB SHELTER and HIDING.

But the early raids, with living curtains of fire thrown into the upper reaches of the heavens by the Russian batteries, and with the *Luftwaffe* tossing off flares which hung in slowly descending clusters like blazing suns, these were celestial sights that might have been directed by an archangel.

During the first few weeks of bombing it required something of a military maneuver on the part of the Caldwell family to be able to see the raids at all. With the exception of our trips to the Radio Center for two A.M. broadcasts, which were specially arranged, Erskine and I, like all citizens not actually on the rooftops for fire-fighting duty, were directed by law to go underground into the shelters. My appointed place under the bed was used so frequently that it became almost a reflex action on my part to roll into it at the first wail of the siren. But my husband did not think this dignified.

His opinion was undoubtedly influenced by the fact that he has an enormous chest and large shoulders, a product of his preliterary days when he was a professional football player; and the space from bed-frame to floor could scarcely be called adequate. Erskine's choice was a corner behind the sofa, and to ensure his invisibility he would draw up the white bear rug until it covered his shoulders. There he would sit in all his dignity, staring from the corner like a big bear, while the hotel wardens came into our blacked-out rooms, called out to us, and prowled about until they finally gave up from sheer weariness.

APARTMENT-HOUSE SHELTER SITUATED IN KRASNOPRES-NENSKY, A MANUFACTURING DISTRICT AT THE WEST END OF MOSCOW

CELLARS UNDER all the apartment houses in this district have been reinforced for shelters with extra pillars added, and many have been equipped with ventilators which serve to purify the atmosphere during long hours of occupation. These were installed primarily as protection against gas attack, in which case the doors may be sealed, making the shelter safe. Most shelters are equipped with chessboards.

This apartment house accommodates 1500 adults and 875 children. About 500 of the children were evacuated to the country. The majority of the people using the shelter are conductors of streetcars and busses, railroad-station workers, textile and metallurgical factory workers.

Discipline is strict so that people may rest. Many were sleeping soundly even though the shooting was very loud the night I worked here. Early in the raid, while people are still wakeful and the conversation rises too loud, one often hears a warden say, "Speak, comrades, but quietly."

Sometimes, with that thoroughness which is a characteristic of the Russian race, the patrol would come back and send us scampering to our respective hideaways again; but finally the hall would quiet down and we could come out and watch the raid.

My own position was made more complicated by the fact that the alarm usually caught me with three or four film packs in the tub, in the process of developing, and while the search went on I would lie under the big bed, counting the seconds and minutes and hoping I could get back to the tub and throw the films into the hypo before they were too badly overdeveloped.

The nights took on a curious routine. First, while the action was still confined to the outer defense rings in the distance, I had a multitude of preparations. All the art objects had to be moved against the far wall and under the piano. After my experience with miscellaneous articles shooting inward at the embassy, I did not wish to be knocked out with a china lamp or agate inkstand. Profiting by the knowledge that eight embassy typewriters had been put out of commission by being dashed onto the floor, I would set both our typewriters under the desk. I never received much encouragement from Erskine during these operations, which he considered old-womanish. Sometimes the concussion works in reverse, he would tell me, and things blow out. But I would explain that when a ventilator has missed your head by inches, you take an entirely different attitude toward movable objects.

In a future world, if wars continue, I believe modern architecture will develop a severity that will surpass anything yet attained. I used to think about modern architecture, as I crawled around under the piano in the darkness, stacking those statuettes and vases. I used to picture rooms with built-in wall seats and sunken lighting fixtures, with recessed cabinets and all surfaces that one might bump into, rounded and smooth, with nothing loose around the place and not a single object in the middle of the floor. If I ever get out of this, I would say to myself, I'll go back and tell those modern architects that they're on the right track but they should carry modernism even farther.

It is strange how in a bombing everything in the room seems to rise up against you and become your enemy. The Napoleon pillar was too heavy to move, and in the darkness and the vibration I feared Napoleon more than Hitler.

But once the bric-a-brac was stowed away, the place was my workshop, and my whole attitude changed. It has always been my experience that a camera in my hands produces a subconscious transformation. A few years ago, for example, I did a considerable amount of photography on some skyscrapers under construction. If the photographic needs of the job required walking over a scaffold eight hundred feet above the street, it seemed as routine as if the sidewalk were only eight feet below. But I felt this ease only when working, when it seemed of some purpose.

Photographing the bombings was much the same. Once I began viewing the skyline through the ground glass of a camera, my world became one of composing streaks and dashes of light, of judging the length of exposures, of trying to make each sheet of film bring out the most intense portions of the unearthly beauty unfolding before the lens.

I had begun making time exposures (varying from a few seconds to eight or twelve minutes each) with one camera in operation. As the raids increased in intensity I worked with four. The size of the raid was measured by whether it was a two-camera, three-camera, or four-camera night. But I never operated all five at once.

My fifth camera, along with a couple of lenses and half my store of films, flash bulbs, and synchronizing equipment, I had transferred to the basement at Spazzo. I was always afraid that the tools I was working with might get smashed up during a raid. The possibility of being left without a single camera grew to be an obsession, so I always took care to divide the risk.

As time went on, our routine was perfected to the point of seeing that our room was stocked with beer and sandwiches well before the alarm sounded; and later, as other journalists moved into our hotel, we used to keep open house during a raid. One after another, when the patrol had completed its round, silent pajama-clad figures would steal into our room. I believe that most of the Moscow raids described in the American press were viewed from our splendid balcony. But during those early weeks we held vigil alone.

People in London and Barcelona used to say that they minded a raid much less if they were in a crowd. I never noticed this, perhaps because my cameras were such absorbing company; but there was one night, early in August, when this objective point of view deserted me.

Usually a raid approaches gradually, and by the time the action has reached the center of the city one becomes adjusted to it, in a way, and the whine of bombs and deafening banging from guns on near-by roof-tops come as less of a surprise. But this night, before I got the first carved-lion ash tray on the floor, the bombs started whining. We had no time to put away typewriters and china lamps, although I did manage to get the four cameras going, two on the broad marble window sill overlooking the Kremlin and two pointing in opposite directions through the grille of the balcony.

Then all time was thrown out of joint. As each finely machined specimen of high-grade steel, streamlined like a bird's wing, was dropped out four miles over our heads, we could hear it screaming its way closer and closer to earth. It seemed as if it would never reach the ground. Erskine would grab me in those strong arms of his and carry me to a little vestibule between two sets of doors, which divided our bedroom from the parlor. We would wait and finally, when the crash came, we could hear that sickening sound of bricks giving way: like toast being crumbled inside your ear. Then we would think: at least that one missed us. Next I would run out and change the films, knowing that such a jar had blurred the exposures then in process. Then another and another would send us back between the doors. But each time, no matter how close the shriek came, I always felt safe when my husband carried me back in his arms.

Even during a raid we could always tell the time, for the Kremlin clock, its gold hands and figures concealed under gray paint, still chimed out each quarter hour. It was Erskine's night to broadcast, and

ANTIAIRCRAFT BARRAGE

THIS WEB of guns on Moscow rooftops indicates how heavily the city was fortified. It would be impossible to fly through such concentrated fire.

What the picture cannot show is the din created by the continuous cannonading. As each shell leaves its gun it jars everything within a large radius—including not only buildings but spectators as well. On this night it went on for six hours with only slight letups. It was the loudest noise I have ever heard.

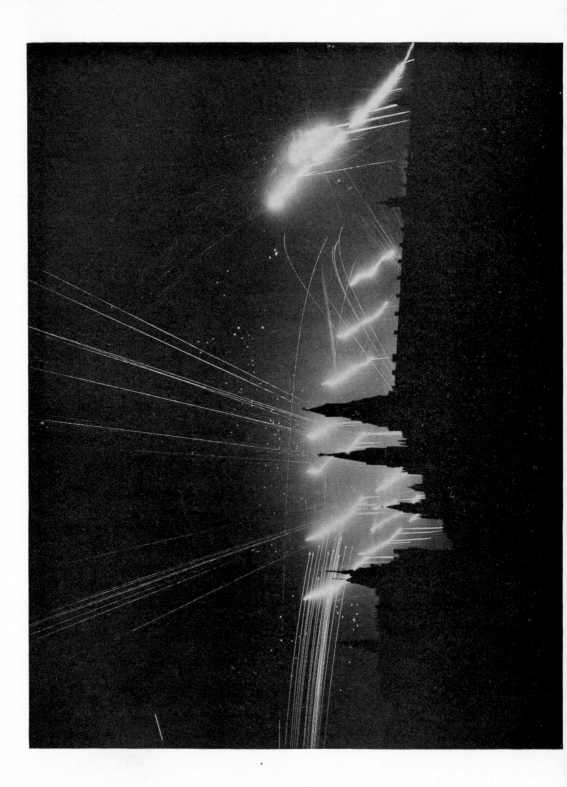

at one-thirty he had to leave for Radio Center. We had been wearing our Russian military helmets whenever we approached the window sills or the balcony, but now he changed his for an enormous helmet which the Mayor of Moscow had provided especially for going to broadcasts. It had a steel visor that projected over his face, and a metal apron that swept around the sides and back, and it might have been designed for a Martian invasion.

"If they set fire to the hotel, you go right down to a shelter," he directed. "And don't waste any time. The Huns are expert at bombing burning buildings."

"I'd hate to get shown up now after all these days of making believe that I'm not here," I said.

"Never mind that. If it gets any worse you get into a basement. Do you hear?"—with which he was gone.

Only a few minutes after he left, the loudest scream of all sounded through the air. I ran back between the double doors, feeling very lonely, while the bomb executed its interminable descent, and when it finally landed I could hear the skeleton of a building across the street give way. I hurried out to the balcony. Just behind the Kremlin wall an enormous plume was rising into the air. It seemed to hang there, frozen against the moonlit sky. Then planks and bricks began dropping out of it. I could hear the shouts of soldiers and patrolmen running toward it across the square.

BOMBING OF THE KREMLIN

THIS WAS an extraordinary night when the German parachute flares, like a string of pearls, were dropped in parallel rows over the Kremlin. Drifting with the wind, they descended slowly to earth in snakelike lines.

Note the short, thick, vertical lines leaving the path of the flare. These are globlets of molten magnesium which drop off the burning mass of the flare itself and fall straight to earth.

The long fanlike rays sweeping upward are Soviet tracer shells to show the gunners where their shots are headed. Every tenth shell has tracer coating.

As to the horizontal lines at the left: these were fired from guns on a near-by rooftop, aiming low at the flares and attempting as well to shoot down the German plane dropping the flares.

Though not as spectacular in the picture, perhaps most important of all are the small white dots which spatter the sky. These are bursting shells from the Zenith guns which are placed densely around the defense rings of Moscow. They burst at an altitude of from ten to twenty thousand feet, and a barrage is constantly set up in an attempt to hold back the German planes from the Moscow area. This was a particularly spectacular display of antiaircraft barrage. Even the Britishers who had watched the defense of London said they had never seen such fireworks.

The damage was concealed behind the wall and it was a week before I was able to find out that a whole Kremlin palace had been blown to bits. It was not the building used by Stalin for offices, but a palace used as a barracks by the Kremlin guard. Not this, however, nor any other hits made on the Kremlin were ever permitted by the censors to be released in news dispatches.

The raid began dying now. The Germans were going away, and the ground fire was drawing into the distance. I rested on the broad window sill.

Air raids affect people in various ways. Some people grow very hungry afterward, others become sleepy. Most of my Russian friends developed an appetite and had to eat as soon as the raid was over, but I was one of the sleeping kind. When the guns grew quieter I would drop off at once, often right on the window sill beside the cameras. Sometimes a wave of planes would come back, and the blasting of guns on rooftops near by would jar me awake. I would start up to see the square below dancing with fireflies as the shrapnel tinkled down on the pavement. But as soon as the sound started to grow softer I would be back in slumber on the marble ledge, my cameras, set for time exposures, still recording any streaks of light that might flash through the sky.

When my husband came back we would get into the wide bed that had held the Lindberghs, and the German trade commissioner, and perhaps Trotsky too, for all I know, and very comfortable under the yellow satin quilt we would doze off, and wake up again if the shooting picked up, watching it through our big windows.

Finally at dawn we would hear the loudspeaker on the roof above us call out, "The enemy has been beaten back, comrades. Go home to your rest." As confused voices rose from thousands of people leaving the subway, we would fall into a deep sleep.

CHAPTER 10

Microphones and a Boudoir Clock

EVERYONE IN radio circles said that to give a live-voice broadcast from Moscow would make radio history. But they always added that it couldn't be done. We heard this in New York, and we heard it again in Moscow. A dubious hope that we might be able to accomplish it had been expressed by Paul White, Columbia's foreign manager, when we left home. "It's a hundred-to-one chance," he said, "but it might come through." When we arrived in Moscow we found that the National Broadcasting Company had been paying a man's salary for three years just to keep him on the spot, negotiating for a live broadcast.

Radio Moscow sends out a continuous stream of music, news, communiqués, and so forth, but any voice which goes live into the microphone must be that of a Soviet citizen. All other material must be recorded, and the records played back to the censors before being put on the air. These records are useless for the United States, as the major chains follow a policy of using only live voice for newscasts.

After a superficial inquiry we decided that the obstacles were insurmountable, and we were so busy with photography and writing that we promptly forgot about it. But the day the war started, Paul White began shooting us cables.

On the first Sunday after the invasion, therefore, our siege against the old order of radio began. We were brought out of bed by a prayer in cablese from White, begging us to try to work the miracle by 6:51:15 P.M., New York Daylight Saving time (which was fifty-one minutes and fifteen seconds after midnight, Greenwich time, and 2:51:15 A.M., Moscow time), so that Moscow could be included in a series of reports being broadcast from world capitals over the nation-wide network that Sunday evening.

125

We hurried to the "Radio Committiet" on Pushkin Square, where we were told that government-issued communiqués were broadcast daily by short wave and that all Americans who wished to could tune in.

"But this is different," we explained. "Americans want to hear about the war from an American point of view, and this is one of the biggest hookups in America. Twenty million persons listen."

The twenty-million figure made an impression, and we were told to go home and expect a telephone call in half an hour. After forty minutes we called Radio Center and we kept on calling at intervals of ten minutes until we were promised a definite answer later in the afternoon.

At five o'clock we arrived at Radio Center and were told that Radio Committiet saw no reason for breaking the rule that live broadcasts be given only by Soviet citizens.

We hurried back through Pushkin Square and spent the rest of the evening calling all the high officials to whom we had access. At ten minutes past midnight the telephone rang, and it was Radio Center, asking us to come immediately. We rushed to the studio and everyone shook us by the hand: the broadcast was on! For one solid hour Erskine pounded away on the typewriter, pausing at intervals to read aloud while I timed him on what he had written. Then the script was sent out to be read by the Narkomindel censors, by Glavalit, the special radio censors, and perhaps by Stalin, too, for all we knew.

At one-thirty o'clock in the morning the script came back, with the report that everything was all right, and we would now proceed to record it.

Two Caldwells reached for their hats. "Live broadcast or no broadcast!" we said, opening the door.

We were urged to wait another fifteen minutes while the Radio Committiet pondered the situation. During that quarter of an hour two telegrams came in from New York, one for us and an identical one for the Committiet. Paul White, to whom long experience with foreign governments has brought much wisdom, had been sending cablegrams all day saying, "Live broadcast or none."

It was eight minutes before broadcast time when the studio director came in and handed Erskine the script, which by then had been O.K.'d so many times it looked like a racing form.

"We will now go into the studio where you can give your broadcast," he said matter-of-factly.

"Live?" we shouted.

"Yes."

As Erskine read, I watched the timing, slowing him down or speeding him up to keep to schedule. I stood behind the microphone, making signals with my right hand and holding his watch in my left. It was a beautiful gold watch. I had given it to him on his last birthday. I was so excited that I put my thumb right through the crystal.

The next morning we began getting cables. The broadcast had come through as though it had been given from Moscow, Idaho. The first Russian broadcast was a reality; history was made; Columbia and the Caldwells had scored a beat.

The next night was my turn at the microphone, and from then on we alternated. But after that first miraculous Sunday, for two solid weeks the reception was so bad that few programs got through.

Later, after the full splendor of the nightly raids began, I discontinued broadcasting; the night hours were so rich in pictures that I felt my most important post was on a rooftop or balcony. But in the meantime I was able to catch a glimpse of the curious life that went on in Radio Center, Moscow.

Radio Center broadcast in all languages and transmitted to all continents. I first realized the scope of these operations when an alarm brought a pack of performers to the cellar shelter. I listened to Italian, Dutch, Swedish, Czech, Bulgarian, and Chinese. Before the raid was over, a Spaniard and a Portuguese came in, fresh from a South American program. With them was a Parisian, trim with waxed mustache, who had been talking to occupied France. They were followed by a couple of Britishers speaking in clipped accents that might have been overheard on Trafalgar Square. In the corner were three Hindus, sound asleep, resting after their broadcast to India.

This heterogeneous collection consisted of foreign Communists who had come to the Soviet Union and become naturalized citizens. Now that the U.S.S.R. was at war, the greatest contribution they could make to their adopted country was to use their native tongue over the airwaves. Sometimes they read news, sometimes they gave accounts of brave deeds

of the Red Army or of guerrilla troops. Often they read translations of
Soviet literature on what Radio Center called its "cultural programs."
Their broadcasts could be heard by people in America and other countries with short-wave receiving sets but were not, of course, rebroadcast
by American networks. These people also broadcast "live," although
the scripts from which they read did not originate with them, but were
prepared by government propaganda writers.

Since Erskine and I talked on one of America's most complicated
programs, "The World Today," there were many problems of detail.
On this program each capital, whether it is London, Chungking, or
Sydney, talks for three and a quarter minutes; and the timing as well as
the transmission must be perfect if the broadcasting chain in America
is to succeed with the pickup, which converts short wave into long wave
for its millions of American listeners. Three and a quarter minutes on
the air is a bit less than two typewritten double-spaced pages, and we
found that careful boiling down of the news was necessary. My practice
was to sift through the communiqués, use whatever "spot news" there
was for my lead paragraph, and devote the rest of my talk to "color,"
of which there was a great deal during those dramatic days. After
Erskine and I got permission to broadcast live for C.B.S., the N.B.C.
man who had been working for so many years on the problem was permitted to broadcast the next night, and regularly thereafter. Occasionally we were able to arrange to put on a guest speaker; but this practice
was not encouraged by the Committiet, which investigated everyone
with fantastic thoroughness before allowing him to speak "live" into
the microphone. Once our guest speaker was a correspondent who had
been in Moscow for six years and had excellent standing—but even he
needed a ten days' investigation. Shortly after we left Moscow in the
fall, and the correspondents were moved to Kuibyshev, direct broadcasting stopped. "Live" broadcasts are seldom heard any more from
Americans in the U.S.S.R.

There were several American expatriates on the staff of Radio Center, men and women who had taken out Soviet citizenship ten years before. The two we worked with the most were Negroes: Mr. Whittaker,
from Harlem, and a South Carolina colored mammy, whose name we
never heard.

It was Mr. Whittaker who announced us to New York, so that the C.B.S. technicians would know when to switch us on their nation-wide hookup. Our relations with the colored mammy consisted in shoving her gradually off the bench in front of the microphone as our time approached, and being in turn shoved off by her as our time ended and hers, to read from her government-prepared script, began again.

Radio Center was such a busy place that each microphone was in continuous use throughout the day and night, and the colored mammy's soft, even voice could be heard, any time we came into the studio, reading endless communiqués and tales of Soviet heroism to be short-waved to the English-speaking world.

The microphones worked on an equally busy schedule for transmission within the country's borders. A system of radio communications was set up for the reading of letters from families directly to soldiers at the front. Precedence was given to brides writing to their soldier bridegrooms. Once I thumbed through a quantity of these letters that had come to the studio for transmission, and picked out several typical ones to include in my broadcast to America. One of my choices read: "I am counting on you, my darling, to pick off those Hitlerite crows with your bayonet, until our beautiful land is free of the Fascist rabble." And another: "My Beloved, I am learning to operate your punch press, so I shall be able to fight on the home front while you go out to annihilate those wild beasts of Hitlerism. Break the necks of those Fascist hangmen!"

There were so many letters in this vein that I wondered whether it was the natural style of Russian brides or whether that particular type of letter was selected by the Committiet for broadcasting. A letter from a mother, which I included in my broadcast, read: "My beloved sonny Misha. You were a perfect schoolboy, and now I want you to attack the enemy as hard as you used to attack your schoolbooks."

Every day the radio issued instructions so citizens would be on the alert for fifth columnists. Children were warned that any stranger who asked directions might be a spy, for if he were a native of the neighborhood he should know his way. To catch a diversionist, as spies were called, became the ambition of every child. A tale was broadcast of a group of children working in the fields when a stranger, speaking per-

fect Russian, asked his way to the next village. The children sent him in the wrong direction and then ran for a militiaman who arrested him. The man was a diversionist and his parachute was discovered in a near-by tree. Another story was broadcast of a militiaman who got on a streetcar in Leningrad and inquired of the conductor, "How much is the fare?"

"Militiamen don't have to pay any fare," he was told.

"I come from Moscow," snapped out the officer.

"But in Moscow the rule is the same," said the conductor. Within a few minutes the militiaman was surrounded and placed under arrest. He was a German spy.

That Soviet citizens took these anecdotes to heart was evident every day of our lives. Once Tatiana and I were traveling in the subway. We came out at the Palace of the Soviets Station, and as we walked into the street we were asked for our papers by a militiaman. Tatiana showed her Soviet citizen's passport, which Russians must carry at all times, and I brought out my Russian and my American passports, my press card, and all my documents. With a smile and a bow we were released.

"Why on earth were we stopped?" I asked.

"A man in the Metro heard us speaking English and didn't know what foreign language it was, so he followed us out and summoned a militiaman to see if we were diversionists."

This incredibly thorough watchfulness on the part of the whole citizen body helps to explain why there are no fifth columnists active in the Soviet Union. My short walk from the hotel to Pushkin Square, on the nights that I went on the air, was a continuous demonstration of this alertness. Before air raiding began I used to go on foot rather than by

---

PROPUSK

THIS IS one of the most important documents in wartime Russia and one of the most difficult to obtain. It is a night pass that allows a car to circulate during curfew, which lasts from midnight to four A.M. Actually a *propusk*—whether for car or person—is a twenty-four-hour pass.

It is not sufficient for the car alone to have a *propusk*. Anybody who drives during curfew must have one, as must all his passengers. It is a dangerous pastime to try to get your *propusk*-less friends home hidden on the floor in the back of the car. Militiamen may stop the car anywhere; but red lights are particularly dangerous, for there the car is always challenged. Traffic lights are dimmed because of blackout, with just a cat's-eye slit to allow the red or green to show through.

car because I loved the strange half twilight of the white nights, the buildings standing like gray blotting paper against a luminous sky, their windows gleaming with the indirect rays of the sun, which traveled only a shallow distance below the horizon each night. I had to have a special night card or pass, called a *propusk*, to be allowed to walk abroad between midnight and four A.M., the hours of curfew. On the walk up Gorky Street to Pushkin Square, citizen watchers would challenge me at every third doorway, draw me into the vestibule, and by the light of a carefully shaded match examine my credentials. When they found that I was an Amerikanka, I was always sent on my way with cordial expressions of regard for my great country and equally great President, Mr. Roosevelt.

Going by car speeded our trips only slightly, for even our car had to show its passport. Getting into the studio required more *propuski*, furnished in slow motion by a wooden-faced girl after she had telephoned to various radio officials to make sure that I was really due on the program. I never saw her show a glimmer of recognition, no matter how many nights this process was repeated. After identification, a separate *propusk* was handed to a militiaman as each doorsill was crossed. The capture of the radio station is a favorite fifth-column tactic, but in Russia it has all the probability of a flock of white rabbits taking over a dog pound.

During our weeks of broadcasting we grappled with frequencies and kilocycles and meter bands. Cables between Caldwell and Columbia posed such problems as whether transmission was satisfactory on meter bands 25 comma 19 point 76 comma 31 point 41 comma 19 point 05 comma 19 point 72 query. And Columbia would reply either that there had been complete silence from Moscow or that our voices were unusable and unintelligible.

I have known few things in my life more demoralizing than the uncertainty of that microphone in Moscow. After boiling down the day's news into the time allotment, running the gantlet first of censors and then of guards demanding *propuski*, rehearsing my talk in front of the studio's key timepiece (a boudoir clock) to check timing, gargling my throat so that anxiety would not make me completely speechless, I would then go on the air over that unimaginable void of ether and oceans—only to find out the next day that I had been heard clearly by two people: Mr. Whittaker and Mammy.

Finally a winning combination was struck. I used to picture it, a rainbow of meter bands arching from Pushkin Square to midtown New York. From then on we had only two things to worry about, sunspots and the boudoir clock.

Sunspots were more than we or the technicians could hope to conquer. There is no cure possible except a celestial change of heart. But the boudoir clock we consistently tried to master, never quite succeeding.

There was no two-way conversation possible between New York and Moscow, and the electrical timing device in the studio had been shut off because of the possibility of power failure during air raids. Therefore the boudoir clock was used, in the absence of wall clocks with second hands, metronomes, and the other timing paraphernalia usually employed by broadcasting studios. Considering that our three and a quarter minutes were being sliced in between such distant points as London, Cairo, or Ankara, Erskine and I always expressed a natural anxiety about its accuracy. Whereupon Mr. Whittaker would cry, "I'll verify it," would carry it to the telephone while he called the post office, reset it, and in a few seconds either Erskine or I, depending on whose night it was, would be reading into the microphone, trying simultaneously to gauge the quarter minutes without a second hand. It was a rare and happy night when American Naval Observatory Time had a meeting of the minds with the Moscow post office.

The mysterious personages who handled the second censorship for Glavalit, somewhere in the upper reaches of Radio Center, remained invisible. Once I outwitted them, but it was more by accident than design. Early on the evening of July 9 the foreign press was electrified by the announcement that Maxim Litvinov was going to broadcast in English at eleven o'clock that night. This was his first official reappearance since the breakup of Anglo-Soviet negotiations in 1939, and the very fact that he was emerging from a two-year retirement was important news. I was in a beautiful position to have a scoop, because my broadcast would reach America on the 5:45 P.M. news roundup and the story, just too late for the afternoon editions, would make only the morning papers in America.*

The time was short, but as soon as the speech was delivered I chose a few extracts, and my paragraph was passed by the Narkomindel censors without delay. This was to be expected since it consisted only of direct quotes from Litvinov.

When I reached Radio Center with my new paragraph, I called for the usual handful of *propuski*, battered my way through the guards, and finally found Mr. Whittaker and thrust the paragraph into his hand. There was a rule that new material must be passed by Glavalit forty minutes before broadcasting time. I was due on the microphone in half an hour, but in as much as my paragraph consisted of the actual words of Litvinov—not even a translation, for he had spoken in English—and had already been passed by the Foreign Office censors, I foresaw no difficulty.

I waited in the studio, rehearsing silently from a carbon copy of my script, while the colored mammy, who was giving a cultural program, read translations from the folk tales of Kazakstan into the microphone.

The time for my broadcast drew closer, but Mr. Whittaker had not reappeared. The minute arrived for him to make his customary announcement that I was due on the air, so the C.B.S. technicians at the receiving end would be ready to switch me on their nation-wide hookup. No Mr. Whittaker. It was fifteen seconds before my starting time—when Mammy stopped reading Kazak literature and rushed into the breach. "This is Moscow calling," she said. "In a few seconds you will hear . . ." and I was on the air. By eliminating several lines of my original material, I was able to read the quotations from Mr. Litvinov into the script and still come out within my three-and-a-quarter-minute time limit. I had just signed off when Mr. Whittaker ran into the room, waving my paragraph over his head. "You can't use it!" he said. "Glavalit say they must have forty minutes, and they haven't had time to pass it yet!"

* To someone used to American ways it may seem strange that the Litvinov address was planned so exclusively for foreign consumption: not only did he speak in English, but his broadcast was not even transmitted to radio sets within the Soviet Union. It was not until the next morning, when *Pravda* and *Izvestia* carried a much condensed report of his speech, that the Russian people knew Litvinov had spoken to the outside world.

"But I have used it," I gasped. "It's just been read!"

The astonishment was so great that I should dream of reading a paragraph that had not been passed by all censors that I was not even reproved.

However, some time later, my luck was reversed. There had been three consecutive nights with no *Luftwaffe*, and I had written a description of Moscow citizens, overtired after many nights of interrupted sleep, at last catching up on their rest. Twelve minutes before I was due on the air the antiaircraft guns began booming so loudly that we had to close all corridor doors and still we couldn't keep the sound out of the studio. I begged permission to write a new paragraph and insert it. Mr. Whittaker went upstairs to intercede for me and came back with the reminder that there was a forty-minute rule for new material, and not a word of my script was to be changed.

I had just signed off, and the cultural program was starting in again, when a five-hundred-pound bomb fell outside in the courtyard. It threw me against the wall, and the colored mammy slipped off her bench as smoothly as though she were sliding down a strawstack.

"Lordy mussy!" said Comrade Mammy.

And then we caught sight of our one casualty. The boudoir clock lay at her feet, and it was plain that it had ticked out its last transoceanic broadcast.

From then on the problems of intercontinental timing were handled by an alarm clock, which, as Erskine remarked, looked as if it had been tossed six or seven times in the early morning from a twelve-story window.

CHAPTER 11

God in Russia

WHEN I HEARD that the priests of Moscow were praying for victory I decided the time had come to go to church.

It was on a Saturday evening in the middle of August that I asked our secretary, Tatiana, to take me to twilight Mass. We went to a great cathedral in central Moscow. It was called Bogoyavlensky, which means God's Resurrection, and as we walked into the huge vaulted interior it seemed as though we had stepped back into another century.

The walls glowed with the rich colors of the oval-faced icons which have hung there for hundreds of years. The air was filled with incense. Hundreds of worshipers lighted slender tapers, knelt on the stone floor worn into hollows, and crossed themselves with the same swift, deft motion that they have used for centuries. While I had known that the Soviet Constitution provides for "freedom of religious worship and freedom of antireligious propaganda," I had never before looked into the subject to see how it worked out in practice.

Against a high altar, radiant with gold halos arched over painted saints, stood a strange little figure. Small in proportions, it looked as though some child, chancing on bits of stiff brocade, had wrapped up its doll, topped it with a crown, and pasted a beard of bleached cornsilk

---

KISSING THE ICON

THE TWO women before the icon are typical of the peasants who worship in the Old Orthodox Church. The churches are filled with icons, and the worshipers choose their favorites. This one is the most popular in the Bogoyavlensky Cathedral. It is called the Madonna of the Resurrection of the Perished. Worshipers are careful to touch their lips to the foot of the Christ child and the hands of the Madonna. They wish only to kiss the sacred flesh and are therefore careful to avoid the clothes. They do not kiss the faces of the Madonna or Child, because that would be presumptuous. The icons themselves are topped with daintily tucked pink pavilions decorated with artificial flowers.

on its wax-pink face. But there was nothing doll-like about the authoritative voice issuing from under that oversize golden coronet.

This was Sergei, Patriarch of the Old Orthodox Church, Metropolitan of the cities of Moscow and Kolomna, Keeper of the Patriarchal Throne for Russian Orthodox believers over the whole world. And he—a priest —was calling on his congregation to defend with arms a country which has stood, in the eyes of the world, for atheism.

"If our Mother Church is dear to us," intoned Sergei, "do we not hold equally dear our mother country—a country where people are building life on the basis of truth and good will! The task of all Christians is to defend the sacred borders of their homeland against the German barbarians. Let God bestow his benediction so that we may destroy and smash the crazy Hitler, the instigator of world slaughter. God will grant us victory."

He made the sign of the cross with double and triple candlesticks, pronounced the benediction, and the people flowed to other parts of the great vaulted church. At one side of the altar a double funeral was being held, with prayers for the dead on paper scrolls across the foreheads of the deceased. The mourners dipped their fingers into a bowl of boiled rice and raisins, which they munched on behalf of the deceased; and a priest threw in handfuls of sand as the two coffins were closed, murmuring, "From earth you come and to earth you return."

At a side altar opposite, a queue of mothers, holding somewhat frightened-looking babies, was forming, waiting their turn for christening. The sacrament was being administered by an archdeacon in a tall

---

PATRIARCH SERGEI

SERGEI'S FULL title is Metropolitan of Moscow and Kolomna, Keeper of the Patriarchal Throne (for the whole world). He is thus the principal figure of the Old Orthodox Church wherever it exists. In Russian, his title is: Mitropolit Moskovski i Kolomenski i Patriarshi Mestoblistitel.

He is seventy-four years old, hears badly, lives in a five-room wooden house, and has a Soviet-made automobile, the M-3 (which is similar to our Ford), speaks a few words of English, as a result of his visit to San Francisco and Brooklyn in 1894.

In the portrait he is wearing three "jewels." From left to right they are:

1. Medallion of gold set with precious stones, showing Christ's face engraved on a cameo;
2. Cross of doctor of theology;
3. Panagia set with diamonds: the Virgin Mary carved on a cameo.

A panagia may be worn only by someone of rank of bishop or higher.

purple cylindrical hat. I had strong doubts as to whether when these babies grew up they would ever see the inside of a church, for the young rarely go to church these days, even in other parts of the world; but they go particularly seldom in Soviet Russia, where their education is in an opposite direction. In fact, I wondered whether these youngsters would ever even hear that they had started their lives with a bath in a font. But there was one touch of modern Soviet life in the baptism, and that was the fact that even the babies must queue up for holy water.

Soviet citizens stand in a queue in crowded stores to buy groceries, in the streets to get a trolley bus, and along the sidewalk to get their morning papers. All throughout the enormous church they were now lining up to kiss their favorite icons. The two longest queues were forming before the Madonna of Unexpected Happiness and of the Resurrection of the Perished. These were popular icons, and their varnish was split and peeling from the pressure of thousands of lips over uncounted years.

"Look how the paint is cracked!" I said to Tatiana.

"Yes," she replied, "and notice how careful they are not to touch the painted clothing. They want to kiss only the hands and feet of the Madonna and Christ child."

BISHOPS BEFORE THE HIGH ALTAR OF BOGOYAVLENSKY (RESURRECTION) CATHEDRAL, MOSCOW

WHEN THE Patriarch steps out of his car and arrives at the church, he is met at the entrance by all the clergy dressed in full regalia. He is led to the middle of the church, where a special space surrounded by a wooden fence is allotted for his movements. Then the robing ceremony takes place, in which he is dressed by four hypodeacons (Russian word: *ipodiakony*) in gold brocade, and the coronet is placed on his head.

Then the service begins, with all the metropolitans, priests, and bishops standing facing the altar. With the Patriarch are the Metropolitans of Leningrad and of Kiev. No one either in the clergy or the congregation ever turns his back to the high altar. They made an exception for me after I was able to impress them with the necessity of getting their photographs.

The Bogoyavlensky Cathedral has its own savings fund, amounting to over a million rubles.

An appeal to the patriotism of all believers, written by Patriarch Sergei, hangs on the wall inside the vestibule of the church. Excerpts: "The Church was never a silent witness of evil being performed. The protection of your country is the sacred duty of every Christian. And so, fulfill it. If our own mother is dear to us, equally dear to us is the mother country. The Orthodox Church has always shared the fate of its people."

It occurred to me that these ancient icons had never before heard such strange prayers. As the worshipers filed up, they murmured petitions not only for their husbands and sons at the front, but for the health of the officials in the Kremlin. In her infinite mercy, the Holy Mother was listening to appeals to protect the leaders of an antireligious government.

When we found the Dean of the cathedral I tried to draw him out on this seeming inconsistency. "No one interferes with us," he told me; "we are quite free. The Church receives a license from the government and, within church walls, the Patriarch and the archbishops are supreme."

As we talked it became plain that he believed if Hitler won the war, the Church would be obliterated altogether, so that a Soviet victory was vital.

"Many Americans believe that there is no religion in Soviet Russia," I began; whereupon I summoned up my courage to ask if I might be permitted to take pictures in church. I received not only his ready consent, but an invitation to tea at the home of the Patriarch, Sergei.

Sergei at close range looked quite real, in his simple black robe, which set off the whiteness of his beard, and with a carved cameo panagia, the jeweled insignia of a bishop, hanging on a gold chain around his neck. He presided over a giant silver samovar at a table set with dishes of chocolates and cherry jam and a tea cozy embroidered like a rooster. Tatiana and I took our places with the Metropolitan Nikolas of

---

TEA WITH ARCHBISHOPS

UNDER THE rooster-embroidered tea cozy is a small china pot in which tea is brewed, and at the left is the large silver samovar for heating the water. On the table were little cakes, cherry jam which was eaten with a spoon or stirred into the tea, and chocolates. In the corner are icons. An icon corner such as this is found in each room in the house. The Patriarch's portrait on the wall is embroidered in thousands of fine stitches.

Reading from right to left are Metropolitan (highest local Church executive) Alexis Simansky of Leningrad; Patriarch Sergei, Metropolitan of the cities of Moscow and Kolomna and chief of the entire hierarchy of the Old Orthodox Church; Metropolitan Nikolas Yarushevich of Kiev; Archdean Alexander in charge of the Bogoyavlensky Cathedral.

The highest officials of the Church, in conformity with the dictates of the Greek Orthodox Church, wear beards and are forbidden to marry. Archdean Alexander is married.

Kiev and the Metropolitan Alexis of Leningrad, who were refugee *
guests of the Patriarch, and our acquaintance of yesterday, Alexander,
the Archdean of Bogoyavlensky Cathedral. In the midst of these flowing
beards and this unprecedented amount of sanctity, I expected to find
tea-table chatter a bit difficult; but my shyness exploded when His Grace
Sergei told me that he had been to Brooklyn. The visit was made in
1894. As the Keeper of the Patriarchal Throne described in broken
English that faraway spot, I began to look on a trip to Brooklyn as one
of the most glamorous voyages in the whole world.

Patriarch Sergei was as deaf and jolly as anybody's great-grandfather.
He kept stirring cherry jam with complete impartiality into my glass of
tea and into his own, while Archbishop Nikolas and Archbishop Alexis
described to me how they had helped Archdean Alexander put out a fire
bomb. The fire bomb, which was the size and shape of a Coca-Cola
bottle, and only slightly torn at the edges, was passed around the tea
table and then replaced carefully in a cabinet containing several foot
bones of saints and a collection of prayer beads made of moon-
stones.

Our chauffeur drove Tatiana and me to church the following Sunday
with somewhat the same feelings as a small boy taking his sisters to
dancing school. The conspicuousness of his position was enhanced by
the fact that no one else arrived by automobile except the Patriarch
himself, who came in his own smart little Soviet-built car. Russian pe-
destrians ask questions of anyone who interests them or puzzles them,
as if it were a hereditary right; and during his long wait, poor un-

---

* Although the Soviet government instructs most of its citizens to stay behind even if their
homes are captured, so as to serve as guerrillas or "partisans," there are certain exceptions—
among them priests and Jews—whom the authorities consider it wiser to evacuate whenever
practicable.

OLD ORTHODOX WORSHIPERS

THE PARISHIONERS cross themselves constantly and automatically from the moment
they enter the church. After each prayer
uttered from the altar the people break in
with a "Gospodi pomilui," God have
mercy.

The congregation is made up largely of
women, usually old. Few young people go
to church. The churches are licensed by
the government and are self-supporting.
Much of the work of the church is done
by volunteer committees.

happy, antireligious Alexander was catechized by the legions of curious unbelievers who passed by. One of his questioners was a militiaman who rushed angrily into the cathedral, saw me taking pictures, and telephoned police headquarters to see if I had a permit.* It is a proof of the authority of the Church over its own affairs that he was instructed that within church walls it was for the bishops and not the militia to say whether I might take photographs.

Inside, a congregation of twelve thousand packed the church so tightly that my equipment had to be passed over their heads. They flowed up on the steps of the altar; on the lowest altar step the Archdean stationed Tatiana and me. I worked with a Speed Graphic and flash bulbs throughout the complete service. It must have looked strange to see the bulbs flashing out among the lighted candles on the altar. The Archdean, however, had instructed me to work away as freely as I wished, for the Church leaders had decided that it was important for American believers to be able to see pictures showing that the faithful still worshiped in Russia. The people must have been astonished, but when they saw their priests helping me they were eager to help me, too.

Some of the priests held my extension lamps when it was necessary to have them held high over the heads of the congregation. In the middle of the service I ran out of flash bulbs—I was using them up by the dozens—and a small altar boy wormed his way to some spare cases I had cached at the side of the church. The parishioners then passed the bulbs to me, bucket-brigade fashion, up to the altar.

Sergei was dressed in jeweled gold robes, even more dazzling than

---

* While my church photographs were taken without making any arrangements through the Soviet authorities, nothing was done to stop me when they found out about it. In fact, when it was learned what a thorough job I was doing, Narkomindel issued a communiqué on religion to the foreign correspondents—an unprecedented procedure for the Soviet Foreign Office.

WORSHIPERS IN NEW ORTHODOX CHURCH

As the archbishop comes out periodically from the altar with *ektenia* (prayers), the people cross themselves rapidly and stoop to kiss the old stone floor. Here the archbishop was leading short prayers for the healing of the sick, for the safety of Red Army soldiers who were fighting at the front, and also for the health of the "authorities of this country"—i.e., for the welfare of the atheistic leaders of the Soviet government.

those I had previously seen, and he conducted the service assisted by the two archbishops, twenty-six priests, and six deacons, all resplendent in gold brocade.

A sort of carbon copy, less brilliant than the original, is the New Orthodox Church, with headquarters in Moscow. It differs from the Old not in any fundamental theology, but in two important particulars. Its higher priests need not grow beards, and they may take wives. In the Old Orthodox Church only the parochial priests could marry. The bishops and higher officials had to remain celibate.

Both of these differences were quickly evident when Tatiana and I called on Metropolitan Vvedensky, head of the New Orthodox Church. He lived in a tiny wooden house with carved, blue-painted window sills, situated near some textile factories in a manufacturing district of Moscow. We rang the bell, and the door was opened by an exquisite blonde creature, his second wife. His Grace was delighted to welcome anyone from the outside world and he chatted at great length in French about his children and his art treasures. Of his five boys we met two, a five-year-old Alexander, the child of the ravishing blonde, and a twenty-five-

---

METROPOLITAN ALEXANDER VVEDENSKY AT HOME

THIS CHARMING blonde is Alexander's second wife, by whom his fifth son, five-year-old Alexander, was born. The walls of his four-room house are crammed with paintings and the tables stuffed with statuary, ivory boxes, carved paper knives, and ivory fans. Crowded in amidst the statuary of this sitting room is a grand piano that the Metropolitan plays.

The portrait above the Metropolitan shows him in civilian clothes. These he wears under his bishop's regalia. He has many sets of ceremonial robes which he changes for different occasions.

The Metropolitan is witty, worldly, and a bit of a flirt. When the Germans were drawing close to Moscow, I called at his home and found the canvases being torn from their frames and piled in stacks, ready for evacuation to the country. Whenever I visited him at his church, he was the center of a large group of women who flocked into his office and begged him to take care of his health, assuring him that they constantly prayed for him. They called even at his home. Indeed, while we were having tea the day I photographed him here, peasants were constantly calling, bringing him gifts of cakes, giant strawberries, homemade wine, and other tributes. Some of them asked his advice about their personal affairs, such as when they should sell their cows and whether they should marry. He treated all of them, especially the ladies, with extreme graciousness.

Parenthetically, I must add that he was extremely courteous to me. He was fascinated with my camera and particularly with the case containing my lenses. He called in his wife and asked her if these didn't remind her of the church jewels.

year-old Alexander, the son of the first wife, and acting Archdeacon of the New Orthodox Church.

Metropolitan Vvedensky, also named Alexander, had lined his four-room house, even the bedchamber, with pictures, the way a stamp collector might continue to squeeze postage stamps into an overflowing album. Paintings of himself, of Venetian canals at sunset, of religious subjects, encrusted the walls and were stacked in the corners.

The young wife brought him a gold-chased chest, which he unlocked so I could photograph the contents. It was glittering with bishops' crosses of golden topazes, diamonds, emeralds, and amethysts. These were his personal property, he told me, not that of the Church. Most of them he had purchased himself; some were gifts; one had belonged to the late Patriarch Tikhon, who had lived in America and was Bishop of Alaska sixty years ago. There were some rare and ancient panagias, with carvings of the Virgin on enormous gems. A panagia is a religious picture, set in jewels, to be hung on a gold chain around the neck. Only bishops are allowed to wear them.

The Metropolitan let the jewels run through his fingers. "These are my *propuski* * into paradise," he said with a smile.

A complete reversal of this perfume-laden atmosphere was found when we called on the Baptists. Mikhail Akimovich Orlov, minister of the Moscow Baptist Church and President of the All-Union Council of Evangelists, sat in a severely furnished office, dressed in a simple Russian blouse laundered to a dazzling white. There were only two pictures on his office walls—one a painting of Christ on the cross, and the other a portrait of Lenin.

"What do you think of Lenin?" I asked.

* *Propusk*—passport.

METROPOLITAN VVEDENSKY GIVING THE BENEDICTION

METROPOLITAN VVEDENSKY is the father of the New Orthodox Church. He is also the father of five children by two wives. In this picture his son Alexander, who is Archdean, stands, wearing a high cylindrical hat, at the extreme left.

The Metropolitan himself stands with his two bishops and archdeacons in front of the high altar, giving the benediction with double and triple candlesticks. The former signify the double substance of Christ as man and God; the latter, the Holy Trinity.

"As a man, we consider him truly great," Pastor Orlov replied, "with a good heart, and exceptionally clever. If this were not so, such wide masses of working people would not be his followers. It is abnormal to have such a difference between rich and poor as exists in capitalistic society. We consider the social program of Lenin very close to that of the Bible."

The Baptists and evangelists have the strongest possible reasons for working to further a Soviet victory. It is only since the Soviet Union was formed that Protestant churches have been able to get a start in Russia. In the days of the czar, Pastor Orlov and a group of Protestant missionaries attempted to spread their faith in the face of continued persecution and great personal danger. This was because the Russian Orthodox Church was so closely allied to the state that the following of other faiths was not permitted. With the coming of the Bolsheviks this government alliance with the Orthodox Church met a sudden end, and it was then that singing Baptists, armed with hymnbooks, began spreading their faith through the land. "Atheists are easier to convert than members of the Old Orthodox Church," said Orlov, adding that Baptist membership has grown in the Soviet Union until it now includes over a thousand communities.

According to census figures given out by Narkomindel, the Soviet Union has 8338 churches. These are self-supporting and self-governing and must be licensed by the state. If attendance falls off in a certain church, that building is closed. Thus the parishioners of functioning churches must frequently travel from distant parts of the city when they gather for worship. In villages a ballot decides whether to keep the

---

BISHOP OF THE NEW ORTHODOX CHURCH

ONE OF the reforms instituted by Metropolitan Alexander Vvedensky is that in the New Orthodox Church high officials may marry and need not wear beards. According to the old-time ideas, any mature man, even though not a priest, believed he had to wear a beard in order to get to heaven.

The Soviet Union has, including both New and Old branches of the Orthodox Church:

active churches	4225
monasteries	37
priests	5665
deacons	3100

The robes being worn are the property of the Church, and are handed down from one group of Church officials to the next.

church open for services or use it for another purpose, and usually the vote is to turn the church building into something else, like a cheese factory or granary. As each younger generation grows up, religion recedes farther into the province of the old. Religion is heard of as little in Soviet schools as alchemy in university science classes.

One of the few occasions when Soviet children hear religion spoken of is when school classes are taken to visit the Antireligious Museum. There they are shown displays supporting the theme that the Church oppressed the peasants during the days of the czar. Paintings and documents illustrated how the priests bled their parishioners, extorting the best of their cattle and crops in the name of the Church, but turning these gifts to the personal enrichment of the clergy. Stress is laid on exhibits designed to show that the Church interfered with the progress of science throughout the world. In a wing of the museum, entitled "The Fight of Religion Against Science," are pictures of Spinoza being stoned, of Columbus being questioned by priests, of Copernicus accused of heresy for his theory that the earth moves around the sun. Despite the antireligious nature of the museum, still it recognizes the art value of the better icons, and many fine examples of religious paintings are kept there for study. In mid-August a bomb endangered the foundations of the museum, and the more valuable of the antireligious paintings and icons were moved to a place of safety, their place being taken by an anti-Fascist exhibit.

The People's Commissariat for Education believes that religion will eventually die out; but in the meantime no one persecutes or interferes with whatever worshipers wish to go to church, for the Soviet Constitution adheres strictly to its provision which ensures to citizens freedom of conscience.

In addition to Moscow's Old and New Orthodox Churches, there are Roman Catholic cathedrals, Moslem mosques, and Jewish synagogues—

MINISTER MIKHAIL AKIMOVICH ORLOV

IN ADDITION to being Baptist pastor, Orlov is President of the All-Union Council of Evangelist Christians. In Russian, the evangelists are called *staroobriadtsy*. Orlov was originally an atheist, a scientific student from St. Petersburg in czarist days. Upon conversion, he toured Russia as a missionary, founding Baptist groups. For this he was persecuted by the Old Orthodox Church and sometimes actually stoned.

all of which conduct their services unencouraged by the government, but unpersecuted. Among the evangelical denominations a bewildering number of sects have members within the borders of the Soviet Union. There are Dutch Reformists, Adventists, Dukhobors, Mennonites, Presbyterians, Shakers, and Rationalists. There are even Holy Rollers in Russia!

BAPTIST CHURCH, MOSCOW

THE BAPTISTS realize more than most religious groups the importance of helping the Soviets to attain victory, for it was the Revolution which gave their believers freedom openly to form communities and worship as they wished. The Old Orthodox Church had been their greatest oppressor.

Missionary work still goes on, by means of preaching at meetings and in the streets. There are between 1000 and 1500 Baptist units over the U.S.S.R., numbering from fifty to five hundred members. Moscow has 2500 members, and there are 300,000 Baptists in the whole country.

Baptists do not accept icons, relics, and the trappings of the Orthodox Church, considering them fetishism and idolatry. They approve of Lenin and consider his social philosophy close to that of Christ.

There are many sects, even Holy Rollers. The latter used to meet in this church, but the church leaders considered them too noisy. Now the Holy Rollers do their rolling in a Moscow apartment.

Religious inscriptions on the wall of the church are in French and German, dating from the time when this branch was established from abroad. The altar is covered with neat crocheted covers for sacramental vessels, on a red altar cloth embroidered in gold in German. The words are: "I am the way and the life" and another quotation stating that the door to heaven is only through Christ.

Excerpts from the Baptist sermon:

Can a Christian not be a patriot! Our country is undergoing a serious and trying moment of its life. A Christian who loves his country must protect it with arms in his hands.

Germany is ruining cities, drowning old people and children in blood, trampling on the sparkling truth of evangelist teachings, persecuting religion and priests.

We will bring everything we have to the altar of our country. The task of a Christian is to bring all his strength to help his country to conquer the enemy.

I took pictures throughout the service, and after it was over, the people thronged up to me, asking whether there were many believers in America. They were delighted when I answered yes and especially pleased when I told them that my grandmother was a Baptist. A group of young people, Baptists from the Ukraine, asked me to take a message of greeting to their co-believers in America. Many of the congregation wept when the minister announced that I would pass on these messages.

DECORATIONS

THE WEARING of great red and gold enameled decorations has assumed a place of the utmost importance in Soviet life. In earlier Bolshevik days, these orders were awarded sparingly and not seen except on the most official occasions.

It is only in the last few years that they have come out of the top bureau drawer and appeared on the streets. New orders have recently been created, and the older ones are now being conferred by the hundreds, perhaps by the thousands. It is probable that their increase is due to official recognition that additional incentives are needed under a socialistic form of society. At any rate, the recipients feel their honor deeply, step up production in their factories or on their farms, and increase their efforts to show that they are deserving of these rewards of merit.

Military decorations, such as the Order of the Gold Star and the Order of the Red Star, are an award for valor, but many civilian decorations exist for outstanding civil achievement, such as those shown here. Military heroes may receive these civil decorations also, and when they do, all the medals are usually worn at once.

Orlova, the movie star, has received both the Order of Lenin and the Badge of Honor, but she does not believe they look well on summer dresses. No one, of course, would appear at an official function without them, but Orlova's omission of these from her daily attire is more unusual than the failure of an American wife to wear her wedding ring. (Soviet wives do not wear wedding rings, by the way, and all stared at mine with great curiosity, and judging by their comments, they seemed to feel a little ashamed of me for wearing something so old-fashioned.)

It is a criminal offense for a person to wear an order who does not have a right to it, and an order can be withdrawn from a recipient who has committed some dishonorable action.

The title of Hero of the Soviet Union goes with the Order of Lenin and the Order of the Gold Star.

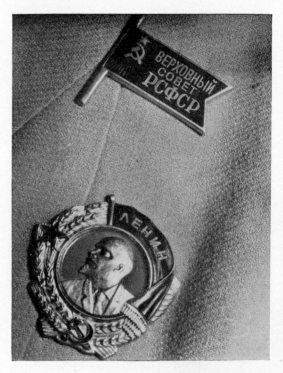

ORDER OF LENIN

THIS IS the highest honor in the Soviet Union. It was established in 1930 and is presented in a Kremlin ceremony by Kalinin to citizens who have shown outstanding merit. Many leading opera singers, artists, writers, engineers, factory workers, and collective farmers may be seen wearing it on the right lapel. It is about two inches in diameter. All these awards carry certain material advantages, and sometimes a lump sum of perhaps 50,000 rubles is presented with them.

Alexandrov, the movie director, has an Order of Lenin, received for one of the pictures in which he starred his wife, Orlova. Alexandrov is the only civilian to possess the military decoration Order of the Red Star. He received this when he did a picture called *Moscow Laughs*, in 1935. Until then, all Soviet moving pictures had been serious. Stalin, when he saw the picture, said: "That director is a brave man to do a humorous moving picture," and it was at the demand of Stalin that Alexandrov was awarded his military decoration.

This Order of Lenin was photographed "on the breast," as the Russians call it, of Barsova, the coloratura soprano. Above the Lenin Order on her ample bosom is a badge of deputy of the Supreme Council of the U.S.S.R. The words on the flag are "Supreme Council of RSFSR" (Soviet Russia proper). This is an elective office. Barsova holds office hours backstage, several times a week, and her constituents may come to her with their problems. Twice a year she attends the great meetings of deputies in the Kremlin Palace.

BADGE OF HONOR

THIS IS one of the largest decorations, about three inches across. The banners are inscribed: "Proletarians of all the world, unite," and with the Russian letters for Union of Soviet Socialist Republics.

The Badge of Honor was inaugurated in 1935 and is given specifically for work well done. Among the recipients are: Polgunov, chief of the Foreign Press in Narkomindel; Eduard Tissé, the famous cameraman who films Eisenstein's pictures and who has worked in Hollywood; Teleshova, director of the Moscow Art Theater and wife of Eisenstein. Among the farmers those who have made important discoveries in seed selection receive the Badge of Honor.

ORDER OF THE RED BANNER OF LABOR

ESTABLISHED IN 1928, it is awarded for exlence in industry and science.

The engraving of Dnieper Dam (in background) became a sad symbol when the dam was dynamited. The Russians looked on the dam as the heart of the Five-Year Plan's achievements. The decoration reads: "Proletarians of all the world, unite."

CHAPTER 12

The Soviet Way

THE MOSCOW INSTITUTE OF TRANSPORT ENGINEERS had an unprecedentedly heavy summer enrollment during 1941, because with the war it became a patriotic achievement for women to qualify as railway engineers. Women flocked to technical colleges all over the country to study for jobs that they might replace men. Russian universities adopted a speed-up system, lengthening the academic day and cutting vacations. The purpose of the educational speed-up, in the words of the People's Commissariat of Higher Schools, was to hasten to meet "the mortal menace of the brown plague to mankind and culture."

I went to photograph the Moscow Institute of Transport Engineers during examination time at the close of the summer session. In one of the laboratories a large troupe, with many girl students, were clustered around a beautifully finished twelve-foot model of the locomotive in use on the Moscow-Rostov railway. It was reproduced in most accurate detail, even to the name STALIN arched over the front under the headlight. The professor wore a little pointed beard, and his embroidered blouse was decorated with an extraordinarily large medal, showing a bronze locomotive in bas-relief and indicating that he was an "Honored Railroad Worker."

I worked quietly with a Speed Graphic, not wishing to distract anyone from the discussion of the dynamics of steam generation. Suddenly some of the feminine members of the class glanced at the clock, folded their notebooks, and hurried out of the room.

"Where are they going?" I whispered.

"To the nursery," somebody said.

Deciding that maternity was as important a subject as the generation of steam, I picked up my equipment and hurried after them across a court and up a flight of stairs. On a straight row of chairs, dressed in identical white coats, sat the lady engineers. Crying bits of humanity were passed out to them, the cries subsiding suddenly into silence as each girl supplied what was wanted.

In the nursery hung the typical ten-times-life-size picture of Stalin, holding a smiling child on his knee. Slogans bordered the picture—for example: "Long live women of the U.S.S.R., to whom Article 122 of the Constitution has brought equal rights with men."

Mealtime over, the mothers handed back their babies, picked up their notebooks, and hurried back to the locomotive named Stalin.

"They are studying to defend * their doctor's degrees," said the head nurse. "So, during the examination time, we keep their children on a twenty-four-hour shift for five days instead of having the babies go home at six o'clock at night, as they usually do. We want the mothers' studies to be as little interrupted as possible. On the sixth day the babies have a holiday at home and then come back here again until exams are over."

These student-wives, I found, pay thirty-five rubles ($7) a month to the crèche for the baby's care—that is, when their husbands are also students. If their husbands are wage earners, they pay from forty to sixty-five rubles, depending on the salary. If they are married to soldiers in the Red Army, they have the benefit of the decreased prices which apply to all expenditures made by Red Army families. It costs an army wife only seventeen rubles, or about $3.40, a month to keep a baby in college.

Student marriages are encouraged, and married students receive an allowance from the government. A "stipend" is also paid by the state to students getting high grades. Those who obtain perfect marks in at least two thirds of their subjects receive an allowance ranging from one hundred and thirty rubles a month for freshmen to two hundred rubles monthly for seniors. Attendance in class is not compulsory, but is sel-

* In Russian terminology students do not "take examinations"; they "defend their theses." The process is verbal and consists of questions put to each student individually by an examining board only two thirds of which are academic specialists. The other third is composed of members of the district party committee, whose questions are to determine that the student's ideology is correct.

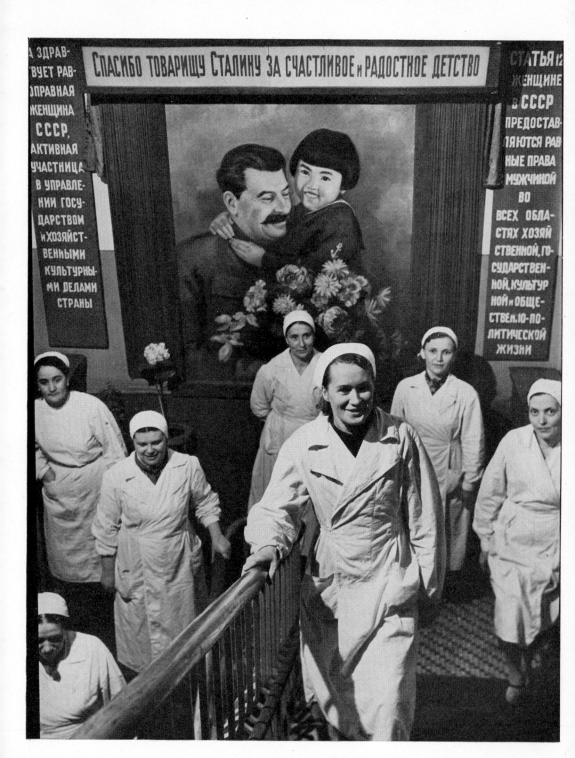

dom missed by students who wish to pass their exams with perfect grades.

The Tomsk Industrial Institute in Siberia had an unusual opportunity to be of service to the country. Students and their professors aided in organization of production in plants evacuated to the interior of the country. Often when we passed near the railroad tracks we saw long lines of freight cars, loaded with basic machinery, moving eastward toward the Urals. Frequently these trainloads of machinery were interspersed with seemingly endless lines of boxcars, with little square windows cut in the top and with men, women, and babies looking out of the boxcar homes. It was plain that whole factories, even to the workers' families, were being moved as a unit.

Certain universities, as well as certain key industries, were evacuated.

THE STAIRWAY OF A TYPICAL CRÈCHE

THE CRÈCHE system exists throughout the U.S.S.R. Every factory, every university, every collective farm, has its own crèche. This is a typical one in Moscow.

When a child is born, it stays at home with its mother for the first three months. Then, when the mother goes back to work, the infant is taken to a crèche. The mother comes in from work to nurse her child at given times throughout the day. After the nursing period is over, the child is put into another crèche, this time a kindergarten. Thereafter the child goes to other crèches and schools, always close to where the mother is working so as to be able to spend nights at home with her.

The rates at a crèche, depending upon the parents' earnings, usually range from twelve to sixty-five rubles a month—cheap enough, with the ruble worth about twenty cents. Red Army families get the cheapest rates.

The nurses in the picture are graduates of the Medical Institute and have worked in this particular crèche during the four years since it was first established. When nursing mothers come in, they put on similar white robes and tie white handkerchiefs around their heads.

Children with any danger of contagious diseases are isolated. Those with tendencies toward tuberculosis receive special care.

This favorite picture of Stalin is seen all over the land. No nursery would be without one. Stalin is supposed to be very fond of children and probably is. The youngsters are brought up to adore him.

The slogan running perpendicularly on the left is Article 122 of the Constitution. The sense of it is that woman, in the U.S.S.R., has equal rights with man in the political, economic, and cultural aspects of life. The slogan above the portrait reads, "Many thanks to Comrade Stalin for a happy and joyful childhood." A summary of the panel at the right: long live women of the U.S.S.R., having equal rights with men—active participants in the rulings of the state and in the economic, cultural, and political sides of the life of our country.

The war and the consequent taking over of many more jobs by women has made nurseries more vital than ever. In England I heard much agitation for similar nurseries, and certainly America should have them if women are to enter factory life with any efficiency.

Kiev University and Kharkov University were transferred to Kazakstan, and the Kiev Industrial Institute was removed to Tashkent, Uzbekistan. Also there were some departments of Moscow institutions of learning which were evacuated to the Urals; but the greater part of these institutions continued to function in Moscow.

When I went to photograph the University of Moscow, the director told me it had been decided that cultural studies must go on. "We are preparing ourselves," he said, "for the great work of reconstruction that will be done when Hitler's hordes have been driven from our land."

The University of Moscow was celebrating simultaneously the one hundred and eighty-fifth year of its founding and the arrival in Moscow of the American writer, Erskine Caldwell. The university library had arranged a display of Caldwell books, translated into Russian, and with evidences of thumbing through by hosts of readers. "We never can keep Mr. Caldwell's books on the shelves," the librarian told me. "They're always in use."

I was urged to bring my husband to the university to speak to the students on the subject of contemporary American writers. Erskine likes to make speeches about as well as he likes to take medicine, but I had been so impressed with the display of his works that I led him to the university on the promise that he would answer questions. "What is Steinbeck doing now," the students wanted to know, "and Dreiser, and Richard Wright?" They showed great curiosity about Hemingway's *For Whom the Bell Tolls*. The existence of his novel on Spain was well known, but his unorthodox reference to Soviet military figures barred its translation.

A number of English-speaking students had read and thrilled to

---

UKRAINIAN FARM WOMEN

WHEN THE war began, these women volunteered to take over in addition to their own work the work of their men. "We have to work three times as hard as we used to," they told me, "once for ourselves, once for our men who have gone to the front, and once for our country." The martial spirit was so strong that these collective-farm women could no longer merely walk to work; they marched. They even began referring to their tools as agricultural weapons.

It is their great pride that they have been able to bring in the harvest as efficiently as when their husbands and sons were working with them.

Gone With the Wind. Its glorification of slavery prevented its being translated, but the original English version was not considered sufficiently damaging for its presence to be banned on the shelves.

The works of a number of modern authors are translated and published in enormous numbers in the Soviet Union. Theodore Dreiser, Jack London, and Upton Sinclair are printed in editions running into hundreds of thousands.

The printing plants of Gosizdat, the State Publishing House, were turning out textbooks by the thousands for college students who were inducted so as to release men for the front. *The Productivity of the Milch Cow* and the *Tractor Textbook* were published in great numbers. Often on the great collective farms during the summer I saw large classes of college girls with an instructor, grouped around a tractor or combine, studying the care, repair, and operation of what they appropriately called "agricultural weapons."

They had the attitude of warriors, these students and the farm women, when they brought in the harvest. The Germans were drawing closer to Moscow, and they knew the deadly importance of bringing in the grain ahead of the enemy. "Every bushel is a blow at Fascism" was their motto. The wheat and rye stood as high as a man's head, and the August harvest, in the Moscow region, was unusually good.

Every farm woman at her threshing machine and every coed on her tractor cast an occasional eye toward the heavens, as the Germans

---

HARVEST ON "SPARK OF THE REVOLUTION" FARM

THIS FARM is on the summit of a hill overlooking a bend in the Oka River, near Kashira, about 125 miles west of Moscow. This year they had the biggest harvest since the beginning of the Soviet Union— almost twice as big as last year's.

Herds of cattle, in enormous numbers, were being driven to the "Spark of the Revolution" when the town of Smolensk was evacuated before the German advance. Usually the women and children evacuated the cattle, led them in constant streams along the road from Smolensk, and pastured them on farms like this near Moscow. As the Germans drew nearer, the cattle were moved closer and closer to Moscow.

"Spark of the Revolution" has more than 2000 acres, of which 700 are planted in wheat, rye, and oats, 350 in grass, 300 in clover, and 100 in vegetables. Improved sowing methods and insect control, for which the U.S.S.R. gives many prizes, are responsible for the increase in the harvests.

These harvests in the Moscow region were carried on between the ninth and fourteenth of August, and the grain was moved before the Germans caught up with it.

moved closer, to watch for parachutists. In his humorous magazine *Crocodile*, Eugene Petrov ran a cartoon showing a farm woman with her pitchfork raised to the sky as down toward it drifts a tiny parachutist. "He doesn't know it," the peasant girl is saying, "but he's about to make a perfect three-point landing." Sporadic parachute landings were attempted in isolated sectors; but where every man, woman, and child is a self-appointed deputy sheriff on the watch for diversionists or fifth columnists, these groups rarely succeed in making undetected landings.

Despite the excellence of the harvest, food rationing was introduced to ensure equitable distribution of meat, sugar, and bread throughout the country. Since there was no real food shortage, and rationing was a precautionary measure, it was possible to buy beyond the ration but at a higher price.

Sugar, for example, was rationed at the rate of three pounds a month for a white-collar worker, and five pounds for an industrial worker. It could be purchased in the form of sugar or candy. However, if anyone used up the tabs on his ration card and wished to buy more, he could go to what were called "commercial basis" shops and purchase sugar without cards. Instead of paying twenty-five cents a pound, which granulated sugar cost under the ration, he would then be charged three times as much. The same arrangement, of purchasing beyond the ration cards at a tripled cost, applied to all goods: cereal, meat, shoes, and rationed clothing.

We foreigners received no ration cards, since we were of course not in the employ of the Soviet state. Therefore we did all our buying at the high cost of three times the ration price, and in addition changed our American currency at the highly disadvantageous exchange rate of 5.3 rubles to the dollar. Diplomats received the better rate of thirteen rubles to the dollar, and even on these terms they found living high in Moscow. For us, it was exorbitant.*

It was seldom that we could get through a day's meals for less than twenty dollars each. A side dish of green peas in our hotel cost eleven rubles, or over two dollars; a main meat dish could be anything

---

* British journalists received the benefit of a semidiplomatic rate of exchange, but for some reason this advantage was never arranged for the American journalists.

between twenty-two and forty-two rubles. The Russians were rather sensitive about having these high costs mentioned outside, and whenever I had to wire for money I always met difficulties if I tried to indicate in my cables the high cost of living. Once I attempted the message: MUST ASK FOR ANOTHER THOUSAND DOLLARS BECAUSE RE-GRET LIVING COSTS RISING ASTRONOMICALLY. (This was to the picture editor of *Life*.) Even private messages of this sort had to be passed at Narkomindel; and the censoring of this cable was a simple matter. All the censor had to do was draw his blue pencil through the objectionable last three words, "costs rising astronomically." I felt a bit foolish, therefore, when the resulting cable went out to New York: MUST ASK FOR ANOTHER THOUSAND DOLLARS BECAUSE REGRET LIVING. I always considered it a remarkable evidence of faith in my honesty, by the way, that my editors never questioned these enormous sums.

Journalists in Moscow have been repeating for years a story about the colorful correspondent Hank Wales, who, when he was stationed in Moscow some years ago, began receiving protests from the New York newspaper for which he was correspondent. His editor reproved him for the size of his expense account and registered particular objections because the accounting showed that he was eating caviar for breakfast. The Hank of Wales cabled to his editor: EGGS IS EGGS.

Even for the Russians the cost of food was rising, but for them it was seldom out of reach, because most Soviet citizens were able to get meals at low rates in the cafeterias of their factories or offices. I ate in some of these cafeterias, and the food was plain, but good, and cheaply priced.

As to rent, that was surprisingly low. In Russia it is gauged to the salary earned, and, in the last analysis, the landlord is, of course, the state. The difficult problem in life for a Russian is not to find a place with low rent, but one with as much "floor space" as he wants. The amount of space is allotted according to the size of family, the importance of a person's work, and the position in life that he has achieved. There is naturally a large element of luck involved, also.

Elisaveta came in to see me one morning, still laughing over a marriage proposal she had received the evening before. With her

prettiness and charm, Elisaveta had received and turned down many proposals. "What do you suppose he told me?" she said. "He promised that if I would marry him I could have all his great big floor space."

Elisaveta had many friends among the writers of the newly established "poster factory," and she took me there frequently to photograph whatever was going on. Tass Windows, as it was called, had been organized for the quick preparation of wartime posters for the streets, and it was a twenty-four-hour beehive of many of the best writers, poets, artists, and caricaturists in the country.

Every morning an editorial board of writers met at the Tass office on Kuznetsky Most to choose items from the last-minute radio reports and communiqués. By noon the poets had translated these into humorous verses and the artists had furnished sketches for cartoons. By midafternoon these ideas, translated into rhyme and caricature, were splashed colorfully in the windows of Tass. All night the artists worked, making reproductions with stencils and water colors, even the best of Russia's artists doing the routine scissoring and brushwork, and by morning copies of the posters, blazing in red, orange, blue, and black, had been mounted on walls and in store windows all over the city. Crowds gathered around each new poster, memorizing the verses to tell their friends. Red Army soldiers passing by jotted down the rhymes and copied the sketches in their notebooks to be reproduced by soldier artists in their own regiments at the front.

The poster factory had a cast of favorite characters, the lead parts taken by Hitler and Napoleon. Napoleon was shown variously as a shadow behind Hitler, as a scarecrow, or represented by his hat hanging on the first of a line of crosses. Hitler (whose name was spelled Gitler in Russian characters) was represented usually by a snake

---

POSTER FACTORY RUN BY MOSCOW ARTISTS

WHEN I saw this scene I thought of the Walt Disney workshop where artists, writers, and poets work together. Here they are shown, to the right, assembling an alphabet series which was released at the rate of one new letter a day. At the left can be seen freshly stenciled copies of Timid Ivan, part of the gossiper series described on page 173.

Posters are reproduced in water colors with stencils, and finishing touches added afterward. Work goes on twenty-four hours a day.

whose contortions followed the shape of a swastika, or as an ape wearing a Prussian helmet, or as a buzzard. When he was shown in human form the favorite representation had him weeping great salt tears to fill up an otherwise empty oil tank.

When the terms of the British-Soviet mutual-assistance pact were announced, a new poster to commemorate the event was hung within two hours in the windows of Tass. It showed two huge fists coming together, the cuff of one bearing the Union Jack, the other emblazoned with a red star. In the process of being strangled by this giant handclasp was a tiny, cringing, swastikaed figure, wearing the familiar mustache.

As the war grew older a new character appeared with such frequency as almost to supplant Gitler. This was a pink-faced citizen named Ivan. Ivan is the gossiper, the rumor spreader. One day a bee whispered into his left ear, and out of his right came a rumor the size and shape of an elephant. The next day he chattered to frightened cooks in a pantry, and, as he talked, a spy with a revolver, dressed in checked trousers like a Chicago gangster, crouched under his chair and copied down everything he said. (Ivan was a factory worker and should not have been talking.) Later in the week, when the Germans were moving closer to Moscow and even foreign journalists were comparing rumors to guess where the Nazis might be, Ivan grew a supernaturally long tongue. It ran right out of his mouth in undulating red folds, curving its way into the street and encircling groups of terrified citizens in its snaky folds. While Ivan's disorderly tongue started a panic, the ever-present Nazi spy hid under this tongue and wrote down everything in his little notebook.

By the time Ivan had become a familiar figure on all the streets of Moscow the moral of these gaily printed posters had been translated

---

POSTER ARTIST WITH STENCIL

WHEN THE old anti-Nazi joke describing an Aryan hit Moscow just after the war started, it was illustrated in a series of posters. Since the Russians interchange the sound of *G* and *H* in foreign names, they captioned these posters:

Pretty, like Hoebbels
Slender, like Hoering
Blond, like Gitler

more severely in the newspapers. The Presidium of the Supreme Council published an order that persons guilty of spreading false rumors were to be sentenced by the Military Tribunal to prison terms of two to five years.

At the same time regulations were published prohibiting the sending of picture post cards, crossword puzzles, or chess problems through the mails. Anyone sending a letter to any foreign country was permitted to write only four pages and must bring the letter to the post office to make sure no messages had been concealed under the stamp. Once there he might have the pleasure of licking the stamp himself, but this must be done in the presence of a post-office official.

Many of the Tass posters were addressed to factory and farm workers. One of them, appearing in infinite numbers about the city, showed a girl at a lathe with a red kerchief bound around her head, and with a face of such familiar features to Americans that our embassy clerks called her Dorothy Thompson. She was saying, "Soviet Patriots! Your self-sacrificing factory work in the rear is molding victory at the front. Erase from the earth the Fascist barbarians."

The war, it seemed to me, had brought about unprecedented unity among the Soviet people. Outsiders who thought the stress of conflict

---

POSTERS IN WINDOW OF DIETETICS SHOP ON GORKY STREET

THESE POSTERS are part of the famous gossiper series. "God's birdie" in posters at left wears a bright-blue suit and vest. The verses are parodies on a poem by Pushkin which all Russians learn as school children: "God's birdie is so serene, so happy, he gets up and sings early in the morning." Using the Pushkin rhythm and rhyme schemes, the story is told of how the birdie carelessly does not put his light out in the blackout, talks to a lovely young lady with ear bent to hear his gossip, chatters about his factory in the presence of spies. He is accused of spreading false rumors, and the verses conclude that he will get what he deserves.

The series on the right is entitled "The gossiper is a good friend for the spy."

In the first two scenes, Timid Ivan, described in text, talks so much that his gossiping tongue comes right out of his mouth spreading panic: when a rumor the size of a bee goes in one ear, it comes out the other the size of an elephant. In the third, the citizen wears rose-colored glasses and does not see that beneath sheep's clothing, a wolf is carrying a revolver and bomb. In the fourth, a huge hand picks up these gossipers.

Simultaneously with the appearance of these posters on the streets, laws were passed listing severe punishment for spreading of false rumors.

would cause the Communist system to crumble were wrong. The Russians gave the impression of being strongly united behind their political system. By now a whole generation has grown up under it. Soviet citizens have seen their standard of living steadily improve, they have had a certain amount of government representation under their constitution, and apparently they have no wish to change. The overwhelming majority of Americans, brought up in a democratic society, would find it difficult to accept the absence of freedom of speech which Soviet citizens take as a matter of course. The Communist system, which apparently works very well for the Russians, would have little appeal to Americans who are accustomed to arguing loudly and vehemently over anything with which they disagree.

Soviet citizens can disagree with safety about certain things—how a factory is run, for example, whether the operation of a store is efficient, whether the collective farm of which they are members is operated to the best interests of everyone concerned; but in matters of major policy they would consider it unwise to lift a dissenting voice.

The unity of the Soviet people has been assured because whatever

---

ORLOVA, THE MOVIE QUEEN OF RUSSIA, AND HER HUSBAND, ALEXANDROV, LEADING CINEMA DIRECTOR

LYUBOV ORLOVA is unquestionably the first movie actress of the Soviet Union. She is also one of the few women in her country to wear slacks. She is so popular that whenever Alexandrov wants to go anywhere, through all the soldiers and guards who have made even small journeys difficult, he takes Orlova. The soldiers wave her through all barriers and say, "Orlova is her own passport."

She is tomboyish and slangy—taught me Russian slang. She is the toast of Soviet Russia. Her husband adores her and builds all his pictures around her. One of her recent films is a Cinderella story which is being released in America under the title *Tanya*. In this she plays a textile worker who, by increasing the speed-up, wins a record as *otlichnik* (most efficient worker) and is decorated with the Order of Lenin. This has a counterpart in real life for Or-

lova, who has been decorated with the Order of Lenin and also with the Red Banner of Labor for her excellent acting. Before shooting the film she took a job in a textile factory for practice. She acts now in many government propaganda shorts having to do with the heroism of the Red Army, in which she is usually a courier who braves the Nazi lines on a motorcycle, carrying dispatches.

Alexandrov is one of the most talented directors in the U.S.S.R. He is known in America, as he came here with Eisenstein, went to Hollywood and then Mexico to work on Eisenstein's famous, ill-fated *Thunder Over Mexico*. Alexandrov used to be a trapeze artist in a circus and starred his wife in a popular picture called *Circus*. He is blond, handsome, and directs with the most graceful hands in the world.

dissension existed during the last few years was wiped out. Thus no organized opposition is left. These drastic measures offer another explanation of why there is no fifth-column movement in the country—one secret of the Soviet Union's strength. But the all-sweeping corrective measures which were taken did leave a wake of fear. Even among the patriotic and loyal, this fear was noticeable.

It was quite evident, for example, when we arrived before the outbreak of war. Ten years before, during my previous visits, the spirit of experimentation was everywhere. It was noticeable in all walks of life, but especially in creative fields, such as the theater. Many of the creative efforts were clumsy and crude, but they were always interesting because the germ of trial and discovery was there.

When I returned in the spring of 1941 I found that a crystallization had taken place. There was less of that refreshing experimentation with new things, and more conformity. No one could afford to make a mistake in ideology.

But in regard to this fear, the war was the great healer. With each month of the conflict, unity became more pronounced and dread les-

---

ALEXANDROV AND ORLOVA ENTERTAINING FRIENDS AT THEIR *DACHA*

SERGEI ALEXANDROV brought back ideas about architecture from Mexico and California and designed his own delightful *dacha*, with studio living room and fireplace, unusual for Russia.

From left to right, Alexandrov, Erskine Caldwell, Orlova, a comedienne, and a stage designer.

Alexandrov calls his wife "Charlie," a leftover from the early days when they first fell in love while working together on a picture, and he had his own secret non-Russian name for her.

A choice of white or red wine was served instead of cocktails, as Alexandrov drinks nothing heavier than wine, although his wife likes Georgian vodka. We exchanged gifts. I brought out an airplane photograph for Sergei, because he loves opening his movies with airplane shots, and a picture of an eagle in flight for Orlova. Imagine my pleasure when I was told that Orlova means eagle. Erskine brought books of his short stories in English (Orlova is studying English) and was given Russian books on the cinema. Orlova presented me with an enameled box, and we exchanged promises to write to each other every three months, she in English and I in Russian. We have been quite faithful in this.

Their *dacha* is situated thirty miles from Moscow on the road toward Smolensk. The road is torn by artillery traffic, their woods are full of antiaircraft guns, and they watch the Moscow raids from their open porch. A thousand-pound bomb fell near by, but did no damage. Alexandrov put out seven fire bombs on the roof of their Moscow apartment.

A *dacha* like this is something which only writers, artists, theatrical people, eminent scientists, or commissars, and others in the high-income group can afford.

sened. Citizens had so many new tasks to do, tasks which demonstrated their loyalty, that they no longer had to fear whether their patriotism might be open to question.

And, despite the lessening of experimentation, the theater, ballet, and opera were still excellent and the acting, dancing, and music always superb. The theaters remained open even through the bombings, although matinee performances became the custom. There was always a performance of Shakespeare running somewhere in the city. In the Moscow Art Theater Sheridan's *School for Scandal* was playing to packed audiences, and the great favorite was, and has been for years, *Anna Karenina*, in which jewel-like sequences and flawless acting build up a perfection seldom matched on any stage.

The Moscow Opera was so crowded that tickets had to be bought far in advance. Whenever Barsova, the leading coloratura soprano of the Soviet Union, or Lemeshev, the handsome young tenor, sang, the workers and collective farmers in the audience stood in the aisles and cheered at the end of each aria. Lemeshev, in particular, had such a following among the younger generation that girls of high-school age cheered and screamed when he appeared. In the middle of the last act

---

FIRE-FIGHTING POSTER IN THE PARK OF CULTURE AND REST

THE FAMOUS Park of Culture and Rest has become a center for defense instruction. This poster shows methods of fire fighting. The fire bomb is being put out on the roof in the approved manner while a searchlight fixes with its beam an enemy plane overhead. Other posters near by carry slogans like: "We will destroy Fascist flying invaders" and "Death to Bloody Fascism."

Moscow citizens have long been enthusiastic fire fighters. Even before the war there was organized citizen participation in fire control, but then it was largely what they call "prophylactic work on fire prevention." Now, everyone says, they do miracles. When the British sent an expert over from London, he said there was almost nothing left to teach them. Children and women take their turns with everyone else on the rooftops. Factory workers do fire-watch duty in shifts, their comrades operating their machines while they are fire fighting on the roof, so production will not lag. Innumerable tales of heroism in putting out fire bombs are told. One woman in charge of fifteen apartment buildings told of one night in which sixty-six fire bombs falling in her district were extinguished. A man told how he put out a fire bomb with his cap. The citizen organization of fire brigades is tremendous. There have been many celebrated fire watchers. Shostakovich put out many a fire bomb on Leningrad roofs; Eisenstein and Alexandrov, the movie directors; Tissé, the famous movie cameraman; opera singers and scientists—all have a heroic record. They keep the dead bombs in rows on their mantelpieces.

The process is known as liquidating the fire.

of *Eugen Onegin,* where Lemeshev in his character of the young poet, Lensky, is killed in a duel, these throngs of girls would pelt the stage with bouquets of flowers and rush out of the theater in a body so as to be able to catch one more glimpse of Comrade Lemeshev as he left by the stage door.

Toward the latter part of the summer, as more members of the British Military Mission continued to arrive in Moscow, the occasional sprinkling of British military uniforms through the opera audiences attracted as much favorable attention as the stars on the stage. During intermissions, when the spectators flocked into the lobby to get tea and big rolls stuffed with cheese and chopped meat, many smiles and friendly glances followed the trim uniforms. Whenever the Britishers appeared, a murmur would run through the crowd: "The British army and the Red Army are now fighting together against Hitler. It is good!"

This approval of the members of the British Military Mission was enthusiastically shared by the Caldwells. We had a standing invitation from big, bluff General Mason MacFarlane, the head of the mission, to drop in for air raids. This was valuable to me, for having used our splendid balcony to the utmost I needed new viewpoints for night pictures. The British Embassy faced the opposite side of the Kremlin from our hotel and was situated at the edge of a mass of roof which became alive with activity when bombing started. Many times when the alarm began sounding we would jump into our car and make a dash for the British Embassy. We had this procedure so perfectly timed that we could reach the embassy, some eight blocks away, before the

---

PTASHKINA AND HER FIRE-FIGHTING BRIGADE

PTASHKINA (at right, in glasses) is a heroine who was decorated for putting out thirty-five fire bombs in a single night. She is a retired worker who lives on a pension from her factory and can no longer do heavy work because of heart trouble. However, when the war began, this semi-invalid refused to be evacuated to the country, and organized schoolboys into a fire-fighting brigade of which she is chief. Her boys are wearing masks and mitts of canvas bags and are using sandbags, and fine spray from a pump, to throw on the incendiary bombs.

Ptashkina's decoration is an award given people who perform exceptional services which help the city of Moscow. On the medal is the inscription: "Outstanding citizen of Moscow city economy." It is a big red-enamel and gold decoration, and with it went five hundred rubles.

siren stopped blowing. Erskine would watch the raid from the embassy until it was time for him to go to the broadcasting station, while I remained to take my pictures.

On one night when we arrived—it was during the third week in August—so much began to happen all at once in the sky that the embassy staff was running back and forth through the darkened house, watching through the windows. It takes a spectacular raid to get Britishers out of bed, they have witnessed so many of them; but on that night even Sir Stafford Cripps was hurrying about in pajamas and fuzzy bathrobe, running to the windows first on one side and then the other, watching the raid.

It was plain that for me it was going to be a "four-camera night." The General led me up to the attic and held a guarded flashlight while I picked out the lenses and film-pack holders I expected to need. We buckled on our helmets. Mine was the regulation Russian-army type, shaped like a mushroom and so heavy that I had to develop a whole new set of neck muscles before I learned to keep it on for more than a quarter of an hour at a time. We filled our pockets with camera equipment and climbed up a little ladder through a trapdoor in the roof.

There is something unearthly about being on an open roof in a raid. The sky seems so startlingly big, with its probing spears of searchlights and flaming onions hurtling their way through space, that a human being appears too small to count at all. But as this raid got under way I had so much to do that I could not think of anything outside the four

---

GENERAL F. N. MASON MACFARLANE, HEAD OF THE BRITISH MILITARY MISSION

HE WAS known to the foreign colony as General Mason Mac and to the Russians as Comrade General. He is a fine fellow, over six feet tall, and looks like the fighting soldier that he is. He was recently (May, 1942) appointed Governor and Commander in Chief of Gibraltar, to which he affectionately refers as Gib. His character reminds you of the rock itself.

He studied Russian four hours a day and learned to speak well in a remarkably short time. At restaurants he carried on long conversations with the waiters, and if there were any Red Army men about, they would come up to chat with him and admire his uniform. This uniform was an object of wonder in Moscow, for he wore the British battle dress, including long khaki pantaloons that went all the way down to his boot tops.

cameras I was trying to operate at once. There are no rules for exposure on a subject like this—at least, none that I know of. The most
I could do was to guess, by the mounting action, which points of the
horizon would be the most interesting to photograph, and then, after
the spurts of firing had taken place, try to estimate whether the illumination had been correct for the exposure of each of the four negatives
in process.

Once I became so engrossed in calculations, as I focused on a group
of cathedral towers with antiaircraft guns sending up decorative spurts
behind their onion-shaped domes, that the General reproved me. "You
can't hesitate over your decisions in war, you know."

"But I'm not a general, only a photographer," I said, so apologeti-
cally that when I completed my focusing arrangements he added kindly,
"Are you sure you are quite happy about that camera now?"

As we started on all fours down the slope of the roof he suddenly
called out, "Get behind that chimney. Those things will be hot when
they come down." I did not realize what "those things" were, as I heard
a swish like satin through the air, and then within less than a minute
a rain of fire bombs had fallen within eye range all over the city. From
a hundred rooftops I could see spurts of flame. Some of them caught
and spread into a steady red glow, but most of them vanished almost
at once. I knew that all over the city, on each rooftop, were stationed
groups of citizen fireguards who had been training for weeks for just
such a night as this; but this was the first chance I had had to see the
results of their work on such a broad scale.

A garage building somewhere off to the side caught into a blaze, and

---

BELFRY OF IVAN THE GREAT
DURING AN AIR RAID

THIS IS the highest tower in the Kremlin, completed by Boris Godunov in 1600. It is one of the many fine old churches within the Kremlin wall.

Shooting up into the sky is a battery of searchlights. Exactly what the crescent lines are I could never determine exactly. I have shown this picture to ballistics experts, who believe that these are antiaircraft shells which just happened to burst as they were obligingly rounding this beautiful curve. Note how the light path tapers off slightly at the left. Apparently these shells went almost straight up from the ground.

a fire truck rushed up and pulled into the drive. By now the grounds were illuminated with red light and I could plainly distinguish the fire engine's crew. It consisted not of men, but of girls wearing firemen's helmets and asbestos suits and mitts.

"May we take a short cut through your driveway?" asked a pleasant woman's voice. "We have come to liquidate the fire."

The blaze was still confined to the corner of the garage, and the liquidation was rapidly effected, whereupon the firewomen took off toward the Lenin Library, near which another spurt of flames was mounting toward the sky.

By this time another phase of the raid had begun. A second wave of the *Luftwaffe* was returning with demolition bombs, hoping, I suppose, to take advantage of the light from the fires that had been set. I wondered how the city looked to them up there and whether the considerable amount of "liquidation" accomplished between waves of planes would annoy them. The peculiar whooshlike whistle of bombs began, caused when a quarter of a ton of steel rushes down through the resisting atmosphere, and at regular intervals we could hear shrapnel tinkle on the roofs and streets about us. The General said, "It's

---

KREMLIN BY MOONLIGHT

THE "white nights of Moscow" is a phrase that Muscovites have used for centuries, but with the war it took on an added meaning. Even without the extra light of the air barrage the summer nights are luminous because of the northern latitude of the city, and the moon shines with surprising brilliance.

The concentrated light thrown on the buildings (center right) is caused by German bombs, both demolition and incendiary, falling into a Kremlin courtyard. The building at the left is the main Kremlin Palace, where the great yearly meeting of the Soviet delegates takes place. It is just behind this, in a similar building, that Stalin and the other government leaders have offices.

The Kremlin windows shown in this photograph are not real windows but are painted on an enormous roll of canvas with fireproof paint. This is part of the multicolored Kremlin camouflage. (Imitation houses were painted on walls; nets covered with artificial leaves were spread about the courtyards, over the great bell and big Czar Cannon; and whole buildings were done over in a bewildering variety of colors.)

In the foreground is the Moskva River and the gateposts of the British Embassy. The slanting lines show where tracer shells swept across the field of the open lens. This picture, a twelve-minute exposure, shows more detail than the other night shots because of the brilliance of the moonlight. The exposures of the other night pictures ranged between one and fifteen minutes, depending upon the amount of action in the sky.

getting too thick to stay out here. Come inside for a while," and we climbed through the attic window.

Periodically I would have to go out to change the films in my four cameras, and as the General helped me out the trapdoor he would say, "Do it as quickly as possible, and if you hear something little coming, stand up, because you're less of a target; but if you hear something coming that sounds big, lie down." I was never able to analyze whether the various descending articles were big or little, so I just buckled my wobbly helmet on tighter, made the rounds, changed films and checked the focus, and then returned for a short breather on the ladder.

We had been joined at the trapdoor by Rear Admiral Miles, a slender, hawk-faced man with the clear eyes typical of all seafarers. He had taken part in many battles at sea but, until he came to Moscow, had never witnessed an attack on land.

Then something began floating down that was so spectacular we all crawled out on the roof and crouched along a railing by a drainpipe to watch it. A flare had been dropped directly overhead and was drifting down toward the Kremlin, close enough for us to count the ribs in the enormous parachute that held it. Suspended from the giant umbrella was a ball of blazing magnesium, so bright that it hurt our eyes to look at it.

"They're certainly looking for something very specific in the neighborhood when they burn up as much magnesium as that," said the General. "That stuff costs plenty."

PATH OF A PARACHUTE FLARE

WHEN FLARES are dropped, like the huge one on the right, it shows that German pilots are looking for definite targets.

While these night pictures appear in black and white, actually the scene is chromatically brilliant: the tracer bullets show a path of bright red; bursting shells may be blue, yellow, or orange; the flares have a color varying from yellow and orange to red, but the big ones look white.

Note how the tracer-bullet lines at the left of the picture seem to begin at a con-

siderable distance above the city. The action of the chemical coating is delayed so as not to divulge to the enemy pilots the position of the guns.

In the foreground are the British Embassy buildings and the Moskva River. The star-topped tower toward the right is the Borovitsky Tower, the main Kremlin gate, where Napoleon entered. Shown dimly in back of it, with modern outlines, is the big new Lenin Library. A fire bomb is just hitting the roof.

"It's not just the cost," said the Rear Admiral. "There's only so much of that stuff in the world."

It took half an hour for the mammoth parasol to drift to earth, and it was a fruitful working time for me. Photographers have for years taken pictures by the light of magnesium, but I certainly never expected to have the assistance of a fleet of German pilots dropping flares from the sky to light up my night pictures of the Kremlin.

It was one of those seemingly endless nights, when all the ammunition that the world has ever made seems to come pouring out of the sky and streaming up from the earth. Just as the sound of guns began dying away we heard a new wave of Nazi planes approaching, and the shooting started up again. The General had taught me how to distinguish between the sound of the Soviet and the German planes. The Russian planes have a kind of steady hum, and the Germans have a peculiar throbbing beat. I set my cameras again, focusing them toward different parts of the horizon and opening the shutters in readiness, and it was then that I heard what I had been too busy to listen to before.

On a cluster of rooftops at the back of the embassy, the fire watchers were calling out to each other. Some of the voices had a surprisingly youthful quality, and I guessed that this must be one of the children's squads which had recently been organized into fire-fighting brigades. While my Russian is not good enough to understand long conversations I can usually catch short phrases, and as the next spattering of fire bombs was dropped I heard boyish voices call out: "Let me have the next one." "The next one's mine!" The General, whose Russian is a bit better than mine, began translating to me, and I to him, as we each caught a phrase, and finally we realized that these schoolboys were arguing with each other for the privilege of putting out the next fire bomb because each child wanted to make a record.

At last the satin-swishing of the fire bombs died down, the throbbing of the Nazi planes fell away into the distance, and the humming Soviet planes took possession of the air over the city, blinking their green and red lights to show the gunner's crews below where they were. I folded up my cameras, and from the square near us we could hear the loudspeaker blaring out: "Comrades, the raid is over. Go to your rest."

The General, the Admiral, and I climbed through the trapdoor, and there, hanging on the ladder like a little furry bat, was Sir Stafford Cripps in his woolly bathrobe, where he had been watching the end of the raid. We all went downstairs and had a whisky and soda, and as the Ambassador settled himself comfortably in a big armchair, his dog Joe pattered in and sat down at his slippered feet.

CHAPTER 13

The Beginning of a Legend

A STRIKING innovation since my previous visits to the Soviet Union, in the early 1930's, was the appearance everywhere of gigantic statues of Stalin. These tower above the populace in post offices, banks, hotel lobbies, universities, parks, and factory lunchrooms. S. Y. Kakabadzne, the sculptor of the favorite version—which shows the leader striding along in military cloak and army boots—was awarded the Stalin Prize of fifty thousand rubles.

Where there is not room for a statue, a prominent wall is usually covered with a banner picturing the familiar mustached face in profile. Sometimes a double profile is shown, Stalin's and Lenin's. Often Stalin is depicted smilingly receiving flowers from a little child.

A parade brings out banners of immense size decorated with the leader's face, and at any mass meeting the speakers stand against a backdrop on which the official portrait is reproduced on such a gargantuan scale that the human performers could comfortably fit into Stalin's eye.

These representations gave me a curious feeling about Stalin. He is so seldom seen, so rarely heard, and yet so much quoted that one comes

---

AGRICULTURAL EXHIBIT, MOSCOW

VISITORS TO the New York World's Fair in Flushing will remember the enormous statue of the Red Soldier which dwarfed the buildings around it. This statue of Stalin had somewhat the same effect at the Agricultural Exhibit. It is Stalin's favorite version of himself and is to be seen in many places—among them, in one of the subway stations and in the lobby of the Moscow Hotel. Replicas of it may be found in the midst of flower beds in the rest homes, in post offices, and in public buildings throughout the country. The sculptor was S. Y. Kakabadzne, who was awarded the Stalin Prize.

The archway in the foreground housed a large number of model tractors. The men and women in the picture are typical city workers.

to think of him as an ever-present yet fleshless spirit, a kind of super-man so big that no human frame can hold him, so powerful that every-thing down to the smallest action is guided by him.

Every time I walked into a public building and was startled afresh by one of those towering marble statues, my determination increased to obtain the difficult permission to photograph Stalin. I wanted to get that massive legendary face on a sheet of panchromatic film, focused through my own lens, to see if he then would look real or superhuman.

Stalin is a mysterious figure viewed across oceans, but he is equally mysterious within the borders of his own country. The very multiplic-ity of his portraits and statues seems to increase rather than dispel this mystery. It is said that the author Lion Feuchtwanger, who had a long, informal chat with Stalin two years ago, asked him, "Why do you permit all this?"

"Do you think I like it?" Stalin is supposed to have replied. "Do you think I enjoy seeing a big funny face decorated with a mustache everywhere I turn my eyes? But if it is for the good of the country, I cannot withhold my consent."

Beyond the myriad replicas of that face few Soviet citizens, and fewer foreigners, ever go. Russians hear less, and probably care less, than the citizens of any other country about the personal lives of their

---

VICTOR V. TALALIKHIN, TWENTY-THREE YEARS OLD— SOVIET AIR HERO

He was born on the Volga, began flying in 1934, when he was sixteen years old. "I am defending Moscow now," he said, "but I hope soon to go to Berlin." The decoration he is wearing is the Order of the Red Star, received during the Finnish war. He had just been awarded the Order of the Gold Star (that makes him "Hero of the Soviet Union") and was going to receive this decoration from Kalinin the day after this picture was taken. His great deed was to ram a German plane with his own. He never expected to come out alive, but managed to parachute down to earth. All three of the German crew were thrown out and killed. This story has become so famous in the Soviet Union that it has even been set in verse. By this time, of course, Soviet ramming tactics are famous, but Talalikhin was one of the first of such heroes. A favorite complaint of these pi-lots is that the German fliers "refuse to accept the battle."

Talalikhin is a little bit of a fellow with blond hair and blue eyes and is extremely good-looking. He has been photographed in newsreels, talking to his mother, painted in oils and water colors, done in sculpture. He has spoken from many platforms to thrilled Soviet audiences.

I took this photograph shortly after one of his early ramming exploits, at which time he was shot in the right hand.

During the first four months of the war he brought down twenty-seven enemy planes.

leaders. What we call "human interest" in journalism is a purely foreign manifestation to them. For example, nine years earlier I had been traveling in Tbilisi and had heard by the purest accident that Stalin's mother was living there. It was not difficult for me to arrange to photograph her. No one made a fuss over her, though she was installed very comfortably in the wing of an ancient palace. The greater part of the palace was being used for government offices, and she had an apartment of two tiny rooms facing a lovely garden. Her small white bed was heaped with the pill-shaped embroidered cushions characteristic of that part of the country, and her walls were covered with cartoons and pictures of Stalin and with snapshots of her grandchildren. One of Joseph's sons,* she told me, was just my age.

The name of Stalin's mother was Ekaterina Dzugashvili, and she frequently referred to her son by his childhood name of Soso. The name Stalin, as is well known, means steel, and was one of the many aliases used by Joseph Dzugashvili. It was Lenin who later selected it as an appropriate name by which he should be known throughout the country.

Ekaterina was a very simple, motherly old lady, who spoke no Russian but talked only in the Georgian language. This is so different from Russian that even the Russian interpreter who was traveling with me at that time needed an interpreter of her own in order to understand. Despite the language barrier, Stalin's mother chatted with me

---

* He is now a pilot in the Red Air Fleet. Although the Germans had rumored him captured, on the authority of a conversation Stalin had with Lord Beaverbrook, in October, 1941, he was at that time indisputably alive.

TALALIKHIN AND THE MAYOR OF MOSCOW AT THE PARK OF CULTURE AND REST

TALALIKHIN MADE a speech in highly oratorical style, with touches of humor which delighted the crowd. Mayor Pronin also spoke. Pronin is young, energetic, and as small as LaGuardia. His official title is President of the Moscow Soviet. Erskine and I arranged a broadcast in which Mayor Pronin sent a message to Mayor LaGuardia.

Behind the speakers' table is a red-felt background showing the usual huge figure of Stalin, also Lenin's Tomb and planes above. The words read: "All Forces of the People to the Destruction of the Enemy." This line is a quotation from Stalin's famous July 3 speech.

Everyone's eyes were on Talalikhin's bandaged hand, with which he gestured eloquently while he talked. "The Fascist pilot missed me when he fired his big-caliber gun," said Talalikhin, "but burned my hand by a tracer bullet that flew near."

in a friendly way. She seemed to have only a vague idea of what her famous son was doing. It was evident that her worries about him, dating from the early days of his underground activities, had never entirely deserted her. When he was young he had studied to be a priest and had been expelled from the seminary when he became involved in the revolutionary movement. This had distressed his mother, who had ambitions for her son to attain a higher place in life than his father and grandfathers had held, all being cobblers. The years of his early manhood were a horror of anxiety to her, for he was frequently arrested and periodically exiled to Siberia. Instead of engaging in recognized forms of work he was always occupied in secret activities which were beyond her understanding.

Shortly after my portrait of her was taken she was brought to Moscow to visit her son in the Kremlin. The delightful rumor which crept out after this visit cannot, of course, be verified. It was reported that the good woman, knowing that under the Soviet regime all citizens must be workers, and that those who do not work may not eat, was seized with worry. She saw her son eating well and was troubled because she could see no visual evidence of what kind of work he did.

In 1937 Ekaterina Dzugashvili died, and it happened that an Amtorg official in New York at that time was about to return to Moscow; so I sent back a copy of his mother's portrait to Stalin. While I never received a direct acknowledgment, I heard through official sources that he had received the picture and liked it.

So little is known about Stalin's family that I was glad to be able to get a firsthand impression of his second wife through the eyes of my secretary. It was more than ten years after his first wife, Catherine, had died of pneumonia that Stalin married Nadezhda (the name means

---

PARACHUTE JUMP IN THE PARK OF CULTURE AND REST

THIS IS the father of all public parachute jumps. For more than ten years Russians have practiced parachute jumping here. Now the parachute tower is practically deserted for the greater attraction of wrecked German planes, which are exhibited in a near-by part of the Park of Culture and Rest.

Leading attractions the Sunday I was there were Junkers, Messerschmitts, Dorniers, Heinkels, also exhibits of dud bombs in denominations of 250, 500, and 1000 kilos.

The parachute jump is a double attraction, for customers may slide down, but must walk up.

Hope) Allilueva, who was the daughter of a leading Communist, a friend of Stalin's. Nadezhda and Tatiana, my secretary, used to go to the same beauty shop. Tatiana described Stalin's wife as a quiet, modest young woman, not beautiful, but nice-looking and having a pleasant, intelligent face. She was in her early thirties when she died, leaving two children, and it is reported that her husband was almost inconsolable. Whether the early religious training which Stalin abandoned as a young man had anything to do with the fact that his beloved young wife was buried in a monastery, no one will ever know. However, he chose a spot for her grave by the wall of the beautiful Novodyevichi Monastery on the outskirts of Moscow, and it is reported from reliable sources that not a week passes in which Stalin does not visit her grave.

In the town of Gori, thirty miles to the east of Tbilisi, Stalin's birthplace has recently been made into a shrine. I had visited the birthplace in 1932 and taken moving pictures of it. When I returned in 1941, I was astonished to find that along with the development of industry and agriculture in the Soviet Union in the last decade, Stalin's birthplace had developed also.

Nine years before, I had been taken, not into the city of Gori proper, but to a tiny village lying in the hills above the town and in the general direction of Tbilisi. In this village of Dedi-Lelo thirty or forty peasants with wide foreheads, deep-set eyes, and strong Asiatic features answered to the name of Dzugashvili. They showed me with understandable pride the house where little Soso was born. It was a primitive structure, consisting mainly of a square hole hollowed into the earth. One entered it by steps cut into the ground. The most elementary sort of covering, with only a chink for the smoke to come out, served as a roof. Vissarion Dzugashvili, Joseph's father, had carried on his cobbling in this cellar. The fact that the future great leader of the Soviet Union had risen from such humble beginnings was something which not only the villagers but all the people of the Soviet Union considered appropriate and praiseworthy.

On my earlier visit I had paid little attention to rumors regarding the rivalry between the citizens of Dedi-Lelo and the people of Gori as to where Stalin had actually been born. But when I arrived in the summer of 1941, I realized that the citizens of Gori had won.

There was nothing pretentious about the house I was shown on this trip. It was simply a different house. It had two rooms with board floors, a porch with carved railings, brick and clapboard walls, and a roof with a chimney. Brick steps led down to the famous cellar where the senior Dzugashvili had cobbled his shoes.

The house was no more remarkable than dozens of other similar houses scattered around Gori and other neighboring towns, but the shrine which enclosed it was extraordinary. Poised on tall marble pillars, a marble and glass roof soared above the wooden house. The skylight was decorated with a hammer and sickle set in leaded-glass panes.

In the corner of the marble terrace that fronted the cottage was a desk containing a large book in which visitors might write their impressions. The Kiev football team, which had arrived just ahead of me, had written that their "first intellectual demand" was to visit this historic spot.

As I took pictures here and there, photographing first the marble and glass exterior of the shrine, and then the narrow bed, carefully roped away from the pilgrims, where little Soso had made his start in life, a group of women arrived in wide peasant skirts and embroidered kerchiefs. After a whispered discussion in the soft lingual syllables of the Georgian tongue, one of them sat down and wrote for all: "With an extreme thrill we looked at the little house where our Dear Friend and Teacher was born. The Women Collective Farmers give thanks to the Great Stalin for the happy life which he has brought to all Soviet women."

They were immediately followed by a delegation of Donbas coal miners, who inscribed: "After looking at this little hut, still brighter and clearer becomes the care of Stalin for the poor people—for all those who were shackled and exploited by capitalism which mercilessly plundered them."

Pilgrims from Kazakstan, in embroidered skullcaps, teachers from the Pedagogical Institute of Sverdlovsk, and finally a professor from the Railway School in Tbilisi filed up and wrote their testimonials.

The professor, who wore a white belted blouse in true Georgian fashion and had a set of handle-bar mustaches, gave me reminiscences of Stalin, whom he had known from boyhood.

"What was he like as a child?" I asked.

"He always wanted his own way," replied the professor, "but we usually let him have it, for he was braver and a better fighter and smarter than any of us."

The professor's father had been one of the early revolutionaries at the turn of the century and had run one of the illegal printshops which played such a large part in distributing information among the secret Bolshevik organizations of the day. In 1901, when it became necessary for Stalin to go into hiding, the professor had hidden him in his father's printshop. The professor was now engaged, he told me, in writing his memoirs for the Institute of Marx and Lenin.

I would have liked to ask the professor why I was shown one birthplace in 1932 and another in 1941, but my intuition told me that the official information was all I would receive.

When I made a pointed effort during the next few days to go to Dedi-Lelo our Georgian friends would say: "Yes, it is a pleasant little village but it won't be very interesting for Americans. There are so many more interesting places to go." When I ventured to remark: "Hadn't Stalin stayed there as a child," I met with "Yes, he stayed there"—but if I wished to do a series of photographs depicting the history of the great leader, there were many more important places they could show me.

Undoubtedly little Soso lived in both places. Certainly Gori makes a more convenient goal for a pilgrimage, for it is along the railroad line—my previous visit to Dedi-Lelo had been on horseback. Probably, too, Gori has a more efficient version of whatever constitutes a chamber of commerce in the U.S.S.R.

"Still, I do wish I could find out where Stalin was really born," I complained to Erskine.

"You might as well stop trying to be a detective," he said. "If they've ukased where Joe was officially born, you can't expect them to undo it all to please you."

CHAPTER 14

I Photograph Stalin

SINCE THERE is no true *h* in the Russian alphabet the pronunciation of foreign names is often subject to charming alterations. When the personal representative of President Roosevelt flew unexpectedly into Moscow early one morning at the end of July, everyone was excited and delighted by the arrival of Garry Gopkins.

President Roosevelt is very popular in the Soviet Union, much more so than was his predecessor, Gerbert Goover. But the President's emissary, Mr. Gopkins, won all hearts. It was partly because the Russians liked Garry Gopkins so very much that my most difficult photograph in the whole Soviet Union was achieved at last.

The day started badly. I made a mistake in protocol. I was sitting in the pantry of the Spazzo House, where the American Embassy had set up its emergency switchboard, and the chief operator was helping me to find Mr. Lozovsky, the Assistant People's Commissar for Foreign Affairs, on the telephone. She was a rather unusual Russian girl who had worked with the American Embassy for years, and she had become an authority on diplomatic etiquette. When we finally reached Mr. Lozovsky, I tried unsuccessfully to persuade him to speak to Molotov. I hoped that he would induce Molotov to grant permission for me to photograph Stalin during the meeting to be held between Stalin and Hopkins that evening. Mr. Lozovsky was as vague as he always was about requests which he was not ready to grant, and, discouraged, I finally hung up the receiver.

"Don't you know that Mr. Lozovsky is very particular about protocol?" said the embassy operator. "You should speak of the head of the Foreign Office as Mr. Molotov, not Molotov, and you should certainly always refer to Mr. Stalin." I had not known, and my bad manners seemed an evil omen.

The whole day was a maze of protocol. The most distressing phase of this occurred at noon, when a telephone call came from Narkomindel with instructions that the request for the photograph must come in writing from the American Ambassador. Getting this document would have been a simple matter if it had not been that Mr. Steinhardt and Mr. Hopkins had just that minute driven out of the gateway for a luncheon being given in their honor at the British Embassy.

Mr. Hopkins had been kind enough to tell me his schedule before he left. I knew that after the lunchon he was to see Molotov—Mr. Molotov —and that later, at some unannounced time, he was to meet with Mr. Stalin for his last talk before leaving Moscow. I was due to go to the British Embassy at the close of the luncheon, where I had an appointment to take a picture of Sir Stafford Cripps and Mr. Hopkins together.

When I arrived at the British Embassy I found that lunch was late. When the guests finally emerged from the dining room, Mr. Hopkins was already behind schedule for his appointment with Mr. Molotov. There was no chance to talk to him and Mr. Steinhardt about a letter regarding the Stalin appointment; I had only a brief instant to get the picture while he sat on a sofa with Sir Stafford Cripps. In the next second he had grabbed his hat and was halfway down the back stairs, following Mr. Steinhardt through a short cut to the car, which was parked in the rear driveway. I followed him down the dark stairwell and breathed my difficulties into his ear. I was not sure he had even heard me.

I went back to the Spazzo House to wait. While I sat in the foyer killing time most of the embassy staff wandered in to see me, expressing concern over whether or not I would get the Stalin appointment. They knew how important and unusual it would be if I could get permission to make the portrait. Finally, at the end of an hour, Mr. Hopkins and the Ambassador returned.

"Let's forget about it and go shopping," Mr. Hopkins said to me,

---

HARRY HOPKINS AND SIR STAFFORD CRIPPS AND JOE

SIR STAFFORD's dog is named Joe, and Lady Cripps has a favorite story in which she cabled her husband, ending up "Love to Joe." Afraid that her husband would think she meant Stalin, she changed it to "Love to Joe Airedale."

and with the Ambassador as guide we drove to the stores, two secret-police cars accompanying us, one before and one behind. Harry Hopkins plunging through the gift stores of Moscow was enough to take anybody's mind off an appointment with Stalin. He examined little ducks carved of Ural Mountain stone. He inspected malachite boxes. He asked my advice on the selection of a peasant-embroidered dress for his daughter Diana, and picked another of white linen worked with Ukrainian roses for Betsey Roosevelt. Mr. Steinhardt led us into an antique-silver store, and when Mr. Hopkins said, "I don't understand this stuff," the Ambassador dived behind the counter, rummaged through a barrel packed with antiques, and brought out an exquisite little teapot engraved with a picture of the Kremlin which he presented to Hopkins as a memento of his trip. When the souvenir hunt was over we went back to Spazzo.

In our absence good news had arrived. I was to be at the Kremlin at seven o'clock! Mr. Hopkins had actually spoken to Molotov—Mr. Molotov.

During the hour that remained I polished my lenses and checked my synchronizers. I go to every important portrait appointment with a conviction that all shutters and synchronizing magnets are going to cease to function—a dread that never leaves me even after years of experience—and this time I had an absolute obsession that nothing would work when I was face to face with Stalin. I also gave a good deal of thought to what I should wear. I had on a blue linen suit, and knowing that Russians like red I drove to the hotel, changed to a pair of red shoes, and put a little red bow in my hair. (I never found out whether Mr. Stalin noticed it or not.) By the time these touches had been added a Soviet-made ZIS car called for me, and it was time to go.

MR. HOPKINS AND THE AMERICAN AMBASSADOR ON A
SHOPPING TOUR

THE EMBASSY car broke down in a square in central Moscow. Russian tires are none too good, and American ones are exceedingly scarce. After efforts to make repairs, the NKVD (Steinhardt's personal bodyguard of secret police, whom we called the YMCA) put us in one of their cars. Hopkins showed great and intelligent interest in everything he saw and was alert in gauging the living standards of the people, in appraising their faces, their clothes, the way they acted.

At five minutes to seven the government car swept me through the Kremlin gate in the Borovitsky Tower—the same gate through which Napoleon had entered. Bells began ringing, the signal that a visitor is entering the Kremlin walls. Soldiers looked into the car to ascertain my identity and, seeing me, saluted and smiled. At each bend in the road there were more soldiers, and more salutes, and so many smiles that I guessed it was not very often that an American girl came to the Kremlin to visit Stalin.

Mysteriously, for I had not seen any other cars approach, I found that our car was no longer traveling alone. A car preceded us, and another closely followed. I am sure that no one who is not definitely expected gets into the Kremlin.

Our procession wound its way through the group of ancient cathedrals, whose onion-shaped domes are just visible over the top of the Kremlin wall, and passed the Bell Tower, completed in 1600 during Boris Godunov's reign. I was surprised to see how high above the city we were. The British Embassy lay below, just across the Moskva River, and beyond was a great stretch of Moscow, the outlines of its soft, rounded domes and hard modern architecture contrasting in the low sunlight.

We drove past the great Czar Bell, set in the middle of a garden, and then we were in a triangular courtyard of the old czarist palace where leading government officials have their offices. At the door more soldiers looked me over, saluted, and smiled, and my equipment was lifted out.

An escort of soldiers took me up in a little gilt, red-carpeted elevator to the second floor.

HARRY HOPKINS' PRESS CONFERENCE AT SPAZZO HOUSE

MR. HOPKINS called this conference after his first meeting with Stalin. From left to right: Hopkins, Llewellyn (Tommy) Thompson, one of the embassy secretaries, Mr. Steinhardt, Alexander Werth of Reuter's, Philip Jordan of the *London News Chronicle*, Erskine Caldwell, and Henry Shapiro, U.P., dean of the American newsmen—there longer than any other American.

The meeting is being held in the drawing room at Spazzo. After declining to answer questions about his personal impressions of Stalin, Hopkins described briefly his mission from the President and then suggested that we had been away from home for so long that we might like to hear about America. "American citizens have no idea of the shortages they soon are to face among consumers' goods," he said prophetically.

I was in a corridor with a narrow red carpet, and from then on I was led along the longest, most branching, most winding hall it has ever been my experience to walk through. I must have passed a hundred doors. It would be impossible for anyone to keep his sense of direction, for each corridor branched off not at a right angle, but at an oblique angle. The ceiling was extremely high and vaulted. There were many windows on my left, looking out on courts. On the right were endless office doors.

At intervals we passed groups of soldiers who telephoned ahead that we were on our way. As we walked, I kept making little speeches to myself. Nothing would be accomplished by being nervous, I told myself reasonably. Just treat Uncle Joe the way I would anyone else. Ask him to sit down and chat and act natural.

Finally we came to big double doors. My coat was taken by an old man with a spade beard. Soldiers let us through the doors, and I was in still another corridor. Here the rooms had numbers. We were passing Nos. 12, 11, 10, and so on, and as the numbers grew lower I wondered whether Stalin would be behind No. 1. However, we paused before door No. 2; the soldiers held it open and accompanied me inside.

No. 2 had a long table, much like the board room of a small Midwestern factory. I was curious to see what books were in the bookcases that lined the walls, but these were curtained. In the corner were three telephones; a long chart of telephone numbers hung on the wall opposite a big portrait of Stalin; blackout curtains were at the windows. On the table were some fresh white pads, a calendar, a small bust of Lenin, and a large jar of big green pencils with green leads. It is probably a dreadful thing to appropriate souvenirs in the Kremlin, but those fat green pencils were irresistible. One of them is on my desk now in Connecticut; the name on it reads in Russian, "Third Five-Year Plan."

In the middle of the table was a tray full of bottles of lemon pop. Hopkins was having a fine talk with Stalin, evidently, for the clock crept onward, and many times I helped myself to a bottle of lemon pop. Every time I stretched out my hand toward a pop bottle, one of the soldiers whisked out the tray and hurried back with a new tray of cold bottles. All the soldiers I saw in the Kremlin wore the big red-enameled decorations which go with the title Hero of the Soviet Union. Those who were waiting with me had several apiece: the Order of Lenin, the Order of the Red Banner, Orders of the Red Star and of the Gold Star.

During the long wait the soldiers questioned me about life in America and about my impressions of the Soviet Union. We discussed the beauties of the republic of Georgia, the pleasures of riding horseback in the Caucasus, what time it was in New York when it was eight-thirty in Moscow, and such nonpolitical subjects.

They were in the midst of teaching me a list of new Russian words when I was sent for. I powdered my nose, took one last glance in my mirror to make sure of the correct angle of the red bow, and started through a vestibule where two men secretaries sat in the midst of telephones. I had just time to remind myself not to be nervous when I was whirled through door No. 1 and found myself in a long bare room. I was conscious of the fact that Mr. Hopkins was standing at one side, but it took me an extra instant to find Stalin.

I think my eyes instinctively went up toward the ceiling, for I remembered those giant statues I had seen; and then I looked ahead at eye level again, and there, standing very stiff and straight in the center of the rug, I saw Stalin. There was nothing unhuman about his size. My own height is five feet five, and Stalin came a fraction of an inch below me. Not only was he short; his whole figure was rather small.

He shook hands with me, and I conjured up my best Russian words for a little chat with him. He still had my picture of his mother, I was happy to discover, and we spoke about how I had photographed her nine years before in Tbilisi. At this disclosure the Kremlin interpreter, a suave young man named Litvinov (but no relation to the Soviet Ambassador to Washington) exclaimed with astonishment: "His very own mother! His real mother!"

It is always a shock to meet someone of whom you have seen a great many pictures. Stalin's photographs make his face look plump, but actually it is rather lean. He looks like a man who has been stout but has recently grown thinner. He has a gray and tired look, an air of almost physical fatigue—which is natural enough, for no one got any sleep during the bombings, and I suppose Stalin got less rest than most. His mustache and hair have a kind of chewed-up, strawlike look. His hands are deeply wrinkled. I observed that Stalin wore no medals; in

fact, he was the only person I had seen in the Kremlin with no decorations. He wore boots and plain, neatly pressed khaki clothes. I noticed that a much more careful pressing job had been done on Mr. Stalin than on Mr. Gopkins. I was astonished to see that his cheeks were pockmarked, for the scars are retouched out of all portraits made by Russian photographers. His rough pitted face was so strong that it looked as if it had been carved out of stone.

I remembered my plan to tell him to sit down and talk and act natural, but one look at that face convinced me that that is not the way to talk to a dictator.

After a few minutes I sank to my knees and opened up my camera, wondering what I could do to make that stone face look human. As soon as I began shooting, the fact that he was the most mysterious and inaccessible figure in two continents faded away, and my subject's name might have been Joe Doakes instead of Joe Stalin—or Ivan Ivanovich, as that character is called in Russia.

I kept changing lenses between pictures, as an insurance that some negatives would be perfectly synchronized, and in my haste I dropped a lens. "Take your time," came the reassuring voice of Mr. Hopkins, who was standing near.

Whoever is unfortunate enough to be within reach of my right arm when I have my head under a camera cloth is apt to find himself a camera assistant. This time it was "Young Litvinov," as he is known in diplomatic circles. As I kept automatically handing out reflectors and flash bulbs, he began holding them for me: first on the far side of Stalin's face, and then above his head for toplighting, which he accomplished easily, for he was much taller than Stalin. Soon Tovarish Lit-

---

HOPKINS AND STALIN

THIS PICTURE, taken from a low point of view, emphasizes the difference in height between the two men. Stalin's short stature comes as a surprise, for the Soviet statues and pictures always give the impression of a tall man.

Both men are extremely heavy smokers. Stalin smokes a pipe as well as cigarettes. Here he and Hopkins are smoking *papy-* *rosi,* Russian cigarettes with a long paper tube at one end. However, Stalin is fond of American cigarettes. His visitors from our embassy know this and often bring him Camels, Chesterfields, and Lucky Strikes. He is equally enthusiastic about American movies and sometimes borrows them from our embassy to show in the Kremlin.

vinov was changing flash bulbs with a single twist of the wrist, as though he had done it all his life.

As I crawled on my hands and knees from one low camera angle to another, Stalin thought it was funny and started to laugh.

When his face lighted up with a smile, the change was miraculous. It was as though a second personality had come to the front, genial, cordial, and kindly. I pressed on through two more exposures, until I had the expression that I wanted.

I got ready to go, and threw my stuff back into the camera case; then I noticed a peculiar thing about Stalin's face. When the smile ended, it was as though a veil had been drawn over his features. Again he looked as if he had been turned into granite, and I went away thinking that this was the strongest, most determined face I had ever seen.

When door No. 1 closed behind me and I walked back through the endless corridor, a little question began forming in my mind. In the Soviet Union there is a custom that appears unshakable. Elevators are made for the purpose of carrying people upward, but not down. As we approached the little gilt conveyance, I thought, "Surely in the Kremlin itself it is possible to ride down in the elevator!" I turned toward it. But no—the colonel accompanying me took me courteously by the arm, and I found that even when one has come from an audience with Joseph Stalin it is still necessary to walk down the stairs.

It was almost half-past nine when I left the Kremlin, and the *Luft-waffe* had been calling regularly at ten o'clock each night. I couldn't risk developing my precious films at the hotel, for there was too much danger of being interrupted by the hotel wardens. To have an air-raid

---

THE PEOPLE'S COMMISSAR OF DEFENSE

JOSEPH VISSARIONOVICH DZUGASHVILI, sixty-two years old, General Secretary of the Communist Party of the Union of Soviet Socialist Republics, a position which he has held continuously for twenty years. In May, 1941, he was appointed Chairman of the Council of People's Commissars, a newly created post in the Soviet Union, corresponding to that of Premier; and twelve days before this portrait was taken (it was made on August 1, 1941) he was appointed People's Commissar of Defense by the Presidium of the Supreme Soviet, an elected body.

His official career in the new Soviet state began immediately after the Russian Revolution, in 1917, when he was appointed the first People's Commissar of Nationalities. This position, as well as the new name of Stalin, was given him by Lenin.

warden break into my bathroom and tear me away from a partially
developed negative of Stalin was more than I cared to risk.

When I reached the hotel, therefore, I had Alexander, our chauffeur,
come in and help me carry my developing tanks and trays of solutions
down the stairs and place them on the floor of the car. We drove to the
Spazzo House and arrived just as the Ambassador and Mr. Hopkins,
along with two of the embassy secretaries, were leaving. They had been
invited to a banquet in the deepest shelter in Moscow. It is a tiled room,
far under the Metro, furnished with upholstered sofas and designed for
the use of the highest Kremlin officials. Few foreigners ever see it, but
the Russians didn't want to take a chance on having the Nazis bomb
the United States President's emissary that night. The party was very
excited about the invitation.

Alexander helped me set up my laboratory in the servants' bathroom
in the embassy cellar. When the alarm sounded and the spears of
searchlights darted up into the sky, the sandbags stacked against the
cellar windows would ensure that my darkroom would be light-tight.

The negatives of Stalin were so irreplaceable, should anything go
wrong, that I did not have the courage to plunge them in, sink or swim,
a whole film pack at a time, as I usually do. I began processing them
one by one. It was a busy night outside, and I could hear the rhythmic
booming of the guns as I worked; and when, finally, long-descending
shrieks began I was glad of that bank of sandbags outside the cellar
window.

Wouldn't it be fantastic to have a negative fogged by a fire bomb, I
reflected, as I dipped Joe's face thoughtfully into the hypo.

As the night wore on I grew hungry. In the excitement of the appointment, I had entirely forgotten about supper and I couldn't remember
whether I had eaten any lunch. But it should be easy to get something to
eat in your own embassy, I thought.

I came out, therefore, and found several embassy clerks sleeping
in the inner part of the cellar, which had been designated as a shelter.
One of them sat up on his cot, and when I whispered that I was hungry
he got up and started on a hunt. But the steward, it seemed, had gone
off to the big shelter in the subway, with all the pantry keys in his

pocket. One rarely used icebox had been left unlocked, but it contained only a bowl of rice of doubtful date.

While I rested, eating cautious spoonfuls of the cold boiled rice, the clerk searched out other articles to speed my work: an extension cord, so a mazda bulb could be draped over the radiator, a box of pins for hanging up wet negatives, an electric fan to shorten their drying time, a couple of soup plates for print developer.

I wanted to be prepared for the possibility that I might have to radio-photo the pictures to America, which meant that I had to have a set of prints made by morning. I had no regular printing apparatus, but an old type of clamp-back printing frame which I had borrowed from the chauffeur would serve. It could be held up to the mazda lamp on the radiator to expose the prints, but I must conjure up a red safelight to develop them.

The most valuable contribution of the U. S. Diplomatic Service that night, as far as I was concerned, was a piece of red muslin. At least, it was a dustcloth of reddish color. With a hand-held flashlight wrapped in the dustcloth it was possible to control the developing time of the prints in the soup plate, and a full set of Stalin prints became an accomplished fact by dawn.

CHAPTER 15

We Go to the Front

THE RUSSIANS are a secretive people, and while this may have its military uses it is a distinct barrier to correspondents who wish to gain a firsthand view of what is going on. Perhaps all the restrictions in wartime are a good thing.

However, regardless of wartime restrictions, Erskine and I felt that it was of supreme importance for us to get to the front and see at first hand the operations of the Red Army. Ever since the beginning of the war we had been begging the authorities to let us go, and the middle of September had arrived with still no result.

Finally, the matter was argued out over a pair of butter horses. The horses, sculptured beautifully in butter, were table decorations at a remarkable dinner given by Narkomindel to the press. First, enormous bowls of caviar were served (with the perpetual cucumbers), then little quail with frills around their matchstick legs, swimming in luscious sour-cream sauce, followed by a dessert of frozen fruit. One hundred members of the Soviet and foreign press were present, including the inevitable Mr. Hatenaka, the Japanese correspondent of *Nichi-Nichi*, and many distinguished Soviet writers, such as Ilya Ehrenburg, author of *Out of Chaos*, Mikhail Sholokhov, author of *And Quiet Flows the Don*, our friend Eugene Petrov, and his novelist brother, Valentine Kataev.*

The last toast was drunk and the party filed into the salon for coffee and apricot brandy, but Mr. Lozovsky and I still sat behind the banks

---

* "Kataev" is the family name of the brothers, and Valentine Petrovich Kataev is the author of *The Embezzlers* and other novels which have been translated into English. Eugene Petrovich Kataev took his father's name of Petrov as his pen name, in order not to be confused with his distinguished brother.

of flowers and the butter horses while the waiters began carrying away
the scraps of the feast.

"I can't go back to America without photographing the front," I said.
"I simply can't. What will I say when my fellow countrymen discover
that I have not seen with my own eyes the heroism of the glorious Red
Army? They will exclaim, 'Why were you not allowed to witness those
noble deeds about which we hear so much? Perhaps, then, they do not
really exist!' "

It sounded a bit oratorical, but continued association with Russians
makes such speech seem natural.

"It is very dangerous at the front," said Mr. Lozovsky. "Aren't you
afraid?"

I get rather tired of being asked if I am afraid when I believe that
the mention of danger may be merely a convenient form of refusal.

"There's only one thing I'm afraid of. That's of going home without
having finished my job."

This seemed to sink in, so I added, "I came here to photograph your
country. If I had wanted to be safe I would have stayed at home. If the
Red Army soldiers can face the danger, why shouldn't I?"

"Fighting is their work," said Mr. Lozovsky.

"And photography is my work."

The waiters were clearing off the champagne ice buckets now and
were removing the screen of flowers. The butter steeds were still rearing
their satiny legs and waving their golden manes as though they were
charging toward victory.

"Hmm," said Mr. Lozovsky, enigmatically, through his mahogany
beard. "You are a very determined young lady."

Two days later we were called late in the evening to Narkomindel
and told to come back the next morning prepared to take a trip. We
were instructed to wear plenty of warm clothing, in preparation for
rough places and cold weather. But beyond that we were given no
inkling of where we would be taken.

There is such a thing as being too happy for speech. What little
communication was necessary, the rest of that night, we carried on in
whispers: not only Erskine and I, but Tatiana and the day chauffeur,
who helped us get ready. They felt that it was their victory too, because

even though they were not going they had known all along how much
it would mean to us.

Tatiana lent me her heavy yellow sweater; the night chauffeur lent
me a woolen scarf. I had no extra socks, because earlier in the summer
I had sold them to Alexander, the day chauffeur, who had admired the
bright colors I wear with slack suits. Now I bought some of my old
socks back from him. I wore the only heavy slacks I owned, a gray
tweed pair. But when it came to a warm coat I had nothing but the
bright-red one which even the Chinese had realized was not the proper
thing to wear at a war. There was nothing to do but wear it, and be
glad that it had a black-satin lining. All during the trip to the front,
I was whipping it off and turning it inside out whenever we came
within the range of guns.

It was cold and dark when we left the hotel to go to the entrance
of Narkomindel. In the half darkness around the bathtub, which was
still filled for fire-bomb duty, a small group of newspapermen had
gathered. They must have been the result of the most painstaking
selection according to Foreign Office protocol. It was evident that great
care had been given to selecting British and American representatives.
There were five Britishers and six Americans. I was pleased to find
that Mr. Hatenaka, the Japanese correspondent, and his Leica were not
among us. The youngest of the three censors came along.

The most weirdly dressed of the correspondents was Cy Sulzberger
of *The New York Times*, who wore his Greek battle dress, a kind of
white shiny tunic of the Isadora Duncan school. The most de luxe was
Alex Werth of Reuter's, who wore a dazzling short coat of white dog
fur. And the most natty was Philip Jordan of the *London News
Chronicle*, in his khaki military outfit worn by British war correspondents in Africa. The other men wore just clothes, and as each muddy
day passed by they were reduced more and more to something that
resembled a uniform, so covered did we all become with the earth
and the mud of the Russian steppes.

We were distributed in a fleet of five cars, with an armed chauffeur
and a military officer-guide packed into each. Around our feet were
disposed various bundles carrying food, and one of them contained
objects of a familiar shape. It seemed incredible to me that we should

be carrying champagne to the front; but that proved later to be the case. The chauffeurs were supplied with their own hand grenades, which they kept in the front pockets along with cranks and tire-mending tools. As Erskine and I pulled out of the Narkomindel courtyard, past the bathtub, our secretary and day chauffeur stood on the sidewalk, waving us off as proudly as though we were their children just leaving for boarding school.

All that day we could feel a good hard roadbed under our wheels, but that was the last day that we were fated to have anything under us more firm than mashed potatoes.

The autumn rains had begun and were drilling their wet needles into the roads and fields. At intervals we drove off the highway into the woods and gobbled down some of the slices of peppery sausage and fistfuls of black bread which we carried with us, eating them between bites of the inevitable raw cucumbers which Russians include in the simplest or most elaborate meal. Cholerton, the British correspondent of *The Daily Telegraph*, who has lived in Russia for almost twenty years—so long that he has grown a long black beard like a Russian—ankled through the wet ferns and picked little white mushrooms which he brought back to the car with him and nibbled contentedly, as we drove on through the rain.

I had known big, bearlike Cholerton on my visits to Moscow in previous years. Most of the other correspondents on this trip were new to the Soviet Union, although I had met some of them on other fronts—in wartime one encounters the same journalists in many parts of the world. For example, I had met blond, slight, whimsical Philip Jordan, of the *London News Chronicle,* on a Cairo balcony overhanging the Nile, at the beginning of the African campaign. In Chungking, Erskine and I had known and liked the *Chicago Daily News* correspondent, Arch Steele: gaunt, sparing of words, Lincolnesque in appearance. Arch Steele was justly respected by his fellow correspondents for his astuteness. We all called him the Admiral.

I had met Cy Sulzberger during the first year of the war, in Bucharest, when we were covering the Balkans, he for *The New York Times* and I for *Life*. Cy, with his prominent light-blue eyes and still more prominent chin, always reminded me of a tightly wound watch

spring. His manner was so quick and positive that everything was usually being done his way before the rest of the crowd woke up to what was happening. He rushed about during our trip along the front as though he expected the Russians to dry up their roads and mop up the mud so that he, Cyrus, could move faster. Whenever his car became hopelessly stuck in the mud, as all our cars did at intervals, he began reminiscing about his fiancée, a beautiful Greek girl, and wondering how soon he would be able to join her in Turkey, where she was waiting for him. (Four months later, the Greek refugee became Mrs. Cyrus Sulzberger in Beirut.) Vernon Bartlett, a roly-poly, elderly British M.P. who was representing the British Broadcasting Corporation, was even more impatient with the discomforts of the roads than Cy.

Alexander Werth, tall, dark, with a rather gloomy face, was a useful addition to our party, for he was half Russian and made a perfect translator of speeches and toasts at banquets. He was a living example of a popular Soviet quip about Leningrad, for he had been born in St. Petersburg, educated in Petrograd, and did not leave for England to complete his schooling until after the city had become Leningrad.

The quietest members of our party were the Associated Press and United Press correspondents. Diminutive Henry Cassidy had been the A.P. correspondent in Moscow for several years, and star-reporter Wallace Carroll had just arrived from other war fronts.

At the end of a stretch of a hundred and forty miles we arrived in Vyazma, a small town surrounding a grain elevator. Its main street was named Boulevard of Karl Marx and was overshadowed by a green-domed monastery which loomed disproportionately large above the tiny peasant homes below. The little plaster houses on the sloping

---

PLOWING THROUGH THE MUD

SOLDIERS IN raincapes, like this one, dug out our cars every time they got mired in the muddy roads. After continual downpours, the roads became even worse than this, until some sections were absolutely impassable. The Red Army soldiers did not mind the mud, for they knew it was making things harder for the Germans.

Russian troops kept hammering away at the mechanized equipment of the Nazis, as it bogged down in the mud. Behind the German lines, Soviet guerrillas followed up every advantage that weather gave them, to disrupt German transport.

With the roads dissolving into mud, the Nazis tried using horses. The Soviets also took to horses, but it was easy for them because they had plenty, and in conformance with their scorched-earth policy, they left none behind for the Nazis.

streets were decorated with the elaborately carved wooden eaves and window sills characteristic of that part of Russia. Things had been quiet in Vyazma, but our arrival there was simultaneous with the starting up of the new German offensive against Moscow. We did not realize its significance at the time.

In the tiny Vyazma International Hotel we had a banquet which included saucers of sour cream with caviar, and excellent small steaks served with slices of raw fish and raw onion placed decoratively loop on loop. After washing it all down with vodka, we went to bed, agreeing that the party was to get up promptly at half-past six.

I am always skeptical about these early-morning arrangements, and anyone who takes photographs has had, I am sure, the same experience as I: that the people who are not photographers never realize the value of every hour of daylight. I didn't think all the vodka the night before would help matters, either.

Nevertheless, Erskine and I were up at six-thirty. As I had feared, everyone else was still sleeping, and neither of us could think of any polite way of waking up a lot of newspapermen and Russian officers. Ten minutes later the two of us were standing in the narrow hallway of our primitive little hotel while Erskine shaved in an affair which looked like a kitchen sink, the one source of running water in the hotel. I was waiting my turn behind him with my toothbrush when suddenly we heard it: the old familiar whine through the air. I was standing at a window, but I jumped away, grabbed Erskine by the shoulder, and in a second we were lying on the floor of the hall.

SUPPER FOR CORRESPONDENTS IN VYAZMA, THE NIGHT BEFORE THE BOMBING

LEFT TO RIGHT: Philip Jordan of the *London News Chronicle*; Cholerton, British correspondent longest in Moscow; Cyrus Sulzberger of *The New York Times*; Erskine Caldwell; General Sokolovsky, Chief of Western Staff under Marshal Timoshenko; Colonel Sudakov, the tank colonel who was our guide and interpreter (Sudakov served three years ago in Washington, D.C., as secretary to the Military Attaché at the Soviet Embassy); Anurov, one of the censors from Narkomindel, who ac-companied the correspondents so as to be able to censor their dispatches upon return; Henry Cassidy of A.P.; Arch Steele (covered up) of the *Chicago Daily News*; Wallace Carroll, of U.P.

General Sokolovsky, like many Soviet military officials, was young for his rank. He was forty-three and a former peasant. The three stars on his collar indicate that he is a general. He was a modest, pleasant man, brisk and intelligent.

That first of several bombs that fell had one practical result. It brought everybody out of bed. All the doors down the length of the hallway opened simultaneously, as though pulled by a single string, and correspondents came plunging out on their hands and knees in various stages of scanty attire. One member of our party did not appear, and when the bombing stopped we went into his room and looked at him. It was the censor, and he was lying in bed, unhurt, but completely surrounded by the window sash, which had fallen in on him so precisely that he looked like a picture in a frame.

I was dressed, fortunately, and I snatched up my camera and ran out into the street. The air reeked with the smell of cordite. After a bomb drops, the atmosphere for some minutes is filled with a peculiar cloud. Bits of plaster, dust, and crumbled brick hang so thickly in the air that it is a little time before one can see just what has happened. I could tell that several buildings directly across the street from our hotel had been demolished, and I started to walk into the flying cloud when I saw something moving toward me. It was a little white puppy, and I marveled that he had come out alive. I picked him up and held him in my arms; I could feel him trembling with fear. Rescue squads were arriving now, most of them girls in the uniforms of medical sisters, and they started searching the wreckage. Four of them climbed over a pile of clapboard that had recently been a house and reappeared, carrying a stretcher between them. On it lay the body of an old man, so covered with powdered plaster that he looked like the unfinished work of a sculptor. The beard and eyebrows seemed to have been merely indicated with a few rough chisel strokes. And then, so suddenly that the girl rescuers were as startled as I, he sat up on his stretcher.

It made me happy that the man and the dog were alive, and I pressed

---

RESCUE SQUAD

RESCUE SQUADS searched the jumble of wreckage for people who might have got trapped when their houses collapsed. Among the victims they found were some who showed hardly a scratch, for one of the peculiar effects of bombing is that the concussion, sometimes rather distant from the blast, can catch people and collapse their lungs, leaving them quite unmarked.

on into the ruins. The plaster cloud was still whirling, and as I walked into a little courtyard it lifted enough to reveal a sight that until then had been veiled. A family of four lay in their doorway, in contorted positions and very still. I set down the dog and began taking pictures.

It is a peculiar thing about pictures of this sort. It is as though a protecting screen draws itself across my mind and makes it possible to consider focus and light values and the technique of photography, in as impersonal a way as though I were making an abstract camera composition. This blind lasts as long as it is needed—while I am actually operating the camera. Days later, when I developed the negatives, I was surprised to find that I could not bring myself to look at the films. I had to have someone else handle and sort them for me.

As I worked, a woman ran up and sank to the ground by the mangled body of a young girl with dust-filled yellow hair, one of the bombed group. I learned from the comments around me that this was her mother. She had been down the street when the bombs fell, and this was the first she knew that her daughter had been killed. Her desperate moans penetrated even my protective shell, and as I focused my camera on this vision of human misery it seemed heartless to turn her suffering into a photograph. But war is war and it has to be recorded.

A larger rescue squad arrived with a truck and shovels. The shreds of blood and hair and internal organs and clothing were scraped up and thrown into the truck, and it removed one more small family that had taken its unconscious stand between Hitler and his *Lebensraum.*

Our party left the tears and spilled blood of Vyazma behind and pushed its way on toward the front over a succession of rivers of mud which had once been called roads. Sometimes the rivers widened into

---

DEATH COMES TO VYAZMA

THESE PEOPLE were killed as an act of revenge.

The night before Soviet pilots from the Vyazma airfield had slipped over to German-held Smolensk, twenty minutes' flying distance away, and, swooping down from a cloud bank at 10,000 feet, had dive-bombed the enemy airport. They had returned to Vyazma with no worse damage than a bullethole through the wing of one plane.

At dawn the Germans returned the visit to Vyazma. Undoubtedly, our hotel, where Russian Air Force officers were known to be quartered, was one of their targets. However, they missed our hotel, and this was the result.

lakes, where the boundaries of the road had blended with the meadows and all were mashed to a uniform consistency by the treads of tanks and heavy artillery which had poured in steady streams to meet the enemy. We might have been traveling over Camembert cheese.

Once when we became mired to the hubcaps and our party had to rebuild stretches with stones and logs in front of each helpless wheel —a backbreaking job which took two and a half hours before all cars were extricated—I remarked that at last I had met the famous General Mud face to face.

"Oh, no," said our chauffeur, "in modern warfare he has been reduced to the rank of colonel."

But it was my private opinion that the Red Army had succeeded in promoting him to the post of generalissimo.

Sometimes while we were negotiating these almost liquid highways, small units of the *Luftwaffe* would appear and put in their own bit of work on the roads. The first time this happened we dashed out of our cars and slithered across the slippery surface to the edge of a meadow, where we threw ourselves down in the low shrubbery.

It is odd what images become engraved on your mind. I remember noticing that we were lying in the largest patch of fringed gentians that I have ever seen. The gentians were at a level with my eyes, and over this blue border I watched three great curtains of mud rise into the air and hang there shimmering, as though suspended on invisible curtain poles in the sky. When these heavenly draperies descended to earth again, there were three large sludgy pits, perfectly round in shape, in the road behind us, and our cars were undamaged, though glistening with a coat of mud laid on thick, like maple icing on a cake.

I began gathering fringed gentians, but the soldiers who were driving

---

NO. 9 TRUBETSOV STREET

THE DEAD family were placed in a truck and driven off, and the ground was scraped with shovels. First-aid girls, dressed in heavy denim coveralls, had reached the spot with miraculous speed. Here they could no nothing for the dead, but they tried to comfort the living.

The house where these victims were killed was almost intact, while in other houses near by which were completely wrecked, some people escaped alive. It was as though this particular small family had rushed to their doorstep when they heard the sound of German planes and had died where they stood.

our cars had something much more practical to gather. They began pulling boughs off the shrubs and trees and tucking them around the fenders and tying them on the tops of the cars. When we moved on again we looked like a nursery on wheels.

At twilight we reached a schoolhouse within six miles of the German lines. The benches where children had sat during the years, studying their arithmetic lessons with beads on an abacus and writing compositions on the life of Lenin and the philosophy of Karl Marx, had been piled against the wall. Their places had been taken by cots packed tightly down the long schoolroom. So thoughtful of our comfort was the Foreign Office which had planned this trip that a barber was even waiting to give the correspondents a shave.

After a supper consisting of slices of salami and Bologna and cucumbers, served with pieces of black bread as big as a fist and portions of creamy butter the size of a deck of cards, we were told to expect a surprise.

In the middle of the schoolroom three chairs were placed. The wick of the single oil lamp which hung suspended from the ceiling was turned up a trifle, its rays blurred by the cigarette smoke in the air. A private tucked the black paper more securely about the window frames to secure the blackout.

Then three men, all very young, were led in between sentries and seated. One had a bandage around his head and around his hand; the second had a bandaged hand supported in a sling; the third, unhurt, gazed at us uncomprehendingly and insolently.

"I believe that you have already made their acquaintance," said the Red Army colonel. "These are the pilots who bombed you this morning."

The German crew had taken off in a Junkers 88 from the Shekalovo Airport at Smolensk that morning and on the way had been chased by Red airplanes. One motor had been pierced, but they kept on, dropped their load, and were within six miles of slipping successfully back over their own lines when a Soviet plane succeeded in shooting holes through the second motor. This forced them to land in a wheat field. All of the crew of four had been captured alive, but the mechanic was too badly wounded to appear. The pilot had a sprained arm, and the bomber, with his bandaged head, was evidently in considerable pain and talked with difficulty, but the radio operator was unscratched and as cocky as any typical young Nazi party member at a political rally.

I don't know how the other correspondents felt as they gravely questioned these men who had dropped their missiles so close that it might have been the end of us instead of those families just across the street. But my habitual impersonality with a camera came to my aid, and if I had any feeling at all it was just a slight sense of gratitude that they should have let themselves get shot down so providentially close to where we were going to spend the night, so that I could have a continued story.

They talked in German, which was translated first into Russian and then into English, but soon the correspondents, most of whom spoke German, abandoned the intermediate languages.

These men had bombed London, and when asked why, they replied quick as a shot that Berlin was bombed first. "War with England," said the pilot, "was inevitable and necessary"; but when questioned about the war with Russia, they admitted it had come like a bolt from the blue and, until they had been brought almost within sight of Russian territory, they had not known they were being sent to fight the Soviet Union.

This coincided with some remarkable statements I had heard earlier in a Moscow hospital where I had photographed German infantry prisoners. It was as though the Nazis had been afraid to let their war-weary soldiers know they were being called on to face a powerful new enemy, until they had them well along the route to the front lines.

Before seeing these pilots, I had interviewed many German prisoners, most of them infantry. The pilots were of a somewhat higher caliber. Undoubtedly, they have to be, for flying a plane is a highly skilled job; but the German infantry captives had impressed me by their resemblance to animals. I suppose prisoners always appear at a disadvantage, and allowances should be made, but these German soldiers gave me the feeling that the Nazis were throwing into battle every man capable of supporting the weight of a gun. They were immature, half-baked young boys, with no ideas of their own, with no enthusiasm for anything. The fervid Führer-worship that we hear about may exist, but it

was something I never saw. Neither did I see hatred. I observed only a blind acceptance of the job that had been mapped out for them. It was a job they disliked. They would rather have been home. As things stood, they were glad to be warm and comfortable, with a handful of Russian cigarettes within reach. But their minds were the minds of automatons. There must be higher caliber soldiers than this, but I had the feeling that all available man power, down to the last dregs, was being poured into the Russian war. Perhaps what I was seeing was typical of a whole new generation which has grown up, pressed into a stifling mold. This, perhaps, is one of the most serious aspects of war and eternal readiness for war.

I am not sure that the German pilots understood why they were being questioned, or that we were correspondents, and I doubt if they knew what our nationalities were. When asked why they had bombed women and children in Vyazma, they said, "We did our duty for the Vater-land." When questioned about their attitude toward America, they said, "America is actually in the war already." And when asked if they knew that American planes were being sent in to help the Russians, they said, "America is a long way off."

There was one question I wanted to ask. We had heard over and over that the clothing of the German soldiers is so poor that, when captured, often they are found to be wearing no underwear. I was curious about the underwear, but felt that such a question should not come from a woman. Unfortunately, it did not occur to anyone else to ask.

Pilot Taüse, a butcher's son, was well poised and sometimes humorous. Radio Operator Trocha, son of a tailor, was as impudent as the neighbor's bad boy, and Bomber Rasek, the janitor's child, who had

---

CAPTURED GERMAN BOMBER CREW

THIS IS the crew of the German Junkers which bombed us in Vyazma and killed the family across the street from our hotel.

Josef Trocha, on the left, was the radio operator: twenty-six years old, son of a tailor, and as cocky as any typical young Nazi-party member at a political rally—perhaps because he was unscratched.

Walther Rasek, in the middle, was the bomber: twenty-four years old, son of the janitor of a Nazi-party building in Germany. His head wound evidently gave him considerable pain; he talked with difficulty.

Rudolf Taüse, on the right, was the pilot: twenty-five years old, son of a master butcher. He seemed the most intelligent and was quickest to answer our questions.

The fourth member of the crew, the mechanic, does not appear in the picture. He was too badly wounded to be present.

released the explosives which had brought death to Vyazma, was silent and dazed with his wound.

As the questioning drew to a close, and the guards started to lead them away, I noticed that Pilot Taüse glanced up and noticed for the first time that he had been sitting under a big poster which showed a caricature of Hitler, a pygmy figure with the enormous shadow of Napoleon looming over it. I did not think he could read the Russian legend: DEATH TO ALL WHO INVADE OUR SACRED SOIL, but I thought he understood.

CHAPTER 16

Star Shells and Vodka on the Edge of No Man's Land

THE NEXT day the wind from the steppes had risen, and a low bank of clouds hung over the wreck of the Junkers 88 which had bombed us the morning before. Its great hulk, painted with swastikas, and guarded by a Red Army sentry, lay in a level field, the black earth pierced with shoots of winter wheat. Erskine, who had developed a souvenir-collecting facility that astonished his wife, filled his pockets with clips of machine-gun bullets and even took the speedometer of the plane, while I made a set of photographs.

The wind-tossed clouds racing overhead showed cracks of blue which raised my hopes for a sunlit day. But soon I found that I was being pelted with hailstones and I climbed back into the car. The hail turned to rain, and our little convoy returned once more to the task of making its uncertain way.

For almost the entire day the rain kept driving little awls and chisels into the roads. We progressed at the average rate of two and a half miles an hour. A truck containing a demolition squad of soldiers, whose regular duties included blowing up bridges and power lines when necessary, had been detailed to accompany us to the front for the exclusive purpose of digging us out of the mud. As we came to each difficult spot, the soldiers lined the road, standing at attention with their shovels, ready to extricate each car in succession as it got stuck.

By this time I was feeling desperate about the possibilities of getting any pictures in such weather; but it seemed important to make the most of every hour, so whenever our caravan was halted for the digging-out process, I jumped out and photographed what I could. If the mud came only a short distance above my shoe tops I could function fairly well,

but when it came up to my knees it sometimes took the strength of both hands to pull out each foot as I made a step. My subjects were limited by what happened along the road, but things of interest kept coming. First it would be a medium tank, which sailed up and down over the slippery hills and soupy valleys with such a jaunty air that anyone in a mere automobile grew envious. Sometimes it would be a group of soldiers with bayonets and helmets, driving cattle to the front lines— for fresh meat is taken to the army on the hoof. Once it was a shepherd tending his flock, with a gas mask over his shoulder. Sometimes a group of infantry would come out of a wood, with their upturned helmets filled with freshly gathered mushrooms.

Once an ammunition truck camouflaged with spruce branches passed us, only to become mired in a bomb crater in the middle of the road just ahead. While it was being dug out, by soldiers who looked like ghosts with the blinding rain dancing on their rain mantles, another truck tried to pass and slithered into the big crater with the ammunition. The new truck was so densely camouflaged, with branches interlaced like a canopy over it, that I was curious about its contents. I coasted into the bomb crater and peeped through the camouflage. There in the truck, looking elegant and somewhat perplexed, was a beautiful horse.

I knew that the Russians were beginning to use sudden thrusts of cavalry to harass German armored units that were bogged down in the mud, and I suppose this was the mount of some cavalry officer.

Our convoy was beginning to move on again now, and as the first two of our cars moved slowly past me one of the British correspondents leaned out a bit cautiously, so as not to get wet, and called, "Don't hold us up this time, Peggy. You delayed us five minutes the last time we got stuck."

As the third car skirted cautiously around the crater rim, the door

---

WRECKED NAZI RAIDER

THIS WAS the plane, piloted by Taüse, which had bombed us the day before. The Red Air Force brought it down within a few kilometers of the German lines. It was a Junkers 88 painted characteristically with swastikas. Correspondent Carroll, left, and Colonel Sudakov, our English-speaking guide, center, are examining the plane, which is being guarded by Russian sentries. It had made a crash landing and came down with its fuselage and even its propellers riddled with machine-gun bullets.

opened, and Erskine jumped out, pulled me up over the running board, and I was inside. To miss the portions of road ahead which were pitted with shell holes, we took out across open fields, and I began the hopeless task of changing one pair of wet socks for another pair of wet socks. I had plenty to choose from, for I had been changing them all day and they were hanging all over the inside of the car. The distinction to be drawn between them was very fine indeed; it took an expert touch to determine which were the least pasty with mud. It must be nice, I thought, to have a job where you can write about the rain and mud instead of taking pictures of it.

The problem of shoes was easily handled because I had only one pair. Fortunately, we had a copy of *Pravda* with us, and some new layers of newsprint inside the soles felt comforting. My red coat I had long since turned wrong side out, so as not to make a target for the Nazi pilots on their occasional flights overhead, and its black lining was beginning to take on the protective coloring of the roads. There wasn't much I could do about my slacks, which remained solid with mud to the knees throughout the whole trip, although I attempted a little scraping with a stick now and then.

"In Soviet Russia we have a proverb," said the driver from the front seat; " 'what is meat for the Russian soldier is poison for his enemy.' "

"That's all right by me," I said, scraping some of the enemy's poison off my most newly removed pair of socks and hanging them through the handles of a camera case.

"And the bloody Fascists will meet a still more dangerous poison when the mud gives way to snow," added the driver. With which I agreed.

Late in the afternoon the clouds began lifting, and when a weak ray of sunlight filtered through, I was delighted. I was to continue to be heartened by those rays of sunlight until the end of the trip, but I never

---

RUSSIAN GUARDING GERMAN PLANE

WE WERE surprised to find that in spite of the countless bulletholes that pierced the plane body, the cockpit was practically intact. The sentry showed us the little plate which read: Dornier Werke-Junkers 88A. He was obviously proud to be placed in charge of such a valuable trophy. "It is good," said the sentry, "to capture such a great bird."

saw one that lasted for longer than ninety seconds by actual count, and usually its duration was less than a minute. I estimate that during a week at the front I had a total of sixteen minutes of sunlight.

However, the breaking up of the clouds helped the Germans, and soon a group of three were over. We were on an exposed hilltop when they appeared on the horizon, but a patch of huckleberry bushes, which looked as though they had grown for just the purpose of sheltering journalists, harbored us all.

From where we lay we had a view of a little village half a mile away being systematically pounded to pieces. First stabs of fire rose, then puffs of smoke, and, in less time than it takes to tell, the planes had left, and angry flames were swallowing up the little log houses. The Germans must have dropped a quantity of incendiaries to burn up the little settlement so fast. I suppose they felt that even a tiny village can harbor troops. I can see no other reason why it should have seemed important to get rid of it.

We had barely left the smoking village behind us when we were at the front. It didn't look at all the way I had imagined the front would look. We drove into a little birch grove that a Sunday-school class would pick for its yearly outing. During our whole course along the front lines we traveled from one little cluster of trees to another, each grove looking more suited to picnic baskets than cartridge cases.

When we first drove under the thick trees, it seemed as though there was not a human being within miles, but as our eyes became accustomed to the filtered green light, we discovered that we were in a thickly inhabited community humming with activity. Soldiers in dugouts talked through field telephones. Sentries guarded ammunition dumps, which were smothered under piles of green boughs. Here and there a tank had been dug into a hollow in the earth, with only the long guns projecting and even the gun barrels tied up with green branches. Trucks had been pushed under the trees, and to ensure their being doubly hidden, additional trees had been chopped down and leaned against them. At twilight, I found, this extra greenery was moved away, and the trucks ran a kind of commuters' service, carrying fresh troops to hot spots that were "in contact" with the enemy. On their return trips the trucks brought back the squads that had been fighting all day.

Near by a separate little grove had been synthetically created. This was because of the necessity of having a level space for the landing of courier planes. Several truckloads of fir trees had been brought from another part of the forest and stuck realistically into the earth to shield a group of planes. After nightfall the trees were lifted away, and the planes could take off for points farther back from the front lines, with messages from the commandant and with the more seriously wounded.

Even though we were within three miles of the Germans, there was a piano. It was in a two-room dugout called "The Red Corner." A rubber plant stood in a pot at the head of a little flight of stairs cut out of earth and leading down into the ground. The roof of the recreation center was only a slight hump above the earth, reinforced with planks and sod, and showing two tiny windows about ten inches square, with glass panes crisscrossed against concussion with strips of brown paper. Down in The Red Corner a medical sister was playing the piano and a few soldiers were singing a song with a chorus which ran:

"The Germans think they will take their breakfast in Leningrad, their lunch in Sevastopol, and their supper in Moscow—but we will feed the Fascist head-hunters iron to eat." Russians are great harmonizers, and the refrain "Iron to eat—iron to eat" was developed in elaborate barbershop harmony.

In the second room, which led from the music room by a narrow earth tunnel, there were three pairs of soldiers bent over the favorite game of the Red Army—chess. Above the chess players was a hand-lettered poster, THE ENEMY IS HUNGRY. HE WANTS TO TAKE OUR BREAD. DURING FORCED WITHDRAWAL DO NOT LEAVE ANYTHING BEHIND. LET THE FASCIST SNAKE DIE OF HUNGER.

We visited the soldiers' mess and saw quantities of this bread which was not to be left to the Germans. The commander performed his daily duty of sampling the soldiers' food, and this evening he asked me to sample it with him. A typical Red Army meal, I found, consisted of borsch, or cabbage soup, with a big piece of meat in the bottom of each soup bowl, another meat dish, usually beef, with potatoes, gravy, and one or two vegetables, glasses of milk or cocoa, and hot fruit compote for dessert. The red-blooded look of the Russian soldiers gave testimony to the efficacy of this fare.

Then we went to our own supper, which was spread pleasantly under the trees on a long table on which fir branches served both as decoration and camouflage. The evergreens were interwoven with asters and with a purple-and-yellow flower called "Anna and Ivan." The presence of the piano within artillery range of the Germans had astonished me less than the banquet that was laid for us. But it was only this first banquet that came as a surprise, for during our week along the front lines I was to learn that the thunder of enemy guns does not dim the hospitality of the warmhearted Russians.

We began with raw fish, salt fish, and pickled fish. We had cucumbers both raw and pickled, and we ate the raw ones as the Russians do, skin and all, like apples. We had woodcock in sour-cream gravy, and slices of ham, cheese and Bologna, served with little hillocks of caviar decorated with crisp circlets of onion and hard-boiled eggs. In the center of the table were large bowls of cookies, chocolate bars, and little tissue-wrapped candies called chocolate bears.

Occasionally German planes passed overhead, but our Soviet hosts hardly glanced up. When we commented on them, the political commissar remarked, "Those Fascist vultures who fly overhead do not know whether we're encamped tonight in this wood or the next one."

Toasts were drunk in three kinds of vodka—the common white variety, which has a slight gasoline taste; Georgian vodka, which is pale yellow and considered a great delicacy; and brown hunter's vodka, which feels after each swallow as though small fires are being lighted inside.

While we were eating, a private came up to the table with a handful of flowers and stood there shyly, until the conversation died down.

MEMBERS OF AN INFANTRY PLATOON

THE RUSSIANS are noted for their fierce courage in hand-to-hand combat where the bayonet is the chief weapon. Most of the time they carry their bayonets in fixed position. I was much interested in this in view of the fact that this is supposed to be a mechanized war. However, the Russians feel that the final mopping up must be done at the point of the bayonet. The rule of the Red Army soldier is to give his life if he can make it cost two of the enemy.

I have watched Russian soldiers at bayonet practice, running along the edges of fences, leaping hurdles, battering away obstacles to the right and left, and plunging their bayonets into targets on all sides as they run.

Then he addressed me and said, "In the name of the entire Red Army, and because of our admiration for your great country, we wish to present you with this bunch of red poppies."

And I, feeling that a speech was expected, replied, "On behalf of the people of our great country, I am happy to accept from the entire Red Army this bunch of red poppies."

When the champagne bottles appeared, I remembered those packages that had been tucked around our feet in the beginning of the trip, and I was more sure than ever that this final touch had traveled with us all the way from Moscow. In Russia, no one touches his glass without raising it in a toast. The toasts over the vodka had been to each other, but when the champagne was reached they achieved an international character. The commander proposed a toast to the friendship among the great peoples of America, Great Britain, and the Soviet Union.

The political commissar, who shared the place at the end of the table with the division commander, offered a toast to Mr. Churchill and to that great President, Mr. Roosevelt. Then a toast was announced to the Red Army and to its great leader "Tovarish Stalin." When Stalin is mentioned in a toast, everyone rises and drains his glass. But the toast which brought ringing cheers was the one proposed to the downfall of that archviper, that super-Fascist centipede, that drinker of the blood of children and of women, that man-eating Moloch of Nazism, that fiendish barbarian, that megalomaniac, their archenemy Gitler.

As we sat at our banquet table we could see star shells rising above the dark outlines of the treetops. The sound of guns from the German lines was growing louder. "A great deal of that noise is psychological warfare," said the commander. "When the Germans begin getting nervous they fire thousands of rockets into the air. They try to turn night

---

ARTILLERYMEN SHAFRAN (right, aged twenty-seven)
AND ZOLKIN (left, aged twenty-six)

ZOLKIN HAS the title of *otlichnik* of the Red Army, which means that he has shown special merit as a soldier. These two men are members of a battery crew on guard over one of the antiaircraft guns concealed in the shrubbery in a meadow. Crossed gun barrels are the insignia of artillery.

The turtle-shaped helmets are strong and heavy, superior to those worn by the Germans. I had one that I wore at the front. It was almost unbearably heavy until I got accustomed to it, but it did furnish good protection against shrapnel.

into day, hoping that it will keep our patrols back. They're shooting off a lot of stuff tonight just to make a noise."

"Do you mean," I asked, "that the Germans are afraid of the dark?"

"They are in deadly fear of our artillery, which may attack them in the dark," he replied. "When you know the weak points of the enemy you can best them. Because they hate the night attacks, we always thrust at them in the darkness. We found out that fear when we began capturing prisoners; some of their comrades had gone crazy under our night barrage. We learned that they have a name for us, too. They honor us by calling us the Wild Division. But *we* call ourselves the Meat Choppers." *

As we sat at the table talking, one of the Meat Choppers came up to invite me to waltz to the tune of an accordion. After being whirled around under the trees I was breathless, but the soldiers begged me to teach them the latest American dance steps. My efforts to impart the nature of the rhumba, in my muddy slacks and earth-caked shoes, to the accompaniment of the accordion, were greeted with more enthusiasm than the performance merited. It was even more difficult to give a one-woman explanation of swing. Swing would be a natural for the Russians, if they could once see a floor full of collegians doing it, but it will take more than one mud-caked photographer to give them the lesson that their talent for rhythm deserves.

When I came back to the table, I slipped into place between my husband and Wally Carroll.

"Fill up the gasoline glass," Cyrus was singing out.

"Cy is murdering himself," Carroll whispered.

The censor and Cyrus Sulzberger were engaged in a vodka-and-brandy contest. "Come on, Peggy," called Cy, "you've got the photographic eye," and I was enrolled to match each drink, vodka alternating with brandy, adding or deleting a few drops from one glass or the other, as the marathon progressed. The censor had broken into flowery speeches in English, and soon Cy was accomplishing miraculous orations in a mixture of English, Russian, Greek, and Turkish.

---

* The Meat Chopper Division won the Order of Lenin for decimating nine Nazi divisions and reconquering a strip of territory several miles wide.

"I wish he'd stop it," said Carroll. "Nobody can drink a Russian down."

But Cy held up like a man until we were driven to the hospital tent at Dedova, six miles behind the lines, where we were to spend the night. The tent was sunk partially underground, the top of it strewn with spruce boughs to conceal it from the air. The floor was covered with straw, and the canvas walls were hung with slogans and posters. Erskine and I chose a couple of cots in the far corner under a blazing poster of red and black. Above our heads a snake, bent into the shape of a swastika, and with Hitler's mustache, was being bayoneted by a looming Red soldier, and the slogan read: DEATH TO THE FASCIST VIPER.

We slept so soundly under the Fascist reptile that we did not know until we were told the next morning that shells from the German guns six miles away had been spattering about our hospital tent.

Our breakfast of raw fish, Bologna, canned sturgeon, and liver sausage was left untouched by the pale representative of *The New York Times*. But the censor appeared, pink and smiling, and blithely poured an eye opener for himself from the flask of vodka which always stood in the center of the breakfast table. This gave the American correspondents the opportunity to teach the censor the one about the hair of the dog that bit you. He was so delighted with this acquisition to his fund of knowledge that he translated it in the greatest detail to the Russian officers who were sharing breakfast with us. In Russian it sounded splendid. The expression became so popular in translation that throughout the remainder of our trip the Russian officers never missed an opportunity to propose a toast to the hair of that Amerikanski dog.

CHAPTER 17

Death and Life on the Battlefields

THE DAYS alternated between trips through the eternal mud and banquets within the sound of enemy guns. The nights were spent in a bewildering succession of field headquarters, sometimes under canvas
and sometimes under thatched roofs. Once we slept on the floor of a
little resort cottage above the swollen Dnieper, near the fire-gutted town
of Dorogobuzh. We slept all together in a room so small that we lay
elbow to elbow, our feet against the heads of the row of men in front
of us. Erskine rolled me in my blanket over against the far wall and
took his place beside me to give me a maximum of privacy. Occasionally
I woke up and saw the sentry, bayonet in hand, guarding us, while a
single candle flickered on his immobile face.

Often at dawn I would slip out ahead of the others so as to use the
valuable early hours before we started on the move. There were always
interesting types among the soldiers: Mongols, Ukrainians, Siberians,
Uzbeks, Kazaks, and Turkmenians, their faces wet under their dripping
raincapes. And it always was raining.

I used flash bulbs to augment the weak light. One by one, my shutters
began sticking in that helpless, half-open way which is the worst sight

---

GUARDING THE RUINS OF DOROGOBUZH

ON GUARD at these ruined steps were two
Red Army sentries, typical in their heavy
boots, wool-wrapped legs, long war coats
and raincapes. Red Army soldiers have
that healthy, red-blooded look that comes
from having plenty of meat to eat. They
are well disciplined, and while all soldiers
are "Comrade" to each other, they salute
their superior officers and address them as
Comrade Colonel, or Comrade General, or
Comrade Political Commissar, as the case
may be.

These Russian soldiers are tough and
come from hardy peasant stock. The Russian peasant loves his land, and therefore
winning back the land from the invader
has a deep and sacred meaning. These men
know what they are fighting for, and that
is one of the secrets of their strength.

253

that ever confronts a photographer. And as each lens in its crippled shutter went out of commission, I drew reluctantly on the dry ones which I was saving in my camera case.

These morning hours were often the only times that we were stationary during daylight long enough for me to make character studies and photograph soldiers doing their daily camp tasks. I usually worked until one of the correspondents would stick his head out between the flaps of the mess tent, coffee cup in hand, and call, "Come on, Peggy. Everybody's starting now. Don't hold us up the way you did yesterday," and I would hurry my equipment into the car and we would be off.

Once we were under way Erskine would slip his hand into his overcoat pocket and bring out something salvaged from breakfast. The morning he handed me the long, strong drumstick of a goose I was pleased indeed.

Sometimes the feast time, later in the day, gave me a little more time, and I developed a certain banquet technique. As soon as the toasts had begun I would steal away with a piece of black bread in my hand, loaded with salt herring or a slab of cheese, and scout around for photographic subjects.

Once, when I came back at the end of a luncheon, there had been such enthusiastic toasting of Anglo-American-Soviet friendship that it was small wonder one of the correspondents had slipped unobtrusively under the table. We were being piled into cars and were about to be taken to a group of field batteries directly on the first firing line when my husband missed him.

"Don't leave him behind," said Erskine; "he'll never get over it when he finds out what he's missed." So my husband raised the unconscious correspondent in his arms and placed him in the back of one of the cars, where he was brought along, quite unaware that he was being carried to the very brink of no man's land.

The completeness of his coma lasted until far into the night, which we were spending, packed tight as crackers in a box, on the floor of a tent. Suddenly we were startled awake, for our reviving companion, still under his spell, was chuckling and laughing to himself.

"Shut up and let us go to sleep," somebody called. "There's only one of you and there's a dozen of us."

"If there's a dozen of you I'll take you all to the baker," he announced, after which there was complete silence until dawn. At breakfast our correspondent could hardly believe he had been taken almost within a vodka breath of the German lines. He wrote up his story from the notes the other correspondents lent him.

Finally, a difficulty developed that worried me more than the weather. Some of the correspondents decided they had had enough of the rain and the mud and the disproportionate amount of time it took to go from one place to the next. They wanted to return to Moscow. It took so long to travel along the front, they argued, that they might as well start back and write up the things they had seen. The things they had not seen they could imagine. The simple solution of dividing forces and letting those who wished to see more of the front do so, and those who so elected go back home, was immediately rejected: that might give a scoop to those who remained.

The front faction and the home faction were about evenly divided. Erskine and two or three of the other Americans, especially Carroll and Steele, were steadfast supporters of the front group; but otherwise the membership fluctuated so frequently that when matters grew crucial I stuck around because my vote might be needed. Whenever I set forth my side of the case, that we had been promised we would be shown many more interesting subjects, and that surely if we kept on I would get my break of sunlight sooner or later, I was reminded that the needs of photographers are different from the needs of journalists. Well, they *are* different. No doubt about it. Quite different. And there was only one of me and ten of them.

The homing instinct reached its peak over one of the raw-fish breakfasts. The discussion grew so lively that the Russian officers accompanying us had retired, along with the censor, to the next room, to allow us to decide the matter for ourselves. (I often wondered what those army officers thought of our discussions. They had been so hospitable.)

And then it was one of the medical sisters who really swayed the vote. We looked up from our plates of raw fish to see her coming into the room with a steaming mound of mashed potatoes. Golden pools of butter were nestling in the hollows. Everyone's spirits rose, and the

vote was cast to continue on through the mud and rain and see whatever the Russians were willing to show us.

I was overjoyed, because I had a deep feeling that I was going to get my break at last.

I always had interesting little adventures on the evenings that I slipped away from the banquet table. Once the soldiers showed me a big cache of captured German mechanized equipment hidden under the fir trees: some Skoda reconnaissance cars, a huge troop carrier with its caterpillar treads blown partially off, a Mercedes gun hauler, field guns, machine guns, and disabled tanks with swastikas painted on their sides.

Once a tankist returning from a battle where several enemy tanks had been surrounded and captured told me how the enemy tank drivers had filled every available bit of space around their feet, inside the tanks, with women's clothing which they had rifled from Russian villages. One tank, he said, was filled with women's underwear and another was crammed full of peasant embroideries, taken, I suppose, as souvenirs for German soldiers' wives. I was glad they had recaptured that tankload of embroidered scarves and blouses, for Russian peasant handiwork has a richness that is hard to match in any part of the world today. I would not have liked to see it go to the enemy.

Frequently, groups of pilots would return from the fight and show me their captured trophies, for a pilot always saves his enemy's medals if he is able to get them. Each of these pilots had his captured Iron Cross, and one of them had seven of them. "All the Fascist pilots want to get Iron Crosses," he said to me, "but we give them crosses of wood."

PILOTS IN MESS TENT AT AIRPORT

THESE PILOTS were photographed at a small landing field of the Soviet Air Fleet, tucked away in the wooded countryside. A handful of planes had been wheeled under the trees, where they were waiting until nightfall.

The Red pilots are fine-looking men, some of them as handsome as any Hollywood movie pilot. Most of them wore deco-rations: the Order of Lenin, the Red Star, the Mongolian Star. The pilot second from left, rear, had just shot down his twenty-seventh plane the night before.

The Russian people speak of their pilots with the deepest reverence, and when Berlin received a token bombing they were overjoyed beyond measure.

I was interested to learn that the Soviet fliers frequently recognized captured German pilots who had parachuted to safety when their planes were shot down. The *Luftwaffe* evidently made full use of the men who had flown passenger planes over the commercial line operating between Berlin and Moscow in peacetime—men who were thoroughly familiar with the route. Sometimes the Russians knew these captives well enough to call them by their first names. The Germans, however, never showed a sign of recognition.

Sometimes I talked with scouts who had penetrated far enough back of the enemy lines to make contact with the guerrillas, for the Red Army maintains connections with partisan troops wherever it can. Wherever possible, the regular army smuggles guns to the partisans. One returned scout told me about a group of villagers who were successful in halting an oncoming munitions train by tossing burning trees across the railroad tracks. When the German soldiers ran up to try to clear the tracks, the villagers shot at them from an embankment with the only two rifles they had, and when those gave out they threw rocks at the Germans. In the end more of the partisans than the German soldiers were killed, but the enemy had been delayed.

Another scout came from a region beyond Smolensk, where a detachment of partisans had hidden in the tall grass along the highway, waited until a group of tanks came opposite, and tossed bottles of flaming gasoline * at them, disabling three tanks. As this scout worked his way back, he passed through a town where a group of partisans had actually fallen on two invading tanks with hammers and axes. Machine-gun fire from the tanks killed several of these villagers, but finally, led by the village blacksmith, they managed to bend the machine guns out of commission and then, beating on the armored walls, they created so much din and dust that the tank crews had to surrender.

One of the scouts had come from a tiny village, nine miles behind the lines, with a report of how when the Germans moved in, the men went back into the woods, believing the Nazis would be less suspicious of the women. The German officers took up their quarters in a log schoolhouse, and at midnight the peasant women set fire to it with

* This is the Molotov Cocktail, used so successfully by guerrillas in the Spanish Civil War.

gasoline-soaked hay. Then, when the officers rushed half dressed out of the burning building, the women set on them with pitchforks.

In the Soviet Union when territory is captured one does not see the swarms of refugees which have clogged the roads of other invaded countries. The government has previously instructed civilians to stay and become partisans. They have been given directions in the art of sniping and in guerrilla warfare, and if their village is captured they know just what they are expected to do. Guerrillas cannot win a war, but they can do a great deal to make the enemy uncomfortable.

The person whom I remember the most vividly among the Russians I came to know at the front was Tanya. Tanya was a nurse, with widely spaced blue eyes, honey-colored curls that spilled down shoulder length, and a strong, chunky little body. We were in the Yartsevo sector when I met her, not far from Smolensk, and Tanya had been born here. She knew every footpath, and at night, as soon as it grew completely dark, she would buckle on her sidearms and go crawling on her hands and knees through the long grass and low shrubbery, across to the German lines. There, behind the lines, she would learn what she could about the movements of the enemy and the location of German guns, and creep back just before daybreak to report on what she had seen. Then she would sleep a few hours, go to the hospital tent to help tend the wounded, and at night if she was needed she would be off again.

The area she was working in had changed hands many times between the Germans and the Russians, so she was much needed. It is a sector that is still changing hands, and as I write this today I believe it is being regained by the Russians. So the experience of scouts like Tanya has great value.

Later, the night that I met her, we were allowed to visit an action point. We were led to the edge of our little wood and told that we could run across an open meadow to another grove of trees about a quarter of a mile away. We were instructed to run single file and keep three meters apart. As we reached the middle of the meadow the whole horizon was ringed with light and there was the sound of thunder above us. It was the Soviet battery firing over our heads, and the Germans began answering toward us with machine-gun fire. We quickened our pace, and as we approached the grove for which we were headed the Germans

began sending up star shells, to light the front lines so as to be able to see scouts who might be slipping across. Even as I ran I could not help but notice what a brilliant glow the star shells threw on the ghost-white birch trunks. I hoped that Tanya, wherever she might be at that moment, was sufficiently hidden. And then, in an instant, we were inside the grove.

The action point was less than a quarter of a mile from the Germans. We had to walk on tiptoe and talk in whispers. Here, of course, I was not able to take pictures, because flash bulbs would have revealed our position. Under cover of the darkness, the battery crew moved like clockwork, loading and operating their big guns.

When we returned and started on to another section of the front, it was a little past midnight, much too early for me to find out if Tanya had made the journey safely. I shall always wonder about her.

The next day, we had left the woods and groves behind. We were approaching the great battlefields of Yelnya, where war had lashed back and forth in all its fury, the land sometimes in enemy hands, sometimes in Russian hands, until at the end of six weeks of some of the most savage fighting that the world has perhaps ever seen, the Russians had reclaimed it again. This was sacred soil, for this was the first land to be won back for the Soviet flag, and we arrived directly on the heels of this victory. Here there were no picnic groves, no little woods of fir and birch. We were entering a man-made desert.

The fields were chewed up with the treads of tanks, and we were

---

WHERE THE GERMANS DUG IN

HERE AT Ustinovo, near Yelnya, the Germans dug in like cave dwellers. They had fitted up their little dugouts so thoroughly that it is evident they expected to spend the winter. On this cliff that occupied a position strategically commanding a stretch of the main road, they built a command and observation post. In the dugouts were telephones and supply dumps. Above on the hilltop were networks of trip wires leading to mines, and heavy cannon camouflaged under woven branches. Tanks, which had been dug into the clay, with the gun turrets projecting to serve as rotating fortresses, had already been salvaged by the Red Army when we arrived.

In this sector, General Field Marshal Fedor von Bock's Second, Fourth, and Ninth Armies concentrated for what they expected to be a victorious march on Moscow.

Wherever they attempted to take a permanent position they put up signposts printed in German and issued a new set of laws to govern the captured people. But the Russian people refused to submit to capture, and partisan bands would steal up in the night to snipe at the enemy.

passing "scorched-earth" villages, with only patches of ashes darkening the ground to show where homes had stood. On the side of a hill, above a small stream and facing the road, was something that looked like a Zuñi village. Just as our American Indians built their holelike houses, tier above tier, up the sides of the mesa, so as to be able to see and face the enemy as he approached, so the Germans had dug themselves into the hillside of Ustinovo. And they had dug in with them several tanks which they could use as pill boxes. Communication trenches had been dug, joining links with forward positions and command posts. Each little cell-like dugout was banked with sandbags and braced with timber, and inside were metal cartons and wicker baskets which still contained hand grenades and land mines bedded in straw. The Germans must have been driven from this hill suddenly, for large stores of ammunition had been left behind for the Russians.

I heard Erskine shouting to me from the top of the hill. He was waving a German helmet, so I picked up one of my own. There were plenty to choose from; hundreds of them, savagely gashed and broken or riddled with bullets, were lying around in heaps. The metal they were made of was thin, much lighter than the heavy mushroom-shaped casques that protected Russian heads. I selected one that was fairly intact. The owner's name, Herbst, was lettered in white inside, and a single bullet-hole over the left ear showed how Herr Herbst had met his end. I have the helmet at home now, in Connecticut.

We went on along the wind-swept road, between bursts of rain and hail, and late in the afternoon we came to Ushakovo, where the great battles of Yelnya had been fought.

LAND MINES

"DON'T TOUCH anything!" the colonel called out from the top of the hill as he saw me edging closer with my camera to these boxes of land mines. Ammunition, left by the Germans in their hasty retreat, lay all over the place. There were thousands of clips of machine-gun bullets, showing good copper, as though the Germans had plenty of that metal. Strangest sight was the many wicker baskets and metal cases of mortar shells and grenades, neatly packed like Florida oranges laid carefully in straw. Thousands of these baskets had been piled into towers along the road, by Red Army salvage crews.

The Russian officers under Timoshenko's command told us that here along the Central Front, the Germans were losing twice as many men and five times as much equipment as the Russians, and from what we saw it may easily have been true.

There was none of the sylvan character we had seen in our earlier views of the front when we reached the battlefield of Yelnya. Here the Germans had poured across the fields, filling up this area like breath being blown into an expanding balloon. After six weeks of fighting, through August and September, the Russians had managed to snip off the balloon and deal with the captives within the Nazi bulge. And now the place looked like the end of the world.

Here were the ghosts of blasted trees, great trunks split and smashed as though a giant hand had picked them up in bundles and dropped them broken back to earth. As far as the eye could reach was wasteland, pitted with shell holes, channeled with trenches, littered with the remains of war which had swept in concentrated fury back and forth across it during those desperate weeks.

The Russian dead had been buried in a common grave, marked with newly planted firs and surrounded by a fence topped with red-painted tin stars. Field asters still showed touches of lavender and purple where they had been laid on the freshly piled mound of earth. The Germans had been hastily shoveled into their own trenches, unmarked—many thousands had been dug into the ten-mile-square battlefield where they had fallen. Like hundreds of empty turtleshells lay the German helmets, some decorated with little swastikas painted in white, many cracked viciously through the top where the metal had given way during battle.

Erskine called me and pointed to a zigzag trench. The bottom was sprinkled unaccountably with dead mice.

GREAT BATTLEFIELD OF YELNYA

FIFTY THOUSAND Germans were killed, wounded, or captured on this ten-mile-square battlefield. Buried under our feet, as we plowed through the rain-soaked earth, lay the German dead, for they had been hastily shoveled into their own trenches and into the big round pits made by the explosion of their own shells. Twenty thousand Russians fell here, and they were buried in common graves marked with the Soviet red star. These fields are at Ushakovo, where the great battle of Yelnya was fought.

The Germans, overconfident, had ex-panded into a bulge, and the Russians, driving ahead by night, finally met the enemy in hand-to-hand combat here and, backed by their tanks, fought for six weeks. Hundreds of tanks entered the combat, and their treads chewed up these rich wheat lands beyond recognition.

When we arrived on this battlefield, immediately after it had been captured back by the Russians, the ground was still littered with mud-caked helmets and still pitted with shell craters which had filled with blood and were filling now with rain.

Everywhere was the paraphernalia of life—a torn sleeve, the piece of a boot, a tattered raincoat, fragments of rain-soaked German newspaper. Erskine stooped over and pulled out a handle projecting from the ground. It was an officer's broken sword.

We had to be careful where we walked because the ground was full of unexploded mines and shells. Once I stepped on something soft, and a green cloud rose into my face. It was a heap of moldy bread which still retained the shape of loaves, so recently had men been breathing and eating there. Near by was a chased-silver samovar, pierced with a bullethole, which raised an image of Russians drinking tea in what seemed like a bygone age.

When we reached the town of Yelnya, fighting was still going on near by. The front was only a few kilometers away, and the rattle of machine guns and the deep roar of artillery sounded restlessly to the west. Yelnya had had an estimated population of five thousand, and now it was a ghost town. When we drove into its ruined streets I knew that here at last I had the pictures I wanted, pictures that would look like war. It was almost twilight, but the clouds, as though they had heard my prayers at last, began lifting, and the rays of the setting sun poured down on the skeletons that had once been homes.

I jumped out of the car and hastily set up a camera. I had just begun work when one of the reporters, a member of the home faction, dashed past me, notebook in hand. "Hurry up, Peggy," he called. "We're clearing out of here in five minutes and we'll be halfway back to Moscow tonight."

GHOST TOWN

YELNYA WAS a silent ruin when the Russians finally snatched it back from the Germans. Many of its families had been divided, half on Soviet soil and half behind the German lines. This was because the Nazis, when they retreated, tried to drive the population back with them to keep it captive. Sometimes posted on these chimneys we found German proclamations ordering civilians back to the rear, on pain of death.

But the Russians who managed to remain in Yelnya, although they had no possessions left—no cattle, no fodder, no crops—still found a great deal of work to be done. They had to start the fall sowing, even though that meant they were cultivating their fields within range of enemy guns. The soldiers helped with the plowing on quiet days in between their job of fighting, for the front was but an easy hour-and-a-half walking distance from the place where this picture was taken.

It was too much—all the hopes and disappointments, all the fighting to salvage something through the mud and rain, all the arrivals at the most interesting places after dark, the tearing away in the mornings before I could complete my job. "I can't work this crazy way," I said aloud to the empty road. And I began to cry.

Crying doesn't do much good, because it interrupts focusing. I knew this, but I only stood there weeping, wasting my time. And then the censor came along and guessed what the trouble was, proving that there is some use for censors after all.

I shall never forget how he gathered a squad of soldiers to help me and instructed the officer in command of the town that I should be given all the help I needed. The plan was to have the correspondents go on to a banquet that was waiting for them sixty miles back on the road toward Moscow. Erskine would stay with me, of course. And the censor put a little pile of chocolates in the back seat of our car, cautioned me not to take too long, because the sound of the guns was rising, and the crowd was off.

Darkness was beginning to fall now, but the soldiers helped me string out my extension cords so we could light up portions of the road with flash bulbs. As it grew darker I brought all three of my flash guns into use, each with extension wires, and the soldiers strung out with them along the road, watching me for signals while I capped and uncapped the lens. It was too late to get instantaneous exposures, but it worked.

I was interested to see that the only building left even partially intact was the cathedral with its coppery-green dome, now being used as a Red Army barracks. But for the most part the town had been reduced to a collection of skeleton fingers, pointed toward the sky. These were the central chimneys, some of them still smooth with the polished tiles that are characteristic of peasant dwellings. Still, wherever two walls

---

THE CATHEDRAL OF YELNYA

THIS WAR-SCARRED shell of a cathedral served as a welcome shelter for the Red Army troops who reclaimed Yelnya. It was converted into a soldiers' dormitory, for it was the largest building still standing within a radius of twenty miles. Food and wheat seeds and even some farm tools were kept stored in the old church. The soldiers gave potatoes and flour from their stores to the newly freed civilians of Yelnya.

came together, or wherever there was a scrap of roof, people were creeping back to their homes, so resilient is the human race. Sometimes they were welcomed back by their cats, which have a way of lingering around the house even after bombing, although dogs turn wild and run away.

It was getting late now, and the garrison commander thought we should be on our way. Erskine was talking with a group of soldiers by the church, and I took one last walk, down a side street, and watched some people cooking food, which the soldiers had given them, over what remained of their brick and plaster ovens. They were setting up housekeeping in the midst of the ruins, and I noticed that they were using strange cooking utensils. I examined these utensils more closely. They were not mere pots and pans bent out of shape from bombing. They were pieces of wrecked German planes, and portions of metal sheeting from captured enemy tanks. Bent into shallow shapes they serve well enough as baking tins or broiling pans.

The officer and my husband were both calling me now, and their voices were almost drowned out with the rising thunder of guns. The star shells that soared over the front lines to the west were gleaming in a cobalt-blue sky. It was time to go.

But as I walked back to the car I paused to look at a woman borrowing some hot charcoals from the fire of a neighbor. "What is she carrying them in?" I wondered, as I watched her heading homeward. The shape was familiar. She was bringing home hot coals in a Nazi helmet.

CHAPTER 18

White Nights in the Arctic

"WHICH DO you think will be quicker," puzzled Erskine, "to go home by way of Australia, or by way of the Arctic Ocean?" We were back in our Moscow hotel suite, and he was lying on the white bear rug, studying all his available maps. To get world coverage it was necessary to use some maps printed in Russian, some in English, and even the enormous one of Asia and the Pacific, which we had bought in Lanchow. The map of Asia covered the entire floor and was printed in Chinese characters.

It was October, just after our return from the front, and we both had lecture tours starting in less than a month, so we had to get home the fastest way possible. We did not know that Pearl Harbor was less than two months away, but we did want to come home. Even the most stimulating travel in foreign countries, I find, sharpens the desire to return to your native land, where, with an instinct deeper than reason, you feel that you really belong.

The Australia-versus-Arctic question was fantastically difficult to decide. It is impossible to get exact information about travel through warring areas, and even after accommodations have been made there is always the likelihood of being tossed out of your places whenever a couple of generals come along. We had already discarded a possible Africa-to-South America course, with the Cape of Good Hope coming in for serious consideration. The Australia route involved a choice between transit through Iran or Turkey, a flight by British-Oceanic Airways across India to New Zealand, and then return by air across the Pacific. The Arctic trip could only be by ship, and this was the most uncertain of all, for the movements of convoys are protected by the deepest secrecy.

It was Sir Stafford Cripps who finally decided us, by arranging with the British Admiralty for us to travel on the first convoy to leave Archangel Harbor. Furthermore, he obtained permission from the Admiralty for me to take photographs en route, and the handsome credentials that arrived from the embassy, beautifully embossed with the seals of the United Kingdom, were irresistible.

But we found that we could not take the trip without a special dispensation from our own State Department, because of an American law which forbids citizens to travel through belligerent waters on the vessels of a nation at war. An exchange of messages thereupon took place between Moscow and Washington, conducted all "in gray" (in code) so that information about the convoy could not be picked out of the air by the enemy. While these negotiations were being conducted, we thought we had missed our convoy.

However, it happened that some German scouting planes had been seen over the White Sea, and the departure of the convoy was delayed in the hope that it might be possible to shake them; and just as news of this delay came from Archangel, the American Ambassador called us over to Spazzo House to inform us that the State Department had granted us permission to take the convoy trip.

It seemed like extraordinary luck that word had come from Washington just in time. Mr. Steinhardt commented, "There is just one thing you have that I envy you, Margaret."

"What could that be?" I asked.

"That horseshoe that seems to hang always around your neck."

And was there anything else that we needed, he wanted to know.

"Oh, yes," I said, gratefully, "there is one thing I need very much. But you're going to be stuck here without supplies, and you must tell me honestly if you can't spare it."

"And what is it?"

"A new toothbrush."

So the American Embassy in Moscow did its last kind deed for its departing nationals. A splendid new toothbrush was requisitioned from the commissary for me, and another for my husband.

We had been instructed not to inform anyone, either at home or in Moscow, how we were going to travel. We had to get some word to New

York, so we cabled: WE WILL DISAPPEAR FOR ABOUT THREE WEEKS DON'T WORRY.

While our visas, toothbrushes, and Admiralty decrees were being obtained, the developing of the films from the front trip proceeded in such numbers that it took both the day and the night chauffeurs, working together, to hang them up as fast as I got them out of the tub. The bathroom overflowed quickly into the bedroom, and soon the edges of the bedspread and the borders of the window curtains were pinned with wet negatives. Then they began filtering into the sitting room; cords were strung between the legs of the grand piano and back and forth among the cupid chandeliers; and finally even Napoleon and Josephine on their revolving pedestal supported their share of dripping squares of celluloid.

When they were dry and sorted, Tatiana took them to Glavalit, the same censors who had passed on our radio scripts. They were all passed —not in a routine way, but in the midst of many speeches to the deepening of Soviet-American friendship and understanding—and were finally done up in neat packages bound in lead seals.

Then there was that job which for a photographer is the worst one of all: packing the endless paraphernalia so that it will not jar, vibrate, or crush. Into the spaces in my cases left vacant by used-up supplies I packed a collection of vividly painted plaster dolls, brilliant in Russian costumes. They had been made in peasant villages, and Elisaveta had helped me shop for them in the Moscow handicraft stores.

Clothes were reduced to a minimum. I kept only the heaviest, to get me through the Arctic. Tatiana received my raincoat, my extra blouses, and all but my sturdiest pair of shoes, which I would need for the homeward trip. My heavy slacks, still showing trench mud, went with me for the convoy; my linen pair I gave to Elisaveta, who had decided to try to make Soviet women slacks conscious. Both girls received nylon stockings. As silk stockings are rather scarce in Russia, and are not very good, when word got around among my acquaintances that I was packing, I had various feminine callers who hoped to make purchases. The few pairs of stockings I still could spare I sold for eight rubles each, the equivalent of the $1.60 which they had cost me in America. (The Soviet department stores sell rather ill-fitting silk hose for thirty-

GERMAN DECORATIONS

THESE WERE found on the pilot shot down
by Victor Talalikhin, with the factory
plate from the German plane he rammed
in the dogfight which made him famous.
Until this was found, the Narvik decoration had not been seen in the U.S.S.R.

Talalikhin declares that when he cut the
cloth out of the shoulder to which it was
sewn, he discovered that underneath the
pilot wore no underwear.

Soviet pilot heroes, most of whom have
captured German crosses by now, speak
disparagingly of the Iron Crosses. "German
decorations are made only of tin and
cheap metals," they say, "while ours are
made of gold and silver."

It is true that the Soviet orders are
manufactured in the mint.

five rubles, or $7, a pair, and since mine were nylon, unheard of in
the Soviet Union, I could easily have charged twice that sum if I had
wished to profiteer.) My millinery collection, if my assortment of little
bright-colored leather beanies could be called that, was divided equally
between the two chauffeurs' wives.

Then there was the last great banquet at VOKS with all our friends
invited: Eisenstein, Alexandrov, and Orlova from the movie colony; Eugene Petrov, Elisaveta, and many others from the Union of Soviet
Writers; the Mayor of Moscow; the director of the Art Theater; and
an assortment of opera singers. Erskine was presented with the most
unique gift that it was in their power to give: a collection of captured
German insignia which included iron crosses of the first and second
class, medals for marksmanship, the insignia of the *Luftwaffe* and Pan-
zer, and the aluminum skull which is the sign of the Death's-Head
Division.

Early the next morning most of the party guests appeared on the station platform to wave us off. There were no "soft cars" * on the train,
so we were to travel "hard class," which means sleeping on a wooden
shelf. Our car had these shelves in tiers of three. We had engaged two
of the lower ones, and those over our heads were already filling up with
soldiers. Our friends shoved great bunches of flowers into my arms, our
long troop train moved slowly out of the station, and soon Moscow was
left behind.

The woman conductor brought me fruit jars of water, and our bed-
shelf blazed with gladioli, zinnias, and roses. During the three days
which it took us to reach Archangel, the heavy boots of soldiers who
occupied the crowded shelves above hung down over my flowers. However, the soldiers seemed to enjoy the flowers as much as I.

We ate sausage, crackers, and salt caviar paste out of our wooden
supply box. Once we had hot food, when the train stopped at the large
station of Vologda long enough for me to run out and get steaming

---

* The terminology, first and second class, was dropped after the Revolution, even when
it applied merely to travel, as it was reminiscent of the hated class system. Instead, the
terms "soft class" and "hard class" were substituted. The soft-class traveler has a separate
compartment, with benches which are upholstered but not very soft. However, soft cars,
wagon-lits, and restaurant cars were dropped from service with the beginning of the war.
On a hard car, which consists entirely of open wooden shelves, bedding can sometimes
be rented from the conductor.

bowls of *kasha*, a rough cracked-grain cereal which peasants eat. Finally we reached the sprawling town of Archangel—clapboard shacks interspaced with a few modern stucco office buildings, lining a marshy harbor.

Our clothes had never been chosen for an Arctic climate, so we found a furrier and bought splendid hats of stiff reindeer fur, which came down over the ears and tied under the chin. My flowers were still fresh, and I carried them onto the cutter, which we boarded in the darkness. After bobbing around in the dim, windy spaces of Archangel Harbor for an hour, searching for the convoy, we suddenly found the flagship. It loomed black above us, not a crack of light showing. We climbed a ladder up the side—cameras, flowers, and all—and we were on board. We were handed life belts immediately and told to wear them at all times, even when eating and sleeping.

The next morning our ships began slipping out, one by one, under cover of mist. It was such a good fog that the captain had decided to take advantage of it very early without waiting for the Russian tugs which ordinarily would have maneuvered the boats out to sea. This meant fast out and fast around the bends under our own steam, but we managed to negotiate the tortuous twists of the estuary successfully.

As the shores widened to form a bay, and the ships swung into their prearranged grouping, we found that we were in a convoy of twenty-two vessels: fifteen were British, one was Dutch, and six were Russian. All the ships except three of the Russian freighters were armed. Ours,

---

CONVOY FORMATION

THE 22,000-ton cruiser that escorted our convoy was too big to get into Archangel Harbor. It waited out in the deep water of the bay and swung into position as we started the homeward trip. Our own ship (lifeboat rigging shown in foreground) was an 11,000-ton British troop ship. It was the largest vessel ever brought into Archangel Harbor—a feat which took considerable skill on the part of the captain. However, he decided that this job was too tight to be repeated and advised the Admiralty to send no more ships of that draft to Archangel. The harbor, however, is excellent for smaller vessels, and well equipped. Much of the loading and unloading is done by Russian women, whom the captain described as strong and willing workers.

Note the silhouette of the plane carried by the cruiser, which took off at intervals into the distance on scouting trips and returned to hover daintily over the convoy, on the watch for submarines.

The cruiser is half a mile away, and the distant freighters are from one to two miles from the flagship, from which the picture was taken.

an eleven-thousand-ton troop ship, which had been used for African cruises and was not insulated against Arctic temperatures, was well armed with machine guns on the upper deck, depth charges strapped to port and starboard sides, and four-inch guns mounted in the stern.

We were escorted by two destroyers, four trawlers, and a cruiser which was startlingly camouflaged with decorative scrolls in smoke and putty shades, interlaced with wavy lines of lime green.

When we reached the White Sea it was evident that those German planes were still on the trail. Most of the time we could not see them, because of the fog, but we could usually hear them. Occasionally we would catch a momentary glimpse of dark specks chasing through the clouds, and then the fog closed them away again. Sometimes they dropped things—we could not tell whether it was bombs or mines. Then we would shoot back at them. But the fog pressed so densely around us that they could not quite find us and we could not quite find them.

For two days this game of hide-and-seek went on. During that time I lived on the top deck, my helmet buckled on in case of shrapnel, and my camera ready, although I knew very well that if events took place which deserved photographic recording, the fog was so thick I wouldn't be able to get good pictures. The Commodore, however, was mightily pleased about the way the fog held, and by the beginning of the third day we had left the Germans behind.

"The Hun doesn't like to attack convoys," the Commodore remarked. "He thinks twice about it." Commodore Dowding, a compact, barrel-shaped Scotsman, was in a position to know a good deal about the habits of the Hun. He had been torpedoed in the Mediterranean in the last war, his destroyer sunk beneath him, and during the present war he had made it twice across the Channel at Dunkirk. "Once those Nazis do decide to attack," he went on, "they've got odd ideas. They shoot you in the water. Even in our most savage moments the British don't get to that. He's an odd chap, the Hun."

I discovered that even Commodore Dowding did not know where we were going. The movements of convoys are directed daily straight from the Admiralty in London, by wireless code. The codes are frequently changed to make translation by the enemy more difficult. The flagship receives the messages, but never replies. She travels "silent," for if she transmitted messages her sending apparatus would act as a direction finder, and she uses it only if she must send "distresses."

So cautious is the Admiralty about the movements of its convoys that before the Commodore left England for Archangel he and the officers and crews of all the ships were told to bring light clothing for tropical weather. Just before setting sail they were informed that warm clothes would be needed, but it was only after they had been at sea for three days that they knew they were being sent to Russia.

A convoy traveling over open sea forms an active little community. There is always a picturesquely conducted conversation going on between ships. They fairly chattered among themselves by means of flags and blinking searchlight signals, the lights for daytime use only. To make sure that the Russian skippers understood the signals, one of the destroyers cruised in broad circles, weaving its way through the convoy, while its junior officer shouted out the directions through a megaphone. Every so often the cruiser's plane was catapulted off the deck to scour the seascape, trying to spot submarines.

On the fifth day, to the astonishment of everyone, even the Commodore, our handsome cruiser ran up signal flags which said: "Good-by, have a good trip," and she was off, no one knew where. We felt rather lonely without her; but exactly one hour later, another cruiser had taken her place. Our new escort was less decorative, for instead of the whorls and curlicues of camouflage she was painted a uniform battleship gray; but she was bristling with fully as many guns.

We were in the Barents Sea by now, and still heading north. In order to skirt around areas which might be infested with submarines, we went so far north that we crossed the Arctic Circle and at one time were within less than nine degrees of the North Pole.

Here, again, we had the unearthly white nights. Through the long hours of darkness an uneasy splendor hung over the sea. Before turning in, Erskine and I would tie on our reindeer bonnets, wrap blankets around our shoulders, and walk around the deck. Between the translucent sky and icy water floated the barely distinguishable shapes of our fellow ships, not a glimmer of light showing as they traveled at their uniform speed of eight knots an hour.

Sometimes we would pass the Commodore, looking like a little rabbit

in his cashmere cloak and hood. "It's strange, way up here," he would say. "It must be the reflection from the ice. But even in the dead of winter it never gets properly dark." And then he would continue on his rounds, straining his eyes through the ghost light, trying to assure himself that all his flock were still there.

Once, half an hour before midnight, we had unexpected visitors. An oil tanker, with a small convoy, appeared out of nowhere, refueled the destroyers, and disappeared into nothingness.

Early each morning my husband and I would hurry around the deck and count, to make sure that all our twenty-two ships were still there. One of the Russian freighters, a slow one, was slipping a little behind.

Then, as we worked back to lower latitudes, near Iceland, there was an afternoon when from the point on the top deck where I was posted with a camera I could hear tense voices from the bridge, "Have they made contact? They're making contact!" Searchlight signals blinked rapidly, and the ships wheeled out into a scattered formation, leaving wide spaces of water in between. The whole sea seemed to shudder under us as the destroyers, several miles away from us now, dropped depth charges. Four hours later the Commodore passed me and stopped to tell me that they thought they had detected a submarine and hoped

---

ACTION STATION

THE GUN crew kept up constant practice, even when we were above the Arctic Circle. Frequently the Polish ex-prisoners were given rehearsals in manning the guns. The Poles had been prisoners in Siberia until Germany invaded the Soviet Union, which was a signal to set all Polish captives free. Arranging to get them out of the country, however, was long and complicated. The first hundred to be released were traveling on our convoy: Polish airmen and gunners who were going to England to join the R.A.F. They had been out of practice for almost two years. The British coached them willingly and found them quick to learn.

The four-inch guns shown here are mounted on the stern, but not on the bow, as they are in the cruiser. According to international law, merchant ships which make up a convoy may be "defensively armed." Defensive arming consists of guns mounted in the stern, which point toward a theoretical pursuing enemy. But guns in the bow pointing forward would be considered "offensive arming." Close examination of these guns revealed the mark "made in Japan."

I was amazed that there were no icebergs here in the Arctic Ocean, for it certainly seemed cold enough for them. Erskine, who has made a study of ocean currents, explained that they would not come at that season of the year because the tail end of the Gulf Stream spills out here, completely cool and exhausted from its long travel around the earth, but of course carrying no icebergs in its path during the autumn.

they had been able to shake it. The ships were being signaled back into their regular formation now, and by twilight all twenty-two were plowing through the water in their customary pattern.

The next morning, however, when Erskine and I made our count, there were only twenty-one of us. The slow Russian freighter was missing. We never knew what became of it. Possibly the Admiralty knows, but we were never told.

The following day we were passing through the Norwegian Sea, and the water was alive with an enormous school of porpoises. Countless thousands of glistening jet bodies cut through the water and skipped briefly through the air. They were racing the ships. For hours the sea was ink black, and boiling with leaping shapes as streamlined as shell casings.

One day more and we were in the North Sea, and again the water was filled with strange objects. This time it was floating mines. Fortunately, we reached their neighborhood by daylight, so that we could steer around them. Like great basketballs, with prongs like porcupines, they bobbed along within a stone's throw of the ships.

After fifteen days we had traveled through literally seven seas: the White Sea, Barents Sea, the Arctic Ocean, the Norwegian and North Seas, across a strip of the Atlantic, then through the Irish Sea; and finally we reached Scotland. Above Scapa Flow the sky was like a dotted-swiss textile, with cumulus cloud puffs and white barrage balloons. The ruins of Scottish castles on the cliffs were as gray as the shapes of battleships which lay everywhere about us. Like chains of beads, submarine traps were strung through the water.

FIRST SIGHT OF LAND

THE SUN began to shine, the weather got warmer, and everyone felt near home when we came down through the Norwegian Sea and spotted islands to the portside. These are the Faeroes group, south of Iceland, rocky and sparsely inhabited. This photograph was taken from the top of one of the machine-gun stations, which had been erected on the upper deck and were being manned at all times by the Polish ex- prisoners. Just below the Union Jack can be seen the corrugated metal that protects the battle station with guns, shown in preceding photograph. The British and the Poles were still on guard, for even though we were nearing home, the dangers of the sea were being multiplied rather than decreased. But with these rocky capes and coves in sight, my husband and I felt as though we were on a North Cape cruise.

At Scapa Flow an excessively courteous Admiralty official came on board to take up the films I had exposed on the sea voyage, for Admiralty censorship. Only half of them came back, but it was to be expected that many naval subjects would be censored out, and permission to take photographs had been given with that understanding.

One day more on through the Clyde, and we disembarked in Glasgow. Erskine had always wanted a glimpse of Scotland because his people came from there, and I had always desired a Scottish kilt. We went into a Glasgow tartan shop and inquired whether there was a Caldwell plaid.

"No," said the clerk, "Caldwell is a fine old Scottish name, but the clan has never had a tartan."

"Is there an Erskine tartan?" I asked.

"Why, certainly," she replied, "there is indeed an Erskine tartan. As a matter of fact, there are *two* Erskine tartans."

So I had a chance to choose between the black and white plaid, and the red and green. I selected the red and green and was measured for the voluminously pleated kilt, which was to be made, complete with huge safety pin, as the Highlanders wear it. We asked the cost.

"Eight pounds and eighteen coupons."

"What are coupons?" we demanded.

"How is it possible," exclaimed the clerk, "that you don't know what coupons are?"

"Well, we've just arrived. How should we know!"

"How can you eat? How do you exist, if you don't have coupons?"

We were to learn soon enough that on the British Isles everything is apportioned by means of coupons. The clothing ration was sixty-six coupons a year. So we regretfully relinquished the idea of the Erskine kilt.

A week later in London we were dining with an official from the Ministry of Information, and I happened to mention the Glasgow episode. "We have been asked for a lot of peculiar things," he said, "but no one ever before asked the Ministry of Information for a kilt."

The next day a deck of complimentary coupons were sent to our hotel, and we were able to order a kilt of the clan of Erskine.

England was restless. Groups of soldiers were being moved from one end of the islands to the other, and they were uneasy with their forced inactivity. Everyone was clamoring for firsthand news about Russia. They had just been promised, in a speech by Churchill, a more comfortable Christmas in 1941 than the last had been. The British people did not want more comforts. If their Russian allies were deny-ing themselves in their efforts to annihilate the Germans, they wanted to help.

The unaccustomed luxury of the Savoy, of the Ritz Bar, seemed strange to us. Going to the movies was an unbelievably vivid pleasure. We walked over the acres of rubble around St. Paul's. British Broad-casting asked us to take part in a program to occupied Europe, so as to try to let the enslaved nations know what was going on in Russia. In the next booth, in the subcellar which B.B.C. is using since its building has been bombed, was General de Gaulle, also talking to occupied Europe.

We visited Lord Beaverbrook at Cherkley, his country home in Leatherhead, and ate apples with him which he had just brought back from Moscow. We found out that the handsomely camouflaged cruiser which had left us on our fifth day out had returned to Archangel for the express purpose of picking up his Lordship and Mr. W. Averell Harriman, who were returning from the Economic Conference. We also learned from the "Beaver" that he had quizzed "Brother Joe" on how he had liked being photographed by an American girl. Lord Beaver-brook had been in the Kremlin with the Economic Mission, shortly after I had made my portrait of Stalin.

Then to Bristol, a scarred patch of desolation, more completely wrecked, block for block, than London. As we entered the devastated town, air-raid sirens began wailing. Bristol, which had been quiet for months, was bombed as soon as we reached the city.

The next morning we took off for Portugal in a sealed plane, the windows blacked out to prevent passengers from watching possible naval operations underneath. On the way I read the last of my stock of detective stories, an Ellery Queen which had traveled with me on the whole trip. (All my heavy baggage, except one small suitcase, was being shipped to New York by Atlantic convoy.)

In Lisbon we stayed in a penthouse hotel suite where Magda Lupescu had stopped during her flight through Portugal. Its enormous violet bathroom, with a purple bathtub set at the top of a flight of gold mosaic stairs, and over it a mirrored ceiling, seemed more suited to the glamorous refugee than it did to a couple of reporters. A screened-in porch, high above the city, was bright with bougainvillaea vines during the day and commanded a brilliant spread of city lights at night. The effect of lights was startling, as it is to all travelers who return from the blacked-out areas of war.

It was in Lisbon that a new word entered my vocabulary. I had heard it before, but had never used it myself—until I came back to America, where I found everybody using it. That word was priorities.

After listening to alarming accounts of travelers through Lisbon, waiting sometimes for weeks to get Clipper accommodations, it was with some trepidation that we entered the office of Pan American Airways. My husband walked up to the counter and inquired about the reservations being held for Mr. and Mrs. Erskine Caldwell. The clerk looked us over indifferently and went back to his filing cabinet, where he shuffled through a bundle of cards. Finally he returned and, looking at me in a condescending way, said, "There is only one reservation being held. And I think, Mrs. Caldwell, that your husband has the priority."

We both had to get home. I had a lecture tour on the East Coast and Erskine had one in the West. If I hadn't been so conscious of that football physique of my husband, who is twice my size, I think there would have been a free-for-all in the Caldwell family right there, and I am not at all sure that the Atlantic seaboard would have won. But I begged the clerk, "Please look once more. There must be a reservation. Please do something to fix it up!"

He went back and looked through his cards once more, and when he returned he was shaking his head. "No," he said, eying me coldly, "there's only one more place being saved. And that's being held for a lady from Russia."

I thought, "Heavens, who's scooping me?" and I asked, "What's her name?"

He said, "Her name is Margaret Bourke-White," and so I was able to come home, too.

Erskine cabled our secretary from Lisbon, ARRANGE SUNDAY DINNER
WITH BOTH STEAK AND FRIED CHICKEN ALSO ALL KNOWN FRUITS AND
VEGETABLES BOTH IN AND OUT OF SEASON, and we flew to the Azores, on
to Bermuda, on across the Atlantic, and arrived home in time for
Sunday dinner. We had completed our trip around the world.

Within less than twenty-four hours I was facing my first lecture
audience. As I began to speak about the things I had seen, it came to
me in a rush what an eventful trip this had been. I had seen history
in the making, had had my cameras in focus when nations were on the
march. I had made new friends among a brave people and had watched
them defending their country, courageously, with that fervor and self-
forgetfulness which people show only when they believe in what they
are working and fighting for. But I was happy to be home again, talking to Americans. These were my people, these listeners in the straight
rows of seats in front of me. They were the kind of men and women
with whom I had grown up, with whom I felt at home.

It was not till two days later, however, that something made me
realize I was indeed in my own country again. I was at the University
of Tennessee. The students had gathered for chapel, and just before
I spoke they rose to sing.

I had heard the music many times before. I must have listened to the
words, and sung them, hundreds of times; but this time they sank into
my mind. "Long may our land be bright, With freedom's holy light."
It seemed to me that never before had I actually heard the words of
America, and suddenly I found I was standing on the platform before
all those university students—crying.

Glossary

commissariat—executive and administrative organ; corresponds to a
government department in other countries

committiet—committee

Council of People's Commissars—an organization corresponding
roughly to the Cabinet in other countries

dacha—country house, villa

diversionist—spy; fifth columnist

Glavalit—main literature committee, which passes on the publishing
program of the country and thus exercises general supervision
over all publications, radio, pictures, plays, etc. A representative
of Glavalit is in the customhouse of every border town to pass
on literature or pictures which may be brought into the country.

Gooney—a large sea bird of the albatross family

Gosizdat—All-Union Publishing Committee, the name taken from the
first syllables of these words in Russian

icon—religious picture of Christ, the Virgin Mary, or a saint.

Ivan Ivanovich—literally John son of John, similar to our John Doe

kopeck—the hundredth part of a ruble, therefore equal to about a fifth
of a cent in U. S. currency

M2 & M3—Soviet-made, low-priced car modeled after the Ford, with
some Plymouth and some Russian ideas; the M2 is comparable
to our 1935 Ford, and the M3 is similar to the 1939 Ford.

metropolitan—high executive of the Orthodox Church; head of an
ecclesiastical province with headquarters in a metropolis.

Narkomindel—Foreign Office of the U.S.S.R., equivalent to our State
Department. The name comes from the first syllables of People's Commissariat for Foreign Affairs.

289

NKVD—People's Commissariat for Internal Affairs, which had taken over the old OGPU; thus its functions include that of secret police. Name taken from the initial letters

Ogiz—State Publishing House

OGPU—State Political Administration, which included the secret police

otlichnik—superior worker or student

panagia—jeweled pendant containing a miniature religious picture and surmounted by bishop's crown, to be worn only by bishops of the Orthodox Church.

partisan—guerrilla; fighter behind the enemy lines

Patriarch—the highest dignitary of the Orthodox Church; somewhat comparable in position to that of Pope of the Roman Catholic Church

Presidium of the Supreme Council—the body in which supreme government power is vested, chosen by election by both chambers of the Supreme Soviet, and meeting in the Kremlin

propusk—pass or passport; a twenty-four-hour *propusk* allows the bearer to travel about during curfew

ruble—about nineteen cents at the current rate of exchange, which allowed 5.3 rubles to the U. S. dollar

synchroscope—mechanical device for testing whether camera shutter is in perfect synchronization with flashlighting apparatus.

Tass—Telegraph Agency of the Soviet Union. The name comes from the initial letters. The government news agency functions within the Soviet Union, having its central bureau in Moscow and branches in all principal cities, as well as in foreign countries, for the purpose of sending information to the U.S.S.R.

Tass Windows—poster factory under jurisdiction of Tass, which was modeled after the Windows of Mayakovsky, the original poster-making project initiated by the late great poet, Mayakovsky, during the Russian Revolution.

Tovarish—Comrade

udarnik—shock-troop brigadier

ukase—decree; administrative order

VOKS—All-Union Society for Cultural Relations with Foreign Countries; name taken from initial letters

Zenith guns—antiaircraft guns

ZIS—better-class car manufactured at the Stalin Auto Works; similar to our 1939 Buick

Appendix

The following cameras were carried on the trip:

1. $3\frac{1}{4}''$ x $4\frac{1}{4}''$ Speed Graphic, a specially built job accommodating five interchangeable lenses, with engraved footage scale for each. The lenses used were Zeiss Tessar, Schneider, and Eastman Ektar, and their focal lengths were respectively 9 cm., 12.7 cm., 15 cm., 18 cm., 30 cm. The right-hand range finder fitted the 12.7, and a range finder had been attached to the left side to accommodate the 18-cm. lens, as these two objectives were the most frequently used. The focusing of the other three lenses was handled by means of a Leitz range finder attached to the top of the camera and used in combination with the footage scales. Masks matched to the field of each lens could be inserted into the view finders.

2. $3\frac{1}{4}''$ x $4\frac{1}{4}''$ Linhof View Camera fitted with Graphic back for the use of film packs. I carried a series of lenses from wide angle to telephoto, which had been selected so that there would be a step of from $1\frac{1}{2}$ to 2 cm. between each focal length. All lenses were fitted into metal front boards which could be quickly interchanged for the Linhof. The five lenses for the Speed Graphic were mounted on similar metal boards, so that all lenses for both Graphic and Linhof, as well as all other parts, such as holders, synchronizing equipment, etc., could be interchanged between the two cameras.

To use with the Linhof I carried two tripods, the Eastman Cine-Kodak and the Quick-Set.

All portraits in the book were taken with the Linhof.

3. A second Linhof, same size, a spare in case of accidents.

4. $2\frac{1}{4}''$ x $3\frac{1}{4}''$ Plaubel-Makina, with three lenses—7.3 cm., 10 cm., and

19 cm. The medium lens had an aperture of f 1.9. Interchangeable backs accommodated either film pack or roll film. I found this camera useful chiefly for quick work at a distance, for on close work the focusing device was sometimes unreliable. It was excellent for night photographs, used on infinity with the fast lens.

5. $3\frac{1}{4}''$ x $4\frac{1}{4}''$ Soho, an English camera of the reflex type, but more compact and more flexible than our Graflex because of its tilting and twisting front board. Unfortunately, this camera is no longer being manufactured in England, and this particular one was to my knowledge the last available in America when I purchased it. Using it in the heavy rains at the front put it totally out of commission, along with some of my other equipment, so now my great hope is that American manufacturers will commence to build a tilting and twisting front board for the Graflex, which would be an invaluable improvement.

All film used on the trip was Eastman Super-XX Panchromatic, size $2\frac{1}{4}''$ x $3\frac{1}{4}''$ or $3\frac{1}{4}''$ x $4\frac{1}{4}''$ film packs.

The developer I carried was a fine-grain type, DK20. I used it entirely in tanks, developing by the time-and-temperature method. I found that it gave more satisfactory results when diluted one third to one half more than the formula calls for, with the developing time lengthened about three minutes to compensate. Since I am fond of a close side light used on faces, a soft developer is necessary. I like to work with contrasty light, then a soft developer to produce a soft, well-graduated negative, and to finish up with a contrast grade of paper. I carried four film-pack developing tanks, and when I stayed steadily by the side of the bathtub, which was my laboratory, I was able to keep all four tanks working in rotation. When I did my developing during breakfast or suppertime, as I did so often, two tanks were all I could manage at once. The water in Moscow was very hard, and the most careful sponging was necessary to keep a whitish deposit from forming on the negatives. This sponging process, which I did with cotton both while the films were in the hypo and again before they came out of the rinse water,

took more time than the actual developing and could never be
entrusted to others because an incautious fingernail could cause
great havoc.

Although I did not dare depend on Russian stores for my films, knowing that my film sizes would not be in use among Soviet photographers, still I believed that I would be able to purchase
hypo, and therefore carried only a small amount. I found
Soviet camera shops well supplied with fixing salts and also
with fine-grain developers. When my own chemicals began
running low, I found the Soviet preparations quite satisfactory.

While I did all my developing in Moscow, I did not attempt to make
finished prints except in the case of the Stalin portrait. The only
need for prints there was to have them to show the censor, and
for this I had contact prints run off in a Soviet printshop.

Exposure Data (for certain of the photographs in this book)

Football Crowd at Dynamo Stadium—Speed Graphic, 15-cm. lens, K 1
filter; *f* 16; exp. 1/30 sec.; soft sunlight.

Kowboy Koktail—Linhof camera, 18-cm. Zeiss Tessar lens; long bel-
lows extension and lens close to subject to get large image. Two
flash bulbs very close, one above and one front slightly to
right; exposure 1/100 sec. stopped down to *f* 32 for depth.

Chairman Nerivny, Head of Collective Farm—Linhof camera, 15-cm.
Zeiss Tessar; exp. 1/200 sec.; *f* 16; one flash bulb on short extension held high left.

Fire-Fighting Poster in Park of Culture and Rest—Soho, 15-cm. Zeiss
Tessar; strong sunlight; exp. 1/100 sec.; *f* 11.

Subway Shelter—Linhof camera, Goerz-Dagor 12.5 cm.; two flash bulbs
used with long extensions; *f* 9; 1/5 sec.

Telalikhin and the Mayor of Moscow at the Park of Culture and Rest—
Speed Graphic, Eastman Ektar 12.7-cm. lens. Subdued daylight, therefore used one flash bulb affixed to camera to increase
speed. Exp. 1/50 sec.; *f* 11.

Religious Pictures:

Kissing the Icon—Linhof camera, 13.5 Zeiss Tessar; *f* 8; two flash
bulbs on extensions, one near camera and one back at left. For

this picture, the camera on tripod was set at some distance in the shadow so that it would be less noticeable, and when the people took the desired grouping the exposure was made by means of a remote control. Although I seldom crop pictures, because I compose out to the very limits of the field, in this shot the left-hand half was trimmed out and only the right side which had the most interest was retained. Exp. 1/50 sec.

Worshipers in Old Orthodox Church, Crossing Themselves—Speed Graphic, 18-cm. Zeiss Tessar lens, f 11; exp. 1/200; two flash bulbs, one front and one high side.

Tea with Archbishops—Linhof camera, 15-cm. Zeiss Tessar; one flash bulb used on long extension at side left; exp. 1/100 sec.; f 11.

Portrait of Patriarch Sergei—Linhof camera, 30-cm. Schneider Tele-Xenar lens, two flash bulbs, one front and one side; exp. 1/50 sec.; f. 11; camera placed several yards from subject because of extremely long focal length of lens; viewpoint low.

Bishops Before the High Altar—Speed Graphic, Angulon 9 cm.; f 8; 1/25 sec.; two flash bulbs, one affixed to camera and one held high at side right.

Metropolitan Vvedensky Giving the Benediction—Speed Graphic, Eastman Ektar 12.7 cm.; two flash bulbs, one in camera and one side right; f 11; 1/100 sec.

Baptist Church Congregation—Linhof camera, Angulon 9-cm. lens, f 8; exp. 3 sec. Picture taken from organ loft. Windows furnished some daylight, therefore made short time exposure, watching crowd for their quietest moment; sent off two flash bulbs from balcony at last instant of exposure, taking care to recap lens immediately in case the light should cause some of the people to make a startled movement.

Night Pictures:

The Beginning of an Air Raid—Speed Graphic, 15-cm. Zeiss Tessar lens, f 3.5; exp. 1½ min. In the later stages of raid, the searchlights moved more rapidly over the sky and it was seldom possible to catch them as distinct streaks on the film.

Row of Flares in Snakelike Lines Over the Kremlin—Plaubel-Makina, 7.3-cm. lens; f 6.3; exp. 6 min.

Antiaircraft Barrage Showing Web of Guns—Plaubel-Makina, 10-cm.
   lens; *f* 2.9; exp. 3½ min.

Kremlin by Moonlight—Linhof camera, 13.5-cm. Zeiss Tessar lens;
   f 8; exp. 12 min. Moonlight and fire bombs added to the illumination, but there was less light in the sky from the ground
   barrage than on some of the other nights.

Belfry of Ivan the Great—Linhof camera, 30-cm. Schneider Tele-Xenar
   lens; *f* 6.3; exp. 15 min. When the telephoto lens was used like
   this on the night shots its long focal length gave a beautiful
   drawing to the buildings, but the gambling element was large
   as to whether the small portion of sky would include fireworks,
   as their position was unpredictable. Thus, many of the negatives I made with this lens during air raids I had to discard
   for lack of interest in the sky, but the few good ones I got I felt
   were worth the effort.

Path of a Parachute Flare—Speed Graphic, Angulon 9-cm. lens; *f* 6.3;
   exp. 8 min. The five interchangeable lenses of the Speed
   Graphic made this camera most desirable for the night shots.
   As it was often necessary for me to change from a long-focus to
   a wide-angle lens when the action became scattered over the
   sky, a device which had been built into the bed made this easy
   to do in the dark. Instead of the usual notch indicating infinity
   on the Speed Graphic, which would be impracticable for so
   many lenses, a small roller-bearing device had been built under
   the track, allowing the newly inserted lens to click into place
   at its correct infinity focus. This made changing from one focal
   length to another easy under blackout conditions.

Citizen Watcher at Entrance to Shelter—Linhof camera, 15-cm. Zeiss
   Tessar; *f* 11; exp. 1/50 sec.; faint illumination from twilight,
   cne flash bulb held at side, high, and back from subject. Low
   camera viewpoint.

Harry Hopkins and Sir Stafford Cripps and Joe—Linhof camera, 15-
   cm. Zeiss Tessar lens; one flash bulb back at right; exp. 1/100
   sec.; *f* 11.

Stalin and Hopkins—Linhof, 13.5-cm. Zeiss Tessar lens; one light at
   right side; exp. 1/50 sec.; *f* 16.

Portrait of Stalin—Linhof camera, 30-cm. Schneider Tele-Xenar lens;
  exp. 1/50 sec.; *f* 16; one flash bulb close left front, a second
  bulb very far back left side on long extension.

Harvest at "Spark of Revolution" Collective Farm—Soho camera,
  13.5-cm. Zeiss lens; exp. 1/300 sec.; *f* 8; E 22 (orange) filter.

Portrait of General Mason MacFarlane—Linhof, 30-cm. lens; *f* 16;
  exp. 1/100 sec.; two flash bulbs within about four to six feet of
  subject, one front high, the other side left.

Wrecked Junkers Plane a. (all-over shot)—Plaubel-Makina, 10-cm.
  lens; exp. 1/200, *f* 8; K 2 filter, fair sunlight.
  b. (close-up of nose of plane)—Soho, 15-cm. Zeiss lens; light
  poor; exp. 1/30 sec.; *f* 11.

Great Battlefield of Yelnya—Soho, 15-cm. lens; light extremely poor;
  f 8; exp. 1/18 sec.; K 2 filter.

Cathedral at Yelnya (distant shot showing two soldiers in foreground)—
  daylight almost gone, therefore gave time exposure of 5 seconds to pick up background, used two flash bulbs on long
  extensions to give some light to foreground, capped lens. Linhof
  camera, Ektar 12.7-cm. lens; *f* 11.

On the Action Station—Speed Graphic, wide-angle lens; *f* 11; 1/360
  sec.; K 2 filter.

First Sight of Land—Speed Graphic, Eastman Ektar lens; *f* 11; exp.
  1/280 sec.; K 2 filter.

A Note About the Author

MARGARET BOURKE-WHITE *was born in New York and graduated from Cornell. Since 1929, as staff photographer for* Fortune *and* Life, *she has taken her camera over most of the globe. Besides her photomurals, her countless pictures of industrial and other subjects, many of which hang in museums, Miss Bourke-White has to her credit two films:* Eyes on Russia *and* Red Republic. *The first of these also appeared in book form. She has collaborated with her husband, Erskine Caldwell, on three books:* You Have Seen Their Faces, North of the Danube, *and* Say, Is This the U.S.A.?